The Really Useful Elementary Science Book

Amongst the challenges that elementary teachers may often face as they introduce their students to science is the need to maintain a solid understanding of the many scientific concepts and details themselves. This essential resource, intended for pre- and in-service elementary school teachers, provides concise and comprehensible explanations of key concepts across science disciplines. Organized around the *National Science Education Standards*, the book tackles the full range of the elementary curriculum including life sciences, ecological sciences, physical sciences, and earth sciences. Although not a methods textbook, the clear and accessible definitions offered by veteran teacher educator Jeffrey W. Bloom will nonetheless help teachers understand science concepts to the degree that they will be able to develop rich and exciting inquiry approaches to exploring these concepts with children.

Perfect as a companion to any elementary science methods textbook or as a stand alone reference for practitioners, *The Really Useful Elementary Science Book* is a resource teachers will want to reach for again and again.

Jeffrey W. Bloom is Professor of Science Education at Northern Arizona University.

Adapted from *The Really Useful Science Book:*
A Framework of Knowledge for Primary Teachers by Steve Farrow
© Steve Farrow, 1999

The Really Useful Elementary Science Book

Jeffrey W. Bloom

Adapted from *The Really Useful Science Book:*
A Framework of Knowledge for Primary Teachers by Steve Farrow
© Steve Farrow, 1999

NEW YORK AND LONDON

First published 2011
by Routledge
711 Third Avenue, New York, New York 10017

Simultaneously published in the UK
by Routledge
2 Park Square, Milton Park, Abingdon, Oxon OX14 4RN

Routledge is an imprint of the Taylor & Francis Group, an informa business

Adapted from *The Really Useful Science Book: A Framework of Knowledge for Primary Teachers* by Steve Farrow

Typeset in Minion by Swales & Willis Ltd, Exeter, Devon

Library of Congress Cataloging in Publication Data
Bloom, Jeffrey W.
  The really useful elementary science book / Jeffrey W. Bloom.
    p. cm.
  "Adapted from The Really Useful Science Book:
  A framework of knowledge for primary teachers by Steve Farrow."
  1. Science—Study and teaching (Elementary)
  2. Elementary school teaching. 3. Effective teaching.
  I. Farrow, Steve. Framework of knowledge for primary teachers. II. Title.
  LB1585.B633 2010
  372.3'5044—dc22
  2010024141

ISBN 13: 978–0–415–99808–6 (hbk)
ISBN 13: 978–0–415–95819–6 (pbk)
ISBN 13: 978–0–203–84840–1 (ebk)

Full Contents

Section 3 Ecology and the Environment

Section 1
Introduction

This book has been written as a resource for K–8 teachers and future teachers. Although this book is intended for elementary and middle school teachers, I have tried to "up the ante" a little bit. In my experiences with children, more often than not, I found that *my expectations* for what they can and want to understand about science fell far short of what they were actually capable. The *National Science Education Standards* and most state standards and curricular documents provide a minimum baseline for what we may expect children to learn. If children are interested and engaged, they are capable of learning fairly complex concepts.

As a result, the science content addressed in this book is at a somewhat higher level. The five basic reasons for raising the level of conceptual content include:

1. Many science concepts and theories need a higher degree of complexity in order for the explanations to make any sense at all.
2. Many children are quite capable of learning more complex concepts in science for which teachers need to be more prepared.
3. In order to design meaningful instructional activities around concepts, teachers need to have more extensive understandings of the subject matter.
4. If teachers are to teach through inquiry, they need to have better understandings of the subject matter in order to generate questions that guide student inquiry.
5. If teachers provide a community for conducting inquiry, such inquiry can move in directions that are completely unexpected. In such cases, teachers may not have prepared for the conceptual territory. This book aims to provide a resource for just such situations.

What this Book Does Not Do

This book maintains a focus on science content. It does **not** provide:

- activities for use in teaching science;
- approaches for planning and implementing science instruction;
- any pedagogical knowledge or recommendations.

A great deal of effort was taken in writing this book to keep the focus on essential content knowledge and to keep the length of the book reasonably short. However, it is hoped that readers of this book will not take the knowledge in this book and just present it to children. Rather, the intent is to help teachers understand science concepts to the degree to which they can develop rich and exciting inquiry approaches to exploring these concepts with children.

For those interested in matters of implementing science through inquiry, read *Creating a Classroom Community of Young Scientists (2ⁿᵈ edition)* from Routledge.

The Structure of this Book

The book is structured around the traditional subject matter headings in science:

- Life sciences
- Ecological sciences
- Physical sciences
- Earth sciences.

Although it was tempting to use a different and more integrated approach, this structure more closely fits with the structure of the National Science Education Standards, with the exception of ecology, which the Standards put into the other three subject matter areas. Throughout this book references are made to other sections where appropriate knowledge is explored in further depth. However, as you will see, concepts from other sciences come into play throughout each of these sections.

Science Language

It has been suggested that science introduces more new vocabulary per instructional day, than do foreign languages. Although it may be nice to have a book on science that avoids much of this language, this book does present the terminology where appropriate. I believe this is necessary for these reasons:

- The terms help if you want to look up further information on the topic.
- Once children understand concepts, they like to use the real vocabulary of scientists.

However, I do have two recommendations:

1. Try not to present the terminology first, but rather bring in the terms after children have developed understandings of the concepts in their own words.
2. Look up the words' roots, which are most often in Greek and Latin. What you find is that many of these words actually have rather simple meanings.

The Tentative Nature of Science Knowledge

Science knowledge changes all of the time. I was quite surprised in doing the research for this book just how much of the knowledge I had learned previously was no longer "true."

Throughout this book, I have tried to bring the most current understandings. However, I am sure that some of this knowledge will change by the time this book is in print.

Units of Measurement

Scientists everywhere use metric units. All countries except the United States also use the metric system of measurement. I do think it is important for teachers to introduce and use metric as much possible. However, in this book I have used the American Standards units with metric equivalents in most situations. I have done this in part to provide more meaning to the measurements, as well as to bring in a certain sense of familiarity to the discussions.

Where to Go from Here

This book is only the start. There are so many interesting areas of science to explore that this book simply cannot cover. My suggestions are to add to your understandings in several ways:

- Read popular books on science. There are many excellent and easy to read books on a variety of subjects.
- There are many good sources of information on the Web. At the same time, there are many awful sites. Look at *where* you are going. *Is the site reliable and easily identifiable?* Sites connected to museums, to certain federal and state agencies, certain universities, and professional organizations are usually good bets. Others may look good, but may not be very reliable.
- Take more classes and volunteer to help scientists during the summer. Build it in as a vacation activity.
- Use some of the computer and internet resources for exploring science, such as Google Earth, Google Maps, Stellarium, and Celestia.

I have tried to provide a few good sources of information at the end of each section. However, there are many more. The sources I have provided are just the beginning.

Let your curiosity take you and your students to new and exciting places!

Section 2
Life Processes and Systems

The National Science Education Standards addressed in this section are:

Content Standard C: Life Science

    K–4:   1 The characteristics of organisms
    K–4:   2 Life cycles of organisms
    K–4:   3 Organisms and environment
    K5–8:   1 Structure and function in living systems
    K5–8:   2 Reproduction and heredity
    K5–8:   3 Regulation and behavior
    K5–8:   4 Populations and ecosystems (in part in this section)
    K5–8:   5 Diversity and adaptation of organisms

Content Standard G: History and Nature of Science

    K–8:   1 Science as a human endeavor
    K5–8:   2 Nature of science
    K5–8:   3 History of science

How do we know that something is or was alive, or is the product of a living thing? The answers to this question may seem obvious, but it probably doesn't surprise you that children struggle with the concept. Young children often consider non-living things, such as bicycles and computers, to be alive. However, the question is a point of contention even beyond the world of children. Biologists are still arguing about whether viruses are alive. In many traditional Native American cultures, rocks, earth, and other natural objects may be considered alive. In some scientific circles, many scientists accept the Gaia Hypothesis, which considers the whole Earth system, including its atmosphere, geology, and life, as a living system.

    While the question of what is living is fairly straightforward for most of what we investigate with children, there are many opportunities for children to engage in their own "theoretical" arguments about life and to explore the diversity of understandings across cultures. In the rest of this section, we will explore some of the basic concepts and theories involved in our current understandings of living things. The major theories and concepts that will be addressed in this section include: the characteristics and basic needs of living things; levels of organization of living things; development of complexity in animals; characteristics of plants; development of complexity in plants; issues of survival of living things; human survival and health; growth and development; the theory of evolution; replication and genetics; and the variety of life.

Key Idea 2.1 Characteristics and Basic Needs of Living Things

When we engage children in exploring what is alive, what was once living, and what is a product of living things, we can begin by exploring some of the basic attributes of living things on Earth. These attributes include ways to:

- acquire, utilize, and/or make *"food"* or *nutrients*;
- acquire and utilize *air*, which usually involves oxygen and/or carbon dioxide;
- convert and store *energy*;
- get rid of waste products (*excretion*) and unused food products (*elimination*);
- *reproduce* sexually and/or asexually;
- *respond* to various environmental, internal, and external factors, including interactions with other living things;
- acquire and keep a balance of *water*.

In addition, other characteristics that are common to many, but not all, living things include the ability to:

- *move*, at least during some stage of the life the cycle;
- *develop and grow* in size;
- *protect* itself and others of its species, including offspring.

All of these characteristics relate to specific structures and functions. However, the most basic characteristic of living things that includes all of the above is that living things are self-generating, self-organizing, self-maintaining, and self-regulating. These processes are broadly known as *autopoiesis*, which is a set of processes or systems that act to perpetuate the whole. As individual human beings, all of our biological systems, such as our circulatory, respiratory, digestive, nervous, hormonal, and immune systems, act together to repair damage, coordinate functions, and, fortunately, keep us alive.

Basic Needs of Living Things

The basic needs of living organisms, which are based on the characteristics just discussed, include:

1. *Food*: each species needs the ability to acquire, ingest or make (as in plants), and utilize food as a source of energy.

2. **Air:** almost all living things need the ability to take in air: oxygen for use in cellular respiration and carbon dioxide for photosynthesis—the exceptions are Archaea, which are bacteria-like organisms that live in extreme conditions in volcanoes and deep oceans and use sulfur for energy production in a process called *chemosynthesis.*

3. **Water:** each species needs the ability to ingest water and/or maintain a proper water balance within cells.

   • *The chemistry of water*—Water is of central importance because of its unique chemical characteristics that affect cellular biochemistry. Water has the ability to:

     – act as a solvent for a large number of substances;
     – transport chemicals;
     – function as part of biochemical reactions;
     – function in the regulation of various physiological processes;
     – facilitate neurotransmission and nerve function;
     – make various cell membrane functions possible;
     – provide a medium for deoxyribonucleic acid (DNA) functions;
     – provide hydrogen and oxygen for photosynthesis;
     – provide hydrogen and oxygen for cellular respiration;
     – provide a transport and functional medium for enzyme function.

   • *Water for organisms on land, in freshwater, and in the sea*—Terrestrial organisms need to acquire water; aquatic or fresh water organisms need to maintain a water balance without too much water coming into cells; and marine or salt water organisms need to maintain a water balance that doesn't allow the cells to lose water.

4. **Reproduction:** each species needs to be able to produce enough viable and healthy young in order to maintain its population.

5. **Protection:** each species needs one or more ways of protecting itself from environmental factors and predation so that enough of the population survives.

These needs can serve as a focus for classroom investigations of organisms and their structures and functions, adaptations, behavior, and other aspects of their natural history and evolution. Whenever studying organisms, it is always beneficial to compare across different types of organisms. For instance, in children's investigations of earthworms, you or they may ask, *which environments do earthworms move towards?* Along with the children you can generate a list of possible soil variables, such as: very wet, moist, dry, sandy, rocky, clay-like, filled with dead vegetation, warm, and cool. The children can use their results and everyday observations of earthworms to infer how these animals get oxygen and water. Since they breathe through their skin, they need a moist environment, but if it is too wet, they drown. Let's take into consideration that earthworms do not like to come to the surface and be exposed to predators, except for at night when they come part way out of their burrows to mate. So, when we find earthworms on sidewalks during and after heavy rain, we are seeing their desperate attempts not to drown. From these findings and observations, children can compare how other organisms deal with the same issues of air and water.

Structure and Function

The concept of "structure and function" is helpful in comprehending how organisms are adapted for meeting their survival needs, and is essential to understanding biological organisms and systems. The basic questions involved in exploring this concept are:

- For what function is this structure adapted?
- For this particular structure, what is the advantage to the organism and its survival?

When we consider these questions, we need to think about how particular functions can be achieved most effectively by specific structures. Some examples include tubular structures that function to transport materials or information, such as those of arteries, veins, digestive tract, plant xylem and phloem, elephant trunks, nasal passages, and nerve cells. Flat teeth or beaks function to crush food, while pointy teeth and beaks are used to capture, hold, and tear food. Flat, sheet-like structures are useful for expanding surface area, such as for broad-leaf trees to capture sunlight, or for elephants' ears to capture sound and radiate heat. Spherical shapes are useful for minimizing surface area to prevent loss of what is inside, such as for many fruits. Eyes are another spherical structure. The functions of an eye are involved in sensing (seeing) so that the animal can communicate, find food, see and escape danger, and move around the environment.

How do the structural characteristics of eyes relate to these functions? In humans, two eyes are pointed in the same direction with some distance in between, which provides for seeing depth of field and for judging relative distances. On the other hand, eyes placed on either side of the head provide for a greater field of vision approaching 360 degrees, which could be advantageous for protection against predators. Owls have a method of dealing with both depth of field and wide field of vision. They have two large eyes, so that their pupils can open very widely to capture as much light as possible at night. Their two eyes are positioned like those of humans, but they cannot move in their sockets. Having their eyes "locked in position" helps them focus on prey as they attack. However, owls have contended with the limited field of vision of eyes that are immovable by being able to turn their heads so that they can see 360° while they sit on a perch.

Why is it that most animals with eyes only have two of them? Three or more eyes don't offer any significant benefit to most animals, and one eye is a disadvantage in terms of depth perception and field of vision.

Why do eyes have the shape they do? The spherical shape of eyes allows for the arrangement of sensory nerve endings, such as rods and, in some animals, cones, that maximize the field of vision and provide for focusing through a lens. Some organisms, such as those of some snails and flatworms, have eyes that can't process images, but are sensitive to light. The compound eyes of insects, where each spherical eye has a large number of lenses, aren't very good at focusing on a single image. However, these multi-lens eyes are exceptionally good at detecting movement—try catching a fly with your hand!

Whenever we think about structures and their functions, we also must consider the environment or habitat(s) in which a particular organism lives. It is important to see how structures and their functions are adaptations for survival in a particular habitat. An accident, conflict, or disease that damages a structure or function will adversely affect the survival of an individual. A loss of one eye may not be immediately life-threatening, but in the long run, the individual with one eye may have difficulty acquiring food or protecting itself from predators. If the environment in which a particular organism lives changes dramatically, the structures and their functions that were adapted for one environment may not be suited for the new environment. For instance, the plants and animals that live in a grassy plain have structures adapted for this type of environment. However, if this environment changes to a desert, the structures adapted for living in grasslands are not likely to be suitable for surviving in this dramatically different environment that has very little water and vegetation. Such dramatic changes in environments affect the types of food, the way in which water is obtained and regulated, and the temperature differential that needs to be addressed. These kinds of environmental changes have occurred in the past and are occurring now from natural processes and from the indirect and direct affects of humans. As a result we are and will continue to see stresses placed on organisms that result in extinction (see "extinction" later in this section).

Key Idea 2.2 Levels of Organization

This section briefly describes the levels of organization of living organisms. We start by examining cells and cell theory, then proceed to tissues, organs, and organ systems. Keep in mind that some organisms are comprised of only a single cell, while others contain hundreds of trillions of cells that make up multiple organs systems.

Cells and Cell Theory

Up until 1655, no one had observed a cell. Then, Robert Hooke, a 20-year old assistant in English chemist Robert Boyle's laboratory, made himself a simple microscope. He placed a thin sliver of cork from the bark of a tree under the microscope and saw the first building blocks of living things, which he dubbed "cells." He incorrectly believed these cells were found only in plants and were the containers for the "noble juices," which probably referred to the sap of the cork tree as some sort of life-giving material. The Dutch scientist Anton Van Leeuwenhoek (1632–1723) perfected the construction of the microscope to where its powers of up to 270x allowed for its practical use. Following these developments, Van Leeuwenhoek was the first person to describe protozoa (1674), bacteria (1676), yeast cells (1680), and blood cells (1702). Despite these advances, it was not until 1838 that cell theory was proposed by two German biologists, Theodor Schwann and Matthias Schleiden.

Cell theory is based on three premises:

- All living things are composed of one or more cells.
- Cells can come only from cells that have existed before (i.e., replication).
- Cells are the smallest forms of life.

These three premises provide a working definition of life. In addition to these premises, a single cell addresses the characteristics of living organisms by absorbing or capturing food, absorbing air and other substances needed for energy production and storage, maintaining a water balance, reproducing or replicating, excreting and eliminating waste, and responding to external conditions. It is from this basis that viruses have been excluded from the classification of living things. Viruses are kind of rogue DNA containers that use cells of living things to replicate, but they have none of the other components of cells.

All cells are characterized by:

- a surrounding *membrane*;
- *cytoplasm*, which is a watery fluid that contains various organelles and other substances;
- *DNA*, which may or may not be contained within a nucleus;
- *RNA*, which carries information within the cell for making and maintaining cell structures and functions.

Figure 2.1 shows simple bacteria, plant, and animal cells. Each of these cells is surrounded by a cell membrane across which nutrients, wastes, and other materials flow. Only bacteria, fungi, and plant cells have *cell walls*, which provide a rigid structure. All cells are filled with a fluid and somewhat viscous cytoplasm that contains the cell structures, or organelles, as well as nutrients and waste products. The various organelles that appear throughout the cytoplasm carry out functions for survival, much like our organs do. All cells have DNA, but only protist, plant, fungi, and animal cells have a nucleus. Various other structures, such as mitochondria, ribosomes, and Golgi apparatuses, are also contained within the cell, as described below:

- *Cell Membrane*: a semi-permeable barrier that allows some substances to pass through, while keeping in others.
- *Cell Wall*: a rigid barrier around the outside of the cell membrane in bacteria, fungi, plants, and some protists. Cell walls are made of different substances in each of these types of organisms. Pores allow substances to cross.
- *Chloroplasts*: have their own DNA and may have been simple alga that ended up becoming a part of some cells. These organelles contain photosynthetic pigments.
- *Cytoplasm*: the fluid between the cell membrane and the outer covering of the nucleus. Its functions include: (a) maintaining the cell shape, (b) securing the position of organelles, (c) moving the cell as with amoebas, and (d) controlling the movement of internal structures.
- *Endoplasmic Reticulum*: a network of membrane-covered canals, some of which have ribosomes attached. Not all functions are known, but they appear to be involved in constructing proteins, transporting ribonucleic acid (RNA) to the ribosomes, and transporting other materials.
- *Golgi Apparatuses*: are found in complexes of flattened sacs. They function as packaging plants where various products are placed within a tiny sac. These sacs can then be used to transport secretory products, such as digestive enzymes, to the cell membrane for secretion outside of the cell. The sacs prevent the enzymes from digesting the cell itself.
- *Lysosomes*: are sacs created by Golgi apparatuses that contain extracellular digestive enzymes that could damage the internal parts of the cells. When we eat, our digestive enzymes come from these sacs.
- *Mitochondria*: are thought to have been commensal bacteria that are now a part of protist, fungi, plant, and animal cells. They have their own DNA, which biologists use

to track lineages where the mitochondrial DNA is passed from mother to child. This is where cellular respiration occurs. As such, they are the "power plants" of cells, where adenosine triphosphate (ATP) is produced and changed back to adenosine diphosphate (ADP) during energy release.

- *Nucleus*: appears in the cells of eukaryotes: protists, fungi, plants, and animals. Nuclei hold the DNA for cell division and for making RNA and ribosomes.
- *Plastids*: are surrounded by a membrane and store starch and occasionally proteins and oil. They are found in plants and photosynthetic protists.
- *Ribosomes*: are not surrounded by a membrane and are where proteins are made.
- *Vacuoles*: are single-membrane storage containers for water, waste products, and food. They can serve to help regulate water balance within the cell. Water vacuoles are easy to see in many single-celled organisms as they slowly grow in size, then disappear quickly as they eliminate the water.
- *Chloroplasts*: plants cells have chloroplasts that contain the chlorophyll that use light energy to produce oxygen and food in the form of sugars.

From Tissues to Systems

Although cells comprise multicellular organisms, it does not necessarily mean that each of these cells has a similar function. When cells do group together to perform similar functions, they become *tissues*. Some examples of tissues include our epidermis (outer layer of skin), groups of muscles, and the thin transparent tissue that appears between layers of an onion. Different tissues can group together to form *organs* that perform specialized functions. Our hearts are organs composed of a several different tissues. The outside of the heart is composed of a layer of connective tissue—the *epicardium*. The layer underneath the epicardium is composed of spirals of smooth muscle cells held together by connective tissue—the *myocardium*. The inner layer of the heart, the *endocardium*, is composed of simple epithelial cells and a layer of connective tissue. The heart also contains valves that prevent blood from flowing backwards. The next level of organization is known as an *organ system*. If we return to the example of the heart, this organ is one part of the circulatory system. The other organs in this system include the arteries, capillaries, veins, and blood.

The next section will combine our earlier discussion of the basic needs and characteristics of living things with our understandings of cells, tissues, organs, and organ systems. We will examine how the life processes carried on by cells up through organs systems serve to provide for the survival of the vast diversity of life on this planet.

Life Processes and Levels of Organization

From living organisms with only a single cell to vertebrates with hundreds of bones, all of these creatures have developed ways of surviving in their environments. They have developed processes for obtaining and utilizing food, air, and water; for excreting and eliminating waste products and materials; for reproducing; for transporting and communicating within the organism; for protecting themselves. All of these processes occur across levels of complexity and scale—from within a cell to the systems of organs to the behaviors of more complex organisms. Processes involved in survival sometimes occur as cooperative actions among individuals within and between species, such as when female lions hunt together and cattle egrets pick off insects from the skin of cattle. Many processes are similar across species, especially at the cellular level. However, there are organisms that have developed unique approaches to specific survival needs.

Some of the basic approaches to meeting survival needs at both the cellular and system or organ levels are described in the list below.

- *Gas Exchange*

    – *Cellular Level*: cell membrane.
    – *Organ Level*: lungs, gills, trachea (in insects), skin/tissues in amphibians and some invertebrates.

- *Elimination of Waste*

    – *Cellular Level*: vacuoles, pores, etc.
    – *Organ Level*: end of intestinal tract; anus.

- *Excretion of Waste Products*

    – *Cellular Level*: waste vacuoles.
    – *Organ Level*: skin (sweat), lungs (CO_2), liver (bile), gut (mucosa cells, etc.), kidneys (urine, urea, etc.).

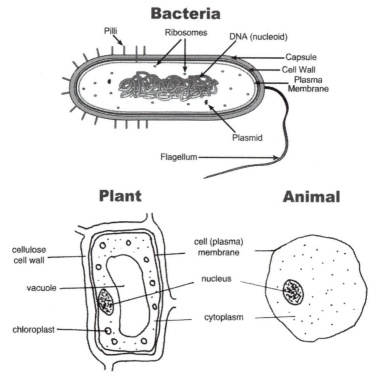

Figure 2.1 The structures of typical bacteria, plant, and animal cells.

Source: Adapted from Farrow.

- *Food Ingestion*

  – *Cellular Level*: transport across membrane; oral pores.
  – *Organ Level*: mouth.

- *Digestion—Metabolism*

  – *Cellular Level*: Golgi apparatus (chemical production), lysosomes (splitting large molecules), mitochondria (cellular respiration–energy production).
  – *Organ Level*: mechanical—in mouth, gizzard (birds, earthworms, et al.), stomach; chemical (enzymes and acids)—saliva, stomach acids, intestinal enzymes; liver.

- *Water Balance (Homeostasis)*

  – *Cellular Level*: osmoregulation.
  – *Organ Level*: hypothalamus (control of blood water).

- *Reproduction or Replication*

  – *Cellular Level*: meiosis, mitosis, fission, cytokinesis.
  – *Organ Level*: sexual organs and cells in most multicellular organisms; asexual budding.

- *Communication and Control*

  – *Cellular Level*: nucleus; nuclear envelope controls permeability; chromatin controls cell metabolism and heredity; nucleolus controls the copying of DNA and the synthesis of proteins.
  – *Organ Level*: nervous system, hormones.

- *Respiration (photosynthesis)*

  – *Cellular Level*: mitochondria (Kreb's citric acid cycle of cellular respiration where food and oxygen are converted to energy); chloroplasts (in green plants) where food is produced from energy (light)—respiration is only at cellular level (see Gas Exchange).

- *Transportation*

  – *Cellular Level*: endoplasmic reticulum (sheets of membranes forming tubular network in cell).
  – *Organ Level*: circulatory system, lymphatic system.

- *Glucose Balance (homeostasis)*

  – *Organ Level*: pancreas (control of blood glucose levels).

- *Temperature Regulation*

  – *Organ Level*: hypothalamus in homeotherms (warmed-blooded mammals and birds). Thermoreceptors in hypothalamus monitor "core" temperature of blood entering brain; thermoreceptors in skin monitor external temperature.

- *Support*

  – *Cellular Level*: vacuoles (pressure for support), cells walls (in plants).
  – *Organ Level*: bones, exoskeletons.

- *Storage*

  - *Cellular Level:* food vacuoles, water vacuoles, waste vacuoles, Golgi apparatus (chemicals).
  - *Organ Level:* stomach (food), bladder (excretory products), fatty tissues (energy stores).

- *Immunity*

  - *Organ Level:* blood—white blood cells (lymphocytes) and other cells; lymphatic system and its lymphocytes—tonsils, lymph nodes, spleen, thymus gland, Peyer's patches scattered throughout the small intestine, bone marrow; skin and other external barriers to invasion by viruses, bacteria, fungi, and parasites; chemical secretions that act as barriers to infection, such as saliva and tears; bacteria—bacteria that live in our digestive system and on our skin, which out-compete infectious bacteria; other organisms, such as mites, that live on the skin and eat bacteria and other invasive organisms.

When we start examining how organisms have developed ways of addressing survival needs across levels of increasing complexity (e.g., from cells to multiple organ systems), we find a separation of structures and functions. For instance, sponges do not have tissues, but they do have specialized cells that secrete digestive enzymes. Instead of these specialized cells being clustered together as tissues, they are scattered among other cells that have different functions. However, in more complex organisms, specialized cells may appear in a separate tissue and organ altogether. The simplest forms of more *complex organisms* appear as colonial organisms, such as the Portuguese Man O'War. In this arrangement, just as in human "colonies," each organism maintains its individual functionality but serves a special purpose within a colony or group. One such organization is a *Volvox,* which is a spherical colony of single-celled green protists with two *flagella. Flagella,* long hair-like extensions, provide for movement of a single-celled organism or for movement of fluids around the outside of the cell. Although each *Volvox* colony is composed of many individual organisms, the whole sphere has some differentiation. The equator cells create daughter colonies asexually, while the polar ends of the colony reproduce sexually. In addition, most species of *Volvox* form either male or female colonies. What's particularly intriguing is how these kinds of separations of function may have been what led to cell differentiation in more complex, non-colonial organisms.

Key Idea 2.3 Development of Complexity in Animals

If we take a broader look at the differences between simple and complex organisms, we move from a few *specialized cells,* as in sponges or Porifera and the newly discovered Placozoa, which are two cell-layer, disk-like organisms, to the development of *tissues,* as in jellyfish and combjellies. From the tissues level of organization, more complex development involves *organs.* The first organs appear in some organisms within a category called Lophotrochoans, which include flatworms, such as planaria and tapeworms. The highest level of complex organization involves *organ systems.* In human beings and other vertebrates, there are *ten organ systems:*

1. Skeletal system
2. Muscular system

3. Circulatory system
4. Nervous system
5. Respiratory system
6. Digestive system
7. Excretory system
8. Endocrine system
9. Reproductive system
10. Lymphatic or immune system.

When you think about the evolutionary development of complexity across the animal kingdom, you may assume there is an unbroken sequence of stages from simple to complex. However, such is not the case. A complex structure or structures may appear in animals that are considered to be lower in the hierarchy of complexity, then not appear again until much higher in the hierarchy. For instance, a closed circulatory system, such as that of humans, first appears among several types of worms, such as horsehair worms, nermerteans, and segmented worms, such as earthworm. However, echinoderms, which include starfish and are in the same major group or superphylum as humans, have only a poorly developed open circulatory system. Such non-sequential development is an intriguing aspect in the evolution of animals, where specific categories of animals "tried out" different structures. Some other examples of developments in complexity appear below. However, keep in mind that there are exceptions to the linear sequences represented here. You also will find some very weird variations on how certain structures work, such as reversible hearts and multiple hearts, which seems to be material of science fiction! In fact, you may find that children could use ideas from the structures of living things to write science fiction stories.

1. *Symmetry*—from asymmetrical to radial symmetry to bilateral symmetry. Characteristics and advantages:

   • *Asymmetry*—reduced or no locomotion; no organs or tissues. All cells contact the external environment for oxygen and food acquisition.
   Examples: Sponges and Placozoans
   ↓

   • *Radial symmetry*—locomotion is slow or non-existent; rapid reactive ability to environment (environmental contact is equally distributed around a central axis).
   Examples: Jellyfish, combjellies, and sea anemones
   ↓

   • *Bilateral symmetry*—allows for distribution of organs in different parts of body; development of centralized sense organs in a "head;" more efficient movement.
   Examples: All other animals, except for echinoderms (starfish, et al.) whose larvae are bilaterally symmetrical and whose adults are pentagonally or radially symmetrical.

2. *Body Cavity (coelom)*—from no body cavity (*acoelomate*) to simple body cavity (*pseudocoelomate*) to complex body cavity (*coelomate*) [*coel* = cavity and is pronounced as "seal"]. Characteristics and advantages:

• *Acoelomates*—organs, especially the digestive tract, are surrounded by cells; the body is solid.
Examples: jellyfish, flatworms

↓

• *Pseudocoelmates*—the digestive tract and other organs are surrounded by fluid in a body cavity.
Examples: rotifers, roundworms, horsehair worms

↓

• *Coelomates*—the body cavity is lined with a layer of cells called the mesoderm (mesentery), which attaches to and suspends the digestive tract and other organs in the body cavity. Advantages:

– allows for extending the growth of organs;
– provides for more efficient circulatory system with an unrestricted heart;
– effective transport of materials that are put into the coelom fluid;
– muscles can use coelom fluid as a hydrostatic "skeleton";
– organ muscles can act independently of body muscles;
– reproductive organs can expand as needed within the coelom;
– provides for much more flexible and rapid locomotion;
– allows organs to be distributed throughout body cavity rather than at specific locations where needed (e.g., mouth does not have to open directly into gut, but can be located in a head with a tubular connection to the digestive tract organs).
Examples: segmented worms, echinoderms, vertebrates

3. *Digestion and Food Acquisition*

• Location and Structure:

– individual cells acquire and digest food
Examples: sponges—have specialized cells for capturing food

↓

– distributed specialized cells
Examples: Placozoans

↓

– *blind gut*, which has only one opening for eating and eliminating waste (imagine having this system!) with specialized tissues for secreting digestive enzymes
Examples: jellyfish, flatworms

↓

– tubular gut, which takes in food at one end and eliminates waste at the other
Examples: combjellies

↓

– multiple specialized tissues and organs
Examples: earthworms, clams, insects, vertebrates

- Function:
  - specialized cells with flagella for circulating water and absorbing food
    Examples: sponges

  ↓

  - passive feeding with food capture tissues and structures and blind gut
    Examples: jellyfish, sea anemones

  ↓

  - active food acquisition with mostly tubular guts
    Examples: roundworms, segmented worms

  ↓

  - active approaches and multiple structures for capturing and ingesting food
    Examples: crustaceans, squid, insects, vertebrates

4. *Circulation and Gas Exchange*

   - *No circulatory system*—all cells are in direct contact with the surrounding environment—cells may have flagella to move water.
     Examples: sponges, placozoa, jellyfish, flatworms, rotifers, roundworms

   ↓

   - *Open circulatory system* with pumping structure or heart that pumps blood out into body cavity where it circulates and returns to heart.
     Examples: mollusks, arachnids, crustaceans, insects, millipedes

   ↓

   - A closed system with one loop.
     Examples: ribbon worms, earthworms, sea squirts, lampreys, fish

   ↓

   - *A closed system with two loops* with one loop to gas exchange organs, such as, lungs, and one loop to the body.
     Examples: amphibians, reptiles, birds, mammals

5. *Blood Pumping Mechanisms—Hearts*

   - The simplest "heart" is one or more non-muscular chambers, which are compressed with the muscular movements of the organism.
     Examples: earthworms

   ↓

   - Variable designs of simple hearts:

     - multiple, simple hearts—gill hearts that pump blood from gills to a single systemic heart that pumps blood to the rest of the body
       Examples: squids
     - 4 atria and 1 pumping ventricle
       Examples: Nautilus
     - reversible heart—pumps in one direction, then reverses direction
       Examples: sea squirts

– series of tubular, muscular hearts
  Examples: insects

↓

- Simple 2-chambered hearts—an *atrium* that receives blood returning to the heart and a muscular *ventricle* for pumping blood out to the body.
  Examples: fish

↓

- 3-chambered hearts (2 atria and 1 ventricle).
  Examples: amphibians and most reptiles

↓

- 3 ½-chambered heart, where a dividing septum between the two halves of the ventricle is almost complete.
  Examples: alligators

↓

- 4-chambered heart (see Figure 2.2) with a double loop system that keeps the non-oxygenated blood and the oxygenated blood separate along with a more muscular left ventricle for pumping blood throughout the entire body.
  Examples: birds and mammals

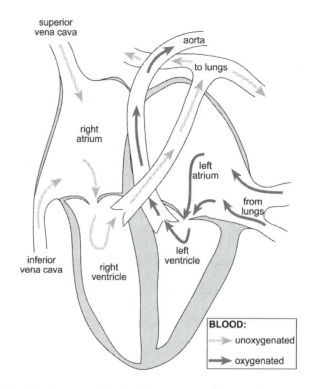

Figure 2.2 Four-chambered heart of birds and mammals. The muscular walls of the left ventricle are much thicker for pumping blood throughout the body.

6. *Nervous System and Senses*

- Sensory mechanisms within individual cells with minimal communication between adjacent cells.
  Examples: sponges

  ↓

- A few specialized sensory cells with primitive nerve "nets" and "rings."
  Examples: jellyfish, combjellies

  ↓

- Centralized ganglia, which are clusters of nerve cell bodies, with specialized sensory tissues.
  Examples: flatworms

  ↓

- Simple sense organs and brain.
  Examples: ribbon worms, segmented worms, clams, snails

  ↓

- Complex brain and sense organs.
  Examples: octopuses, squids, crustaceans, insects

  ↓

- Complex brain and central nerve chord with increasingly specialized nerves.
  Examples: chordates, which include sea squirts, lancelets, and vertebrates

There are many other aspects to the development of complexity in animals with an amazing variety in how different structures accomplish the same function. Some spiders build webs with special "silk" producing glands, and then they wait for prey to get caught in these sticky nets. Other spiders jump on prey, while others build trap doors in the ground and wait for prey to approach. After catching their prey, most spiders inject venom to immobilize the creature and then inject digestive juices onto and into the body of their victim. The animal world is full of such strange, gruesome, and wonderfully unique approaches to survival.

Key Idea 2.4 Human Characteristics

Although we share most of our characteristics with other animals, there are some distinctive features and characteristics that are important to understand. In this section, we will explore the skeletal, muscular, nervous and sensory, and endocrine systems of our bodies. Health and survival issues will be addressed in Section 2.8.

Skeletal System

As with all skeletal systems, our bones serve to protect our internal organs, provide structure, and provide anchor points for muscles. Although we have most of the same bones as other vertebrates, our bones have been adapted for walking around on two legs, for holding and protecting a large brain, and for manipulative use of arms and hands. Simplified sketches of our skeletal system appear in Figure 2.3 and 2.4.

There are 206 bones in the human body. Those that are not shown in detail include those of the head, vertebral column, and pelvis. The head is shown as one bone in the figure, but it's actually made up of 28 bones. Eight of these bones are plates that fit together like a jigsaw puzzle around the space that holds the brain. When a baby is born, these plate bones in the skull

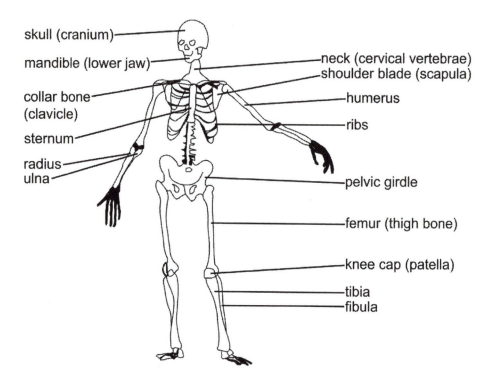

Figure 2.3 A simplified view of the human skeletal system.

Source: Adapted from Farrow.

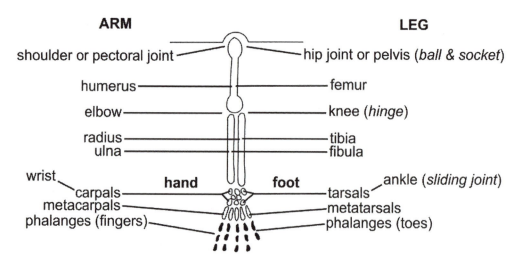

Figure 2.4 A more detailed comparison of our arm and leg bones.

Source: Adapted from Farrow.

have not yet completely developed and joined together, which allows the head to squeeze slightly during birth. These movable skull bones prevent skull fractures during birth and makes birthing a bit easier. There are also 14 bones that make up our facial structure, including the mandible or lower jaw, the maxilla or upper jaw, the cheekbone, and the nasal bone.

The vertebral column is made of 33 vertebrae which provide structure for an upright posture along with the ability to bend and twist. The vertebrae also protect the spinal cord (the central nerve fibers from the brain) and provide tiny holes for these nerves and blood vessels to exit the vertebral column and extend out to different parts of the body. Our ribs that extend out from joints with the vertebrae provide protection for our heart and lungs, while providing anchors for muscles that help to expand and contract our ribcage for breathing. If you've ever broken a rib, you will have realized how much they move with every painful breath. Our bones are held together by *ligaments*, which are fibrous tissues much like that of tendons (see below) that can stretch, but are firm enough to hold our joints together.

Many diagrams of the skeleton do not show cartilage, which surrounds the ends of bones in joints. The *cartilage* protects the bones and provides a smoother surface for joint movement. In the vertebral column, rings of cartilage separate each vertebra. These rings or "disks" also provide a cushioning effect. Around each moveable joint in our body are sacs that contain a thick oily fluid that helps to lubricate the joints and prevent damage to the cartilage. In some instances, this fluid pushes out the sac (or *bursa*) at a weak point. These hernias of the bursa can create little lumps called *ganglia* that push out the skin around the joint. In addition to cushioning the joints, cartilage also provides a somewhat flexible structure to certain parts of our body. Our outer ears lobes and about half of the outer part of our noses are made of cartilage.

Muscular System

There are three types of muscles in our bodies:

- *Skeletal muscles* help us to move. Most of these are attached to bones.
- *Smooth muscles* are controlled by the autonomic nervous system or hormones. They may function rhythmically or as needed. Examples are those in the digestive tract that help to move food through the system.
- *Cardiac muscles* are involved in pumping blood through the heart.

Muscles can only contract with force. When muscles extend, they stretch out by a muscle that performs the opposite action. Take for example, the *biceps* and *triceps* in our arms. When the biceps contract, our arm flexes or bends upward. When this occurs the triceps are extended. When we stretch out our arm, the triceps contract, which in turn extends the biceps. All of our muscles are arranged in pairs or clusters of opposites. Even muscles that are not anchored to a bone, such as those around our lips, are arranged so that when one set of muscles contract others relax or extend.

Most of the skeletal muscles are attached to *tendons*, which in turn are attached to bones. These tendons are advantageous in that they are strong and take up little space. This space reduction is important especially in some areas such as our fingers. Our fingers do not have any muscles in them. If they did they would be far too big to be of any use. Instead, the muscles that operate our fingers are in our forearm, and are attached to tendons that are attached at various points in our fingers. Look at your forearm while you bend your fingers in different ways. You can see the tendons in the wrist and the muscles in the forearm move. The base of our thumb is the only location of muscles in our hands. This muscle is used for grasping tightly with our thumb. The tip of our thumb, however, is still controlled by muscles in the forearm. The points at which each muscle attaches to a bone are referred to as the anchor and insertion points. The *anchor* is where the muscle attaches to a bone that doesn't move. The *insertion* point is where the muscle attaches to the bone that is moved. If you flex your left arm (contract your biceps), you can feel with your right fingers approximately where the insertion point of your biceps is on your forearm. Although it's somewhat more difficult to feel, you can find the anchor point of your biceps at the top of your humerus bone (below the elbow).

Nervous System and Senses

Our nervous system is composed of the *central nervous system* and the *peripheral nervous system*. The central nervous system includes the brain and the spinal cord. The central nervous system is responsible for:

- coordinating movement, including those of the skeletal, smooth, and cardiac muscles;
- monitoring the internal environment;
- monitoring the external environment;
- reacting to messages from the internal and external environments;
- regulating various internal processes, such as heart rate, digestive system function, and breathing rate;
- coordinating sensory information and responses to that information;
- learning and cognitive functions.

Each nerve cell consists of:

- a *cell body,* where the nucleus and other cell organelles are contained;
- *dendrites,* which receive information from other cells and transmit that information to the cell body;
- *axons,* which transmit the information from the cell bodies to the juncture with other nerve cells or muscle fibers.

This juncture is called a *synapse.* The axon that leaves the cell body is a tube of varying length. Near the end of this tube, the axon branches out (like the dendrites). At the end of each branch, there is a "terminal" end that is situated next to the dendrite end of another nerve cell. These ends of different nerve cells do not touch each other: Instead there is a tiny gap across which information must be transferred. The synapse is this area where the two ends meet. Nerve cells or neurons come in three basic types:

- *Sensory neurons*—they carry messages from sense receptors to the central nervous system. They typically have a long dendrite and a short axon.

- *Motor neurons*—they carry messages from the central nervous system (brain and/or spinal cord) to muscles or glands. They typically have short dendrites and long axons.
- *Interneurons*—they only occur in the central nervous system and carry messages from one neuron to the other.

In addition, the peripheral nervous system is divided into two other systems: the *somatic* and *autonomic* nervous systems. Some parts of the nervous system are used to carry out commands from the central nervous system that may or may not be under conscious control, but have to do with skeletal muscle movement and coordination. This is called the *somatic nervous system*. For instance, if you decide to get up and walk, this involves receiving information from one area of your brain to another that controls movement, then sending out information to motor neurons to get up and walk. If you touch something hot, your sensory nerves send this message to the spinal cord, which sends information to the brain at the same time it sends out information on motor neurons to move—and to move quickly! This type of reaction is called a *reflex action*, similar to when a doctor hits the tendon in your knee with a hammer. Even though you notice the sensation, you react more quickly than it would take to register in your brain then respond.

The *autonomic nervous system* controls all of the automatic processes that involve smooth and cardiac muscles. This system senses the status of the internal environment and sends messages that control glands and muscles. When you eat something, this system senses that food has entered the digestive system once it has left the mouth, where the somatic nervous system controls chewing. It stimulates muscular movement called *peristalsis*, which is a rhythmic movement of contraction that moves food forward in the system. This movement looks very similar to earthworm movement. The autonomic nervous system also stimulate various glands to secrete digestive enzymes. The same sort of control and coordination occurs with the heart and cardiovascular system. However, the heart has several mechanisms to keep itself beating, as sets of backup mechanisms. Some of these mechanisms are in the central nervous system and others are in the heart itself. In most cases, the primary message from the central nervous overrides all other messages. In certain circumstances, people may have a problem where these other messages are not overridden. In such a case, called pre-ventricular contractions (or PVCs), the heart starts to beat from one message, then another message starts it again midway through the first one. The result is a kind of double beat that feels like a skipped beat, while the heart recovers its rhythm. Little is understood about this fairly common condition, but it seems to be related to stress.

The autonomic nervous system is further divided into two different systems: the *sympathetic* and *parasympathetic* nervous systems. These two systems operate somewhat like the oppositional muscles of our skeletal muscular system:

Sympathetic Nervous System		Parasympathetic Nervous System
provides reactions to stress	← →	controls normal functions at rest
dilates pupils of eyes	← →	contracts pupils of eyes
inhibits digestion	← →	stimulates digestion
inhibits nasal mucous production	← →	stimulates nasal mucous production
dilates inside of lungs	← →	constricts inside of lungs
stimulates glucose release by liver	← →	inhibits glucose release by liver

inhibits salivary glands in mouth	← →	stimulates salivary glands in mouth
relaxes bladder	← →	contracts bladder
stimulates sweating	← →	inhibits sweating
increases heart rate	← →	slows heart rate
increases blood flow to skeletal muscles		
constricts peripheral blood flow		
reduces blood flow to digestive system		
releases glucose from liver		
causes "goose bumps"		
increases strength of muscles		

The *sympathetic nervous system* tends to control reactions during stressful and emergency situations that require rapid response. The *parasympathetic nervous system* typically functions as a kind of brake or counter-control for the sympathetic nervous system and for normal and at rest activities.

The human *brain* is the most complex of any animal. Figure 2.5 provides a simplified diagram of the brain. The functions of the major parts of the brain are listed and described here:

- *Cerebral Cortex*—thought, voluntary movement, language, reasoning, and perception
- *Cerebellum*—movement, balance, and posture
- *Brain Stem (Pons & Medulla)*—breathing, heart rate, blood pressure
- *Thalamus*—sense processing, movement

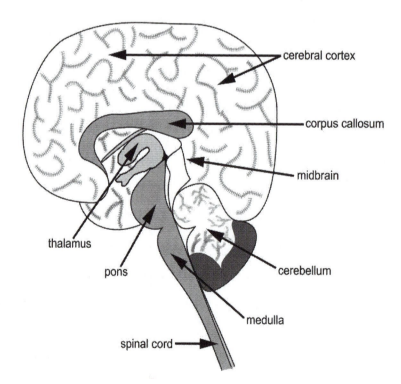

Figure 2.5 The basic parts of the human brain.

- *Hypothalamus* (not shown—near the thalamus at base of brain)—body temperature, emotions, thirst, hunger, circadian (daily) rhythms.
- *Midbrain*—vision, auditory senses, eye movement, body movement
- *Hippocampus* (not shown; part of Limbic system)—plays role in memory and learning
- *Amygdala and other parts of the Limbic System* (not shown)—control of emotional responses.

Our *sensory input* comes from a variety of specialized neurons for sensing specific types of information. These specialized sense neurons include those for:

- *Mechanoreceptors*—hearing, balance, stretching, movement, orientation, gravity, pressure
- *Photoreceptors*—light, color
- *Chemoreceptors*—smell, taste, internal digestive and circulatory chemicals
- *Thermoreceptors*—heat, temperature change
- *Electroreceptors*—electrical currents in environment.

These general categories of sense receptors are further specialized. As with the chemical receptors for taste, there are five separate receptors. Each taste receptor is located in a taste "bud," which is a cluster of nerve endings in a sac that opens through a pore on the surface of the tongue. The five tastes are:

- *Salty*—important adaptation for maintaining an electrolyte balance
- *Sour*—acidic
- *Sweet*—assessing levels of potential energy in food
- *Bitter*—assessing potential natural toxics substances
- *Umami*—taste of amino acids (protein source in meats and cheeses).

A sixth basic taste has recently been suggested, but enough evidence is not yet available. This sixth taste is for fatty substances. Up until recently it also was thought that each type of taste receptor occurred in a different region of the tongue. However, this has been disproven. All of the taste receptors are distributed across the tongue.

Endocrine System

In contrast to the rapid response nervous system, the endocrine system relies on the circulatory system to carry "messages" in the form of hormones. Although hormones travel and take effect more slowly, they tend to have longer lasting effects. It has been suggested that if you get angry as in a verbal altercation with someone, the hormones released in this process may take up to 24 hours to dissipate. If you have a "fight" with your significant other, it may be worthwhile to wait at least several hours before trying to make amends. With the heighten levels of adrenalin in the bloodstream, it may be difficult to have a calm and rationale discussion. Some of the common hormones and their effects are listed in Table 2.1.

Table 2.1 Common Hormones, their Originating Glands, and their Effects

Hormone	Gland	Effect
Growth hormone	Pituitary	Increases growth in young. Maintains size in adults.
Thyroid stimulating hormone	Pituitary	Stimulates thyroid, which controls metabolic rate.
Prolactin	Pituitary	Mammary gland development and milk production.
Thyroxine	Thyroid	Controls cellular metabolism.
Insulin	Pancreas	Controls absorption of glucose from blood into storage. Deficiency is sugar diabetes.
Adrenaline	Adrenal	Raises blood sugar levels for flight or fight responses.
Estrogen	Ovaries	Controls female sexual development and menstrual cycle.
Testosterone	Testes	Controls male sexual development and sperm production.

Key Idea 2.5 Characteristics of Plants

We have been talking at great length about the structure, function, and life processes of animals. The other multicellular organisms—*plants* and *fungi*—have to contend with many of the same issues, although there are some unique differences. Animal cells are contained within a cell membrane, while the cell membranes of plants are surrounded by a cell wall made of cellulose and other carbohydrates. Fungi cell walls are made of chitin, which is the same material in the exoskeletons of insects and crustaceans. Where animals have to acquire food (e.g., filtering, grazing, scavenging, or hunting), plants produce their own food (nutrients) through photosynthesis, but fungi have to find food, since they cannot make their own.

Photosynthesis is a biochemical process that uses energy from the Sun to combine water and carbon dioxide to make sugar and release oxygen (i.e., energy + $6CO_2$ + $6H_2O$ → $C_6H_{12}O_6$ + $6O_2$). The formula for photosynthesis is roughly the opposite of the formula for animal cellular respiration, which uses oxygen and sugars (food) to produce water, carbon dioxide, and energy. The chemical energy is created when a phosphate molecule is combined with a particular chemical, called *adenosine diphosphate* (ADP), to create a high-energy bond when the third phosphate is added. This process is known as changing *ADP to ATP* (adenosine triphosphate). Although plants use photosynthesis to manufacture their own food, they also *respire*. Plants can photosynthesize only when exposed to light, but they respire all of the time to slow-"burn" food to produce energy. Plants do not have the high-energy requirements that animals have, since they do not move, but they do grow, reproduce, and repair themselves, which requires energy. An important point to remember is that *respiration at the **cellular** level* is for the production of *energy* for all cellular processes. *Respiration at the **system** level* is for taking in oxygen and getting rid of carbon dioxide.

Photosynthesis takes place in a green pigment called *chlorophyll*. There are three forms of chlorophyll (*a*, *b*, and *c*). However, chlorophyll *a* is the primary site of photosynthesis. There also are other pigments in many plants, algae, and cyanobacteria. The *carotenoids* are the red, orange, and yellow pigments we often see in the fall as tree leaves change color. This changing of color occurs when the amount of sunlight diminishes as the days get shorter and the green chlorophylls, which "mask" the other colors, decay revealing the other pigments. In addition to diminishing light, other factors can contribute to the timing of leaves changing color, which include water and temperature. The carotenoids are not directly involved in photosynthesis, but pass their absorbed energy on to chlorophyll. Other pigments include the phycobilins. They only occur in red algae and cyanobacteria, which are photosynthetic and were probably involved in the initial creation of the oxygen atmosphere on Earth.

Most flowering and land plants photosynthesize in their leaves. Broad, flat, sheet-like leaves provide enough surface area to "capture" the energy from the Sun. However, these kinds of leaves also provide more surface area from which water can be lost. In arid conditions and in environments where freezing may occur and the Sun is low in the sky, flat leaves can be problematic. These larger leaves contain more fluids, which can freeze and kill the leaf. They are also not as effective in "capturing the sun" when it's low in the sky. This type of leaf often grows parallel to the direction of the Sun when it's low in the sky, and therefore the surface of the leaves are not exposed to as much direct sunlight. However, trees with needles, such as firs and pines, have a reduced surface area to volume ratio (i.e., less surface area for the volume of the needle), which is better for arid and cold climates. Needled trees also tend to have limbs that bend downward along with the needles, so low sun angles are not as problematic since more direct sunlight hits the tubular surface of more needles no matter which direction they point.

Once plants produce food, how do they get that food from the leaves to other parts of the plant? How can plants get water from the ground to their leaves and flowers? Both of these problems involve transport. As in animals with more complex structures, some sort of system of tubes is necessary for transport in plants. Larger land plants have two basic types of tubes. One set of tubes takes food from the leaves to other parts of the plant, while another set of tubes takes water from the roots to other parts of the plant.

How do plants move these materials without pumping mechanisms like animals' hearts? For water transport upward, which can be quite high in tall trees, the narrow tubes take advantage of the chemistry of water. Hold a glass of water, and notice how the edges of the surface of the water move up the side of the glass. If you place a very thin tube in a glass of water, you will see the water move up the tube even further than in the glass. This process is called *capillary action,* which is related to the *surface tension* (see Section 4) of water. Plants have very narrow tubes called *xylem* which travel from the roots to its tallest parts. Water, along with dissolved minerals and other substances from the soil, are virtually sucked up the tubes with no effort needed on the part of the plant. This process of "sucking" is assisted by pores (i.e., *stomata*) on the bottoms of leaves. The stomata are surrounded by "guard cells" that swell and shrink to regulate the size of the opening. This opening (a) allows carbon dioxide to enter the leaf for use in photosynthesis, (b) allows oxygen to leave the plant, (c) helps to prevent bacteria from entering the leaf, and (d) allows water vapor to escape. This escape of water vapor helps draw water up through the plant, which is similar to the process of drinking through a straw. Water crosses into the plants' cells by osmosis, which also assists the "sucking up" of water. Transport of food takes place in tubes with sieve-like structures, called the *phloem.* The phloem utilizes pressure to transport food. In areas of high concentration of sugar, more water is drawn into the tube creating more pressure and "pushing" the material through the tube. When the phloem contains more sugar the increased flow of water is due to *osmosis,* where water moves from one area to another through a permeable or semi-permeable membrane to try to balance the concentration of water. In this case, the higher concentration of sugar in the phloem causes more water to flow into the phloem, much in the same way that sprinkling salt on a slug or snail will draw out the water in these animals' cells and kill them from dehydration—which is not recommended! The phloem can transport material in either direction. In trees, the phloem is located in the inner layer of bark. This location of the phloem can be problematic for trees if deer eat the bark or people cut through the bark. Such events will kill the tree.

Plants can "sense" environmental conditions and automatically respond to these conditions. However, rather than containing a system of nerves, they use the reactions of individual cells, such as when stomata open and close depending on to the amount of sunlight, carbon dioxide, and water. In other instances, they release specific chemicals for transport to other parts of the plant, such as when they react to gravity to send roots downward and the shoots upward. Heavy granules of starch in the *root cap cells* are pulled downward by gravity and start a series of reactions that stimulate cell growth downward. Plants also react fairly rapidly, in plant terms, to sunlight. A plant growth hormone called an *auxin* regulates plant growth. Auxins are broken down in intense sunlight, so a larger concentration of auxins is left on the shady side of the plant. This increased growth on one side pushes the plant toward the Sun. Golfers encounter this problem when putting on the green; they talk about putting with or against the "grain," which refers to the direction in which the grass is growing. When the grass growth follows the Sun, making a putt to the west in the late afternoon is "putting with the grain" (and the ball rolls further with less friction). You can experiment with this by placing a plant in a maze of boxes; the plant will wind its way through the maze by following the light.

Although plants and fungi do not move as do animals, the direction of growth is controlled by various biochemical substances and processes. However, plants and fungi do have to manage the distribution of pollen (male germ cells), seeds, and spores. To attend to that need, a number of unique adaptations have developed:

- attracting insects to inadvertently carry the pollen;
- producing fluffy seed coverings to assist in wind dispersal of seeds (e.g., dandelions);
- snapping open the cones to "toss" out the seeds;
- producing hooked projections on seeds so they attach to the fur (or clothing) of passing animals;
- producing wing-like projections, such as maple seeds that fall with a helicopter action to ride the wind;
- producing fruits that are attractive to animals so they are carried away by animals and buried or dropped, such as with squirrels and some birds that bury nuts and seeds.

Plants also have developed numerous adaptations for surviving in a wide variety of environmental conditions, including those that range from very arid, where cactuses and succulents thrive, to very wet, such as where mangroves, whose roots are underwater, are found. Some plants live entirely under water, while others live partially submerged (e.g., water lilies). Other plants have adapted to very salty conditions near oceans, while others cannot tolerate excessive salt in the soil. Some plants live in cold, arctic conditions, while others thrive in hot and humid tropical conditions. Some plants and trees live in areas where wild fires stimulate healthy growth. In the southwest United States, wildfires used to be necessary for the growth of plant life.

The major organs of flowering plants are roots, stems, leaves, and flowers. Each of these organs are comprised of various tissues that work together to perform different functions in the particular organ.

- **Roots** can penetrate into soils and crevices in rocks, as well as into sewer pipes and through concrete. Their web-like branching not only increases the surface area for water and mineral absorption, but also provides an anchor to keep the plant from falling over.
- The tubular **stem** provides a strong column to hold the leaves and flowers up and off of the ground so that they can compete for more sunlight. The stem or trunk of trees, as mentioned earlier, also provides layers of tubes for the transport of water and minerals throughout the plant.
- **Leaves** contain chlorophyll and other pigments for the manufacture of food and stomata for gas and water exchange.
- In the Anthophytes, **flowers** (see Figure 2.6) are the reproductive organs containing one or both of the sex organs and germ cells. *The stamen* produces the male sperm or pollen. The female *pistil* is composed of the *stigma* to which pollen sticks, the *style* that supports the entire structure, and the *ovary* that contains the eggs. Once the eggs are fertilized, they develop into seeds surrounded by a "fruit," which supplies water, food, and protection.

In the conifers, there are no flower organs. The sexual organs in these plants are the cones. The smaller male cones produce pollen and the larger female cones contain the eggs, which become seeds once fertilized. In *fungi*, the organs include: the sexual organ or *spore producing structures* (which include the "gills" of mushrooms that dramatically increase the spore-bearing surface area), and *food acquisition* organs. Such food acquisition organs include: tissues for the manufacture and external secretion of digestive enzymes and for absorption of the digested material; and in some mushrooms, the carnivorous structures for capturing microscopic organisms or for the capturing small nematodes with a filament loop. They also use filaments for penetrating dead bodies of animals where digestive enzymes are secreted and where the digested material is absorbed.

Other fungi have to get their food through symbiotic relationships with plants, such as in lichens, which are comprised of fungi and algae. Some fungi are parasitic, such as those that cause athletes foot. However, in general, fungi are the *primary decomposers* in ecosystems.

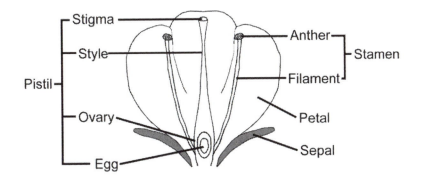

Figure 2.6 Anatomy of a typical angiosperm flower.

Key Idea 2.6 The Development of Complexity in Plants

The *Plant kingdom* includes mosses, ferns, conifers, and flowering plants. These categories of plants show differences in the complexity of their adaptations for survival. Table 2.2 summarizes these adaptations as an increase in complexity.

Table 2.2 The Development of Complexity in Plants

Plant Category	Structures	Functions
Bryophytes Mosses Liverworts Hornworts	• No roots • No tubular or vascular transport system • No cuticle on leaves • Eggs and flagellated sperm (no seeds) • Simple leaves	• No water absorption from soil • Cannot transport food or water • Easier absorption and loss of water • Sperm swim through water to eggs of other plants • Photosynthesis
	↓	
Pteridophyta Ferns and relatives	• Root-like structures or rhizoids that are one long cell • Stem or rhizomes mostly underground and parallel to surface • Leaves or fronds • Spores and sperm-egg stages (no seeds)	• Absorption of water from soil • Transport of water and nutrients • Photosynthesis • Produce more reproductive cells with less energy
	↓	
Pinophyta and others Conifers Cycads Sago palms Gnetums Ginkos	• Seeds (no spores or swimming sperm) • Seeds not in a fruit • Pollen • Vascular system with xylem with tracheids (elongated cells) only and phloem • Roots • Trunk and stems • Leaves	• Resistance to harsh conditions, more energy to produce • Less protection and food • Air-borne dispersal over long distances • Increased transport efficiency and separation of function • Water absorption from soil and anchor for plant • Raise plant further off of ground • Increased photosynthetic efficiency
	↓	
Anthophyta Flowering plants	• Fruit covered seeds • Flowers • Vascular bundles with *xylem* consisting of tracheids and vessel elements and *phloem* with companion cells	• Protection and nutrients for seeds • Reproductive efficiency • Increased efficiency of water and nutrients transportation

Mosses do not have tubular (vascular) transport systems. They absorb water from the environment into each cell. As a result, they need to live low to the ground in very moist environments. They reproduce by producing spores, which contain the basic genetic material for the development of new organisms. Fertilization occurs after the spore leaves the plant. Ferns, on the other hand, use a vascular system of tubes to transport fluids. However, they also reproduce using spores.

The conifers have an extensive vascular system and reproduce using seeds. The seeds of conifers are not contained in an ovary, but are usually contained within a cone. Their seeds are fertilized by pollen that happens to enter the cone. Flowering plants, on the other hand, have their eggs in an ovary, which is located at the base of a flower. They also embed the seeds within a fruit, which provides additional protection and food for the developing embryo.

Key Idea 2.7 Issues of Survival for Living Things

Up to this point we have examined the basic needs of living things and the development of complexity in animals and plants. The list below provides an overview of how organisms of varying complexity have developed approaches to addressing their basic needs and other issues of survival.

- *Regulation*—With increasing complexity, organisms need to regulate an increasing variety of variables, including temperature, heart rate, blood pressure, growth rate, and reproductive cycles. Such regulation can occur with: hormones or other chemical compounds; neurological control; or some combination of the two.
- *Acquisition or Production of Nutrients*—In single-celled organisms, food acquisition can occur through absorption or by envelopment of some sort. Plants make their own food, while fungi externally digest and absorb food. In animals, food acquisition ranges from filter-feeding in sponges to grazing on plants or capturing prey. Many different behavioral and structural adaptations have developed to help with a wide variety of approaches to getting food. Pointy teeth help with capturing and holding prey and with tearing flesh. Flat teeth are useful in crushing and grinding plant material. Pointy and flat-shaped beaks of birds have similar functions.
- *Maintaining Optimal Levels of Water*—All living organisms need water. Those that live in water need to have ways of maintaining optional cellular levels of water, so that the outside "fresh" water does not explode the cells through osmosis. Those that live in saltwater need to have mechanisms to keep the water from leaving and drying up the cells. Organisms on land need to be able to find, ingest, and store water to varying degrees.
- *Acquiring Air and Other Materials for Respiration (and/or Photosynthesis)*—All organisms with the exception of some bacteria and the Archaea need oxygen for respiration. In addition to respiration, plants use photosynthesis to make food from carbon dioxide, water, and energy from the Sun. More complex animals need a way to efficiently take in and absorb oxygen and expel carbon dioxide. Gill and lung structures serve such purposes.
- *Protection*—The concept of protection is important for the survival of organisms. However, we need to be sure to keep in mind the difference between protection of the

individual, and protection as a set of adaptations for the survival of the species. Protection as a set of adaptations involves not only structures, but also behaviors. The ability to move quickly is useful to escape predators. However, this ability is enhanced by specific behaviors. Some birds that nest on the ground will attract a predator so that it chases the adults. If you see a small bird chasing a big bird, this may be a case where the adult small bird is chasing away a hawk, crow, or raven whose intention is to eat the eggs or babies in the nest. There are a number of structures and behaviors that help to provide protection, and at the same time, these abilities have multiple functions. The fast movement of a bird can help with protection, predation, establishing and maintaining a territory, migrating, and so forth.

- *Movement*—Not all organisms have the ability to move. Some may have the ability to move as larvae, but not as adults. Others may appear to be sessile or permanently attached to some surface, such as rocks and coral. Examples include hydra and sea anemones, which you may see slide or somersault across some surface. There are plants and fungi that do not move, except for the possibility of algae that float and move with water currents. The problem for plants and animals that don't move is that they need to combine genetic material with as much variation as possible and to disperse their young so that the adults do not out-compete the young for sunlight and water. Even plants and fungi have abilities to spread genetic material, as with male pollen or spores, which can be done by hitching a ride on insects and other animals or by riding the wind.

- *Efficiency and Effectiveness of Functions Needed for Survival*—From the simpler structures of bacteria and single-celled organisms to highly complex multicellular organisms, all organisms have ways of meeting the basics needs for the survival of the species. As complexity increases, there is a need to coordinate and maintain the entire living system or organism. This need is not the function of any one organ system, but rather a function of the interactions among all organ systems.

Key Idea 2.8 Human Survival and Health

As discussed previously, there is an incredible array of strategies for individual and species survival. For human beings, we have a number of adaptations and other features that have provided for our survival as a species (some of which also have the potential for leading to the demise of the species). We have opposable thumbs, which allow us to grasp and manipulate objects with precision. Our fingertips have a high density of touch nerve endings, which allow for fine discrimination of surface features on objects. We have brains that allow for high levels of cognitive functioning, including an ability to think about thinking, a well-developed ability to conceive of self, and emotions with an ability to integrate them into our thinking and sense of self. Recent research has been investigating the depth and extent of intelligence, emotions, and consciousness (as sense of self) in a wide range of animals (from invertebrates to other primates). The combination of these cognitive functions and our ability to manipulate objects with fine detail have resulted in our unique abilities to survive. Among our abilities, we can manipulate our environments, make shelters, make clothing, cultivate crops, and construct objects for hunting. However, our existence as a species has become very complex. As a result of our abilities to manipulate the environment and make "things," we are adversely affecting local and global ecology, individual health, and the quality of our food, water, and air. In the rest of this subsection, we will focus on human health and well-being.

The human body is incredibly complex. All of our complex organ systems interact with one another in ways we still do not fully understand. As we explore human health, we need to keep in mind that our health depends on organ systems that work well and work together.

Air

Obviously, we need air, water, and food. Air needs to contain enough oxygen for our bodies to extract and use in cellular respiration (energy production). It also should not have too much carbon dioxide or other potentially toxic substances. At sea level, the atmosphere contains about 78% nitrogen, 21% oxygen, and about 0.036% carbon dioxide. Oxygen concentrations decrease with an increase in altitude. Normally, if you have ever had the oxygen concentrations of your blood measured (often called pulse-ox, which uses a little fingertip clip), the normal percentage of oxygen saturation is 96–98%. However, anything over 90% is considered normal. At an altitude of 10,000 feet, the atmospheric pressure drops by 30%, atmospheric oxygen concentrations drop to 15%, and the arterial saturation of oxygen drops to 87%. At this level, a person may become dizzy, get headaches, and feel tired, especially with exertion, among other symptoms. However, after a period of time (from 1 to 3 days or even months for some individuals) most people can acclimate to this altitude. Humans acclimate to high altitudes by breathing more deeply, increasing blood pressure, increasing red blood cell production, and increasing the production of an enzyme that helps the release of oxygen from hemoglobin in the red blood cells.

Although having enough oxygen is a critically important factor, too much carbon dioxide can be very problematic. In the real incident and the movie depiction of the Apollo 13 mission, the astronauts had an adequate supply of oxygen to return to Earth. What they did encounter was an increase in carbon dioxide concentration that could have been fatal had they not been able to filter out the CO_2.

Water

Water is essential to providing a medium for the transport of essential materials, for many biochemical processes in our bodies, and for cells to maintain their form and function. The amount of water we need depends on a number of factors, such as how and where we live and the types of activities in which we engage. In general, we need to drink between 1 and 7 liters (or quarts) of water per day to maintain our hydration. Drinking too much water can lead to "water intoxication" and possible death. This problem usually occurs when people are engaged in an intense physical activity and feel the need to continue to drink water. To keep from drinking too much water, we should drink water with added electrolytes (packages are available) or sports drinks. By drinking too much water, our electrolyte concentrations are diluted to the point where our biochemical processes can no longer function properly.

Food

Food, of course, is essential for our survival and health. We can survive longer without food than we can without water, but we do need food. The old and still promoted "formula" for a balanced and healthful diet includes carbohydrates, fruits and vegetables, meats, and dairy products. However, many people cannot tolerate dairy products and other people have taken on vegetarian diets. Others have allergies or sensitivities to various food products. Some people have genetic diseases that prevent certain foods from being used and even turning these foods into toxic substances. In addition, there are other concerns with certain foods, such as tuna fish and other seafood that have high levels of mercury.

Although the traditional food groups may be helpful, it is more important to stress the eating of specific types of food, such as in the list below. Keep in mind that the amounts of some nutritional needs can vary day by day. At the same time, too little or too much of certain needed vitamins and minerals can lead to serious health problems. Researchers are also finding that greater amounts of some of these vitamins and minerals are beneficial. In general, a proper diet should include a balance of *proteins* that contain the nine essential amino acids, *carbohydrates*, and *fats* and *fatty acids*, as well as sources of *vitamins* and *minerals*, which may be included in the same sources as proteins, carbohydrates, and fats.

List of Foods—Nutrients

- *Protein* or the *essential amino acids*: histidine, isoleucine, leucine, lysine, methionine or cysteine, phenylalanine or typrosine, threonine, tryiptophan, and valine

    – Found in red meats, fowl, seafood, milk products, eggs, nuts, grains, soy, and other vegetables.
    Recommended daily amount: 45–50 g (< 2 oz)

- *Carbohydrates*—sugars, starches, and fibers

    – Found in fruits, grains, syrups; fibers in whole grains and vegetables.
    Recommended daily amount: 300 g (10–11 oz) of carbohydrates; 25 g (1 oz) fiber

- *Fats* and *fatty acids*

    – Found in meats, fowl, fish, oils, and dairy.
    Recommended daily amount: < 65 g (2.4 oz); saturated fatty acids: 20 g (0.75 oz)

- *Cholesterol*—*HDL* (high density lipoproteins or "good cholesterol") and *triglicerides*

    – Found in plant oils, nuts, seeds, flax, etc.
    Recommended daily amount: < 300 mg

- *Minerals:*

    – *Potassium*—Found in certain grains, seeds, nuts, bananas. 3,500 mg/day.
    – *Sodium*—Found in salt, salted foods, certain sauces, canned and packaged foods. 2,400 mg/day.
    – *Calcium*—Found in dairy products, certain beans, certain nuts, sardines, certain grains, turnips, bok choy, broccoli, green leafy vegetables, oranges. 1,000 mg/day.
    – *Iron*—Found in liver, mussels, sardines, anchovies, beef, certain spices, certain cereals, certain nuts, certain beans. 18 mg/day.
    – *Phosphorus*—Found in milk, yogurt, certain cheeses, eggs, beef, chicken, turkey, certain fish, whole wheat breads, almonds, peanuts, lentils. 1,000 mg/day.

- *Iodine*—Found in iodized table salt, seafood, kelp. 150 μg/day.
- *Magnesium*—Found in halibut, nuts, soy, dairy, avocado, beans, whole grains, milk chocolate. 400 mg/day.
- *Zinc*—Found in oysters, beef, fortified cereals, yogurt, flounder, some beans, nuts. 15 mg/day.
- *Selenium*—Found in tuna, cod, beef, fowl, enriched foods, rice, walnuts. 70 μg/day.
- *Copper*—Found in shellfish, whole grains, beans, nuts, potatoes, organ meats, dark leafy greens, dried fruits, cocoa, black pepper, yeast. 2 mg/day.
- *Manganese*—Found in breads, nuts, cereals, green vegetables, tea. 2 mg/day.
- *Chromium*—Found in meats, whole grains, lentils, spices. 120 μg/day.
- *Molybdenum*—Found in peas, leafy vegetables, cauliflower. 75 μg/day.
- *Chloride*—Table salt. 3.4 g or 3,400 mg/day.

• *Vitamins:*

- *Vitamin A*—Found in cheese, eggs, oily fish, milk, fortified foods, liver. 5,000 IU/day.
- *Vitamin C*—Found in peppers, broccoli, Brussel sprouts, sweet potatoes, oranges, kiwi, and fortified foods. > 60 mg/day.
- *Vitamin D*—Body produces vitamin D in reaction to direct sunlight on unobstructed skin. Found in fortified milk and other foods, herring, trout, mackerel, salmon, tuna, egg yolk. < 400 IU/day (probably more in the range of 1,000–4,000 IU/day).
- *Vitamin E*—Found in plant oils (soy, corn, olive), nuts, seeds, wheat germ. 30 IU/day.
- *Vitamin K*—Found in green leafy vegetables, vegetable oils, cereals. 80 μg/day.
- *Thiamin (B_1)*—Found in pork, vegetables, milk, cheese, peas, fruit, eggs, whole grains. 1.5 mg/day.
- *Riboflavin (B_2)*—Found in milk, eggs, fortified cereals, rice, mushrooms. 1.7 mg/day.
- *Niacin (B_3)*—Found in beef, pork, chicken, wheat flour, eggs, milk. 20 mg/day.
- *Vitamin B_6* or *pyridoxine*—Found in pork, chicken, turkey, cod, bread, whole cereals, eggs, vegetables, soy beans, peanuts, milk, potatoes. 2 mg/day.
- *Vitamin B_{12}*—Found in meats, seaweed, salmon, cod, milk, cheese, eggs, yeast extract, fortified foods. 6 μg/day.
- *Folate* or *folic acid*—Found in broccoli, Brussel sprouts, asparagus, peas, chickpeas, brown rice. 400 μg/day.
- *Biotin*—Found in kidney, eggs, some fruit and vegetables. 300 μg/day.
- *Pantothenic acid*—Found in chicken, beef, potatoes, tomatoes, kidney, eggs, broccoli, whole grains. 10 mg/day.
- *Beta-carotene*—Found in carrots, spinach, red peppers, mangos, yellow melons, other yellow and green leafy vegetables.

Disease Defenses

A proper diet is important for general health, as well as for an effective immune system and other health defenses. White and other blood cells are produced in bone marrow to attack invasive viruses and bacteria. These cells circulate through both the blood stream and lymphatic system. If production of these cells is suppressed, our ability to fight off diseases is compromised. On the other hand, extremely large numbers of white cells can be an indication of diseases, such as leukemia. Over the past couple of decades, we have become increasingly aware of autoimmune diseases. These diseases involve white blood cells attacking one's own body. We do not understand very much about these diseases as of yet. However, they can range from mildly uncomfortable to very painful. In some cases, these autoimmune diseases damage tissues and organs to points beyond repair, which can result in death. Some types of autoimmune diseases include: fibromyalgia, rheumatoid arthritis, lupus, Hashimoto's thyroiditis, celiac disease, Crohn's disease, multiple sclerosis, and over 80 others that have been identified so far.

Other defense mechanisms include optimal communities of bacteria living in our guts. These bacteria not only help with digestion, but they can out-compete invasive bacteria. However, when antibiotics are taken for the treatment of bacterial infections, they can kill off the "good" bacteria. During and after antibiotic treatment, it is recommended that people eat salads, raw vegetables, and yogurt (natural sources of these bacteria), as well as take bacteria that are available in capsule form. *E. coli*, a bacterium that can make people very sick and even lead to death, is a natural resident in our large intestines. However, if we ingest these bacteria by not washing our hands thoroughly after using restrooms, by swimming in contaminated water, or eating contaminated foods, we can become very ill. Our skin is also covered with bacteria and other small organisms, such as mites, that help as a line of defense against invaders and to "clean" various parts of the body. These mutually beneficial organisms live in very large numbers almost everywhere in and on our bodies.

Hygiene

Even though many bacteria and small organisms are beneficial, it is important to have good hygiene. Washing our hands after using restrooms can prevent a variety of infections, such as infectious diarrhea, flu, colds, pneumonia, and streptococcus (strept) infections. These viruses and bacteria can be spread from hand-shaking and other physical contact, touching water fountain controls, and doorknobs, where these microbes can live for hours or days. Washing hands thoroughly will kill or remove most of the bacteria and viruses and reduce our risk of infection, especially during cold and flu season. Antibacterial soaps do not work any better and could build up bacterial immunities to the substances used in these soaps. Hand sanitizers that contain alcohol can be even more effective at killing bacteria, but do not deal with "dirt" on the hands. If you buy hand sanitizers, be sure they contain alcohol, which is the active ingredient and is more effective than ingredients found in other products. In addition, keep in mind that bacteria will remain on our skin and that they reproduce rapidly. As time progresses, the bacteria that were "cleaned off" of our hands will return to the same population size within an hour or two.

Hand washing is very important to prevent getting sick. However, we also need to promote other aspects of proper hygiene, which include:

- Bathe or shower regularly.
- Brush and floss teeth at least twice daily (morning and before bed).
- Keep bandages on wounds until healed (or, for more serious injuries, clean wounds daily and replace bandages until healed).
- Avoid sharing drinks, food utensils, and towels.

Proper hygiene can not only prevent contracting a wide variety of common illnesses, but also prevent spreading or becoming infected with the antibiotic-resistant *Staphylococcus* (staph) bacteria, which is referred to as MRSA (methicillin-resistant *Staphylococcus aureus*).

Parasites

The other potential health problem involves parasitic and related types of infections, which include some bacteria, single-celled organisms, and multicellular organisms. Biting insects and arachnids (e.g., mosquitoes, ticks, etc.) can spread bacteria and other organisms that cause a number of diseases, such as Rocky Mountain spotted fever, relapsing fever, Lyme disease, Malaria (not in the United States), and many others. Water supplies may contain organisms not killed by chlorination, such as Giardia (a protist), a variety of enteroviruses, and others. Hookworms can be contracted by walking barefoot outside in southern parts of the United States. Other common parasites and their common sources include:

- *Pinworms*—contaminated clothing, sandboxes, toilets, towels, food, etc.
- *Ringworm* and other skin fungal infections—mostly airborne spores.
- *Tapeworms* (a flatworm)—contaminated meats and fish that are not well-cooked.
- *Threadworm* (a roundworm)—walking barefoot on soils containing the larvae.
- *Schistosomiasis* (a flatworm or fluke)—swimming or wading in contaminated fresh water.
- *Babesiosis* (malaria-like disease)—deer tick bite.
- *Dengue fever* (virus)—*Aedes* mosquito bite.

There are also many other parasites common to the United States. Further information can be found on the National Institutes of Health website (http://health.nih.gov/result.asp/499/12). Some strategies for minimizing the risks of parasitic infections include:

- cooking meats and fish well and avoiding raw or very rare meat and fish;
- wearing hats, long pants, and long-sleeve shirts when in the woods and other areas where ticks and mosquitoes live, and then afterwards checking all parts of your body for ticks;
- using insect repellants when outside in areas with biting insects;
- swimming in water that is known to be reasonably safe;
- wearing shoes when walking outside.

Allergies and Environmental Sensitivities

Many people have a variety of allergies and sensitivities to various substances and foods. Allergies are immune system problems, where immune cells (e.g., white blood cells and certain antibodies) are activated in response to some environmental substances (allergens) or food. The results can range from hay fever type symptoms (sneezing, watery and itchy eyes and throat) to more severe reactions, such as hives, asthma, and swelling of the throat and airways.

Swelling of the air passages can be fatal, if not treated quickly. Epinephrine injections (epi-pens) followed by antihistamines are the usual treatments. Some allergies can be very subtle, such as fatigue and "bags under the eyes," which are thought to be from food allergies. Some common food allergens include peanuts, nuts, sesame, and shellfish. If people are allergic to such foods, they need to be careful of the ingredients in cookies, crackers, and other food products. There also has been an increase in the number of cases of environmental sensitivities. Little is understood about these problems, but they can be quite debilitating. In general, it is good not to wear perfumes and scented deodorants, and to avoid using cleaning products with strong odors or scents in any indoor environment. The other problem that can be quite serious involves molds. Some molds are reasonably harmless, while others can be very dangerous. The common black mold that grows in homes around water leaks and other moist places is dangerous. Cleaning these areas with bleach may eliminate the "black" areas, but it does not kill the mold spores. Wood, wallboard, and other surfaces on which mold is growing need to be replaced, if possible. There are products that will kill the mold and its spores, but these products are usually more difficult to obtain from local sources.

Exercise and Sleep

Exercise and sleep are also important to the health of individuals. The benefits of exercise include:

- improves oxygen delivery to cells for cell metabolism;
- decreases body fat;
- improves joint and muscle movement;
- builds strength and endurance;
- may improve restful sleep;
- helps reduce the effects of stress on body and brain;
- improves immune system;
- lessens anxiety and depression.

At the same time, some activities have the potential to cause injuries, such as tennis elbow; stress fractures; and pulled or torn muscles, tendons, and ligaments. Some sports and other activities can also cause more serious injuries.

Sleep is important for mental activities and general health. People with sleep disorders, such as sleep apnea—where breathing stops for extended periods of time and results in reduced levels of oxygen reaching the brain—don't sleep well and are frequently aroused from sleep. Other sleep disorders are insomnia (inability to fall asleep), narcolepsy (falling asleep at any time during activities), restless leg syndrome, sleepwalking (somnambulism), sleep terrors (sudden awakening from slow wave sleep with various manifestations of fear), teeth grinding, fibromyalgia (discussed above), excessive sleepiness, and various problems with sleep cycle timing or with sequence and lengths of sleep stages. Lack of sleep or poor sleep quality can affect: memory, ability to concentrate, ability to do mathematical calculations, daytime drowsiness, body temperature, immune system function, growth hormone release, heart rate (increase and irregularity), emotions, and social relations.

Drugs

A recent news report stated that the United States has the largest percentage of drug (illicit or recreational) use in the world. However, alcohol and tobacco are not included in this list. We commonly think of the dangers of drugs in relation to the popular illegal and legal drugs. However, common drugs like aspirin and acetaminophen and prescription drugs all have effects and potential dangers. Some people are allergic to certain antibiotics and other prescription drugs. Some drugs are processed through the liver. In some cases, these drugs, including acetaminophen, can cause liver damage in certain individuals or with excessive or long-term use. Aspirin and its relatives can cause stomach bleeding and reduce the ability of blood to clot. This latter effect on clotting is why doctors recommend that certain at-risk individuals take aspirin to help prevent heart attacks and strokes. However, taking too much aspirin can inhibit blood from clotting after injuries or surgery (doctors will instruct patients to stop taking aspirin and its relatives at least a week prior to surgeries). Any drug, no matter how safe one may think it is, can have problematic effects. A complete treatment of this topic is not possible in this book. However, there are numerous internet sites that provide information on specific drug effects.

Key Idea 2.9 Growth and Development

The complex systems that keep organisms alive and provide for their survival begin life as a single cell. From this single cell, entire multicellular organisms grow and develop. All individuals within species start their lives from new individuals, such as larvae and babies, then grow to adulthood and eventually die. From the scientific perspective, an "individual" organism's *life is an arrow*—from new organism, which could be a fertilized egg, to its death. However, if we think in terms of the "species," we see a *life cycle* that perpetuates that particular species. An individual is born, grows and develops, contributes to the birth of new individuals, grows old, and dies, as new individuals begin and continue their lives. The approaches to this sequence and cycle have many similarities, but also many unique differences across the vast diversity of organisms.

The simple cell division of bacteria and single-celled organisms produces an "adult" very quickly. Eventually, the organism is either eaten or dies from some external condition or from "old age" as the complex cellular physiological processes start to break down. As we move into more complex multicellular organisms from invertebrate animals to higher plants, fungi, and vertebrate animals, the initial processes involved in the development and growth of young have to contend with a number of additional issues. These issues include:

- providing the materials and energy for growth and development;
- ensuring the survival of enough individuals to maintain the continuity of the species;
- regulating the speed and sequence of development at the embryonic, larval, and pre-adult stages.

In terms of providing *food for growth and development*, organisms, such as bacteria and protists that reproduce rapidly by forming new organisms, do not have to contend with providing "food" or protection for the offspring. At birth, the offspring are complete organisms capable of carrying on all of the activities of the species. More complex organisms have ways of supplying food for the developing embryo. More complex plants have fruits and most verte-brate animals lay eggs, which also contain a food source around the developing embryo, such as with a chicken egg's yolk. Mammals and a few sharks have placentas that allow the develop-ing embryo or embryos to obtain food from the mother's blood.

Animals that lay eggs have come up with various strategies for *ensuring the survival of the species*, since their offspring are much more vulnerable. Animals that lay a small number of eggs either guard and tend their young, as in birds, or bury or hide the eggs, as in sea turtles. The other strategy is to "play the odds" by laying large numbers of eggs to increase the chances that offspring survive, such as in frogs, some fish, and snails. Other strategies include camou-flaging or dispersing the eggs. Some fish produce a fairly large number of eggs and aggressively protect them, such as sea horses whose fathers carry around the developing eggs. However, once the young emerge, they are on their own, so the larger numbers help the odds of survival. Many animals, such as horses, some sharks and other fish, do not give birth to young until they are developed enough to survive mostly or entirely on their own.

Most plants and fungi play the odds by producing large numbers of offspring. However, some fungi and plants have multiple ways of reproducing. Aspen trees can reproduce sexually, but rarely do. Instead they "sprout" new trees from their extensive root systems. When you walk through an aspen forest, you may only see one tree with dozens or hundreds of intercon-nected clones. If one above-ground "tree" dies, the roots can sprout new trees. However, in adverse conditions, such as forest fires that may prevent survival, these trees can reproduce sexually. A number of plants, invertebrate animals, and protists can reproduce both sexually and asexually. If conditions make it difficult for either sexual reproduction or survival of off-spring, these organisms can start reproducing asexually. Hydra, which are small freshwater

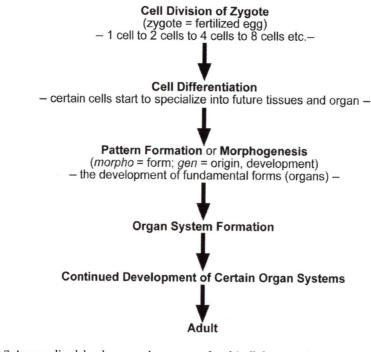

Cell Division of Zygote
(zygote = fertilized egg)
– 1 cell to 2 cells to 4 cells to 8 cells etc.–

↓

Cell Differentiation
– certain cells start to specialize into future tissues and organ –

↓

Pattern Formation or **Morphogenesis**
(*morpho* = form; *gen* = origin, development)
– the development of fundamental forms (organs) –

↓

Organ System Formation

↓

Continued Development of Certain Organ Systems

↓

Adult

Figure 2.7 A generalized developmental sequence of multicellular organisms.

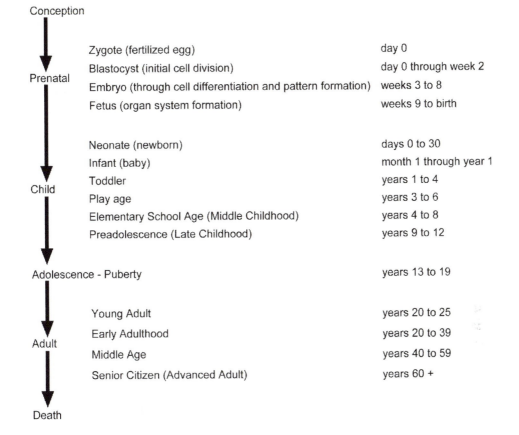

Figure 2.8 The developmental sequence and stages of humans.

organisms related to sea anemones and jellyfish, can produce sperm and eggs, but also can develop buds that fall off and live on their own. Some organisms, such as earthworms, contain both sex organs. They cannot self-fertilize, but no matter what other earthworm they meet, they can get together and fertilize each others' eggs.

The *speed of development* is controlled by the DNA in the new offspring. Each species has its own regulatory code. The following two figures depict a generalized sequence of development for multicellular organisms (Figure 2.7) and the sequence of stages in human development (Figure 2.8). The earlier stages in both sequences tend to be fairly consistent. However, as development proceeds, some variation in timing can occur. The early embryological development of vertebrates (all chordates) and echinoderms (starfish and relatives) have very similar stages of early development.

Key Idea 2.10 The Theory of Evolution

Evolution is the major unifying theory of biology that provides a cohesive and coherent framework for all biological facts, principles, and laws. Although we think of evolution as more of a recent phenomenon, this theory was discussed as long ago as ancient Greece. During this time, Greek philosophers did not use the term "evolution," but they did discuss notions of descent with modification over time, which is the same as the contemporary conception of evolution. At the same time, thinkers in early China and India suggested that all living things originated from a single simple source, which then acquired new properties over time. Later in Medieval times, when the Catholic Church was the dominant social and political force in much of Europe, the theory of evolution was seen as incompatible with the Christian notion of special creation. The Church maintained that creatures did not evolve, but rather were created by a higher power. Despite this religious viewpoint, a number of European thinkers advanced evolutionary ideas in the 1700s, such as some of the following philosophers and scientists:

- **Immanuel Kant** (1724–1804) was a German philosopher who noticed a number of similarities among different organisms, and thereby concluded they must have a common ancestor.
- **Carolus Linnaeus** (1707–1778) originally thought all species originated as described in Christian notion of special creation, but later plant hybridization experiments led him to modify his view. He developed the pattern of naming and classifying living things that we use today. This taxonomic or classification scheme included an explanation that new species arose as hybrids between existing species, which he thought was consistent with "God's plan."
- **Erasmus Darwin** (1731–1802), Charles Darwin's grandfather, believed all life had a common origin, but he struggled with explaining the mechanisms for descent. He did discuss the effects of competition and sexual selection, as well as notions that the use or disuse of structures could lead to their growth or disappearance.
- **Jean-Baptiste Lamarck** (1744–1829) made the major advance in establishing evolutionary theory, when he contended that species were in constant change. Lamarck believed the use or disuse of structures affected their inherited size or shape. This notion, which is not consistent with contemporary understandings, is known as the "inheritance of acquired characteristics." For example, if we lived in complete darkness and didn't need eyes, Lamarckians believed that our eyes would become smaller or disappear as a direct result of the environmental conditions. By contrast, a Darwinian perspective would say that we would keep our eyes as they are, but that if blind or eyeless individuals were born by some mutation they may survive and pass on those traits. However, in this case, the eyed or eyeless individuals have no distinct advantage over the other to cause any rapid replacement of the other.
- **Alfred Russel Wallace** (1823–1913) independently from and concurrently with Charles Darwin developed the idea of natural selection as the defining concept of today's theory of evolution. *Natural selection* refers to the processes involved in survival of species based on how well suited their characteristics are for specific environmental conditions.
- Even though Wallace developed the core understandings of contemporary evolutionary theory, **Charles Darwin** (1809–1882) is considered the grandfather of the contemporary theory of evolution. Darwin and Wallace published a paper together, but Darwin's book, *The Origin of Species* (1859), became the major reference for evolutionary theory. Darwin's theory of evolution through natural selection was based on his observations of different species during his scientific voyage on the *Beagle* (1831–1836). While conducting observations on the Galapagos Islands west of

Ecuador, he noticed that although the animals inhabiting this isolated island were similar to species found elsewhere, they were not varieties of the same species. Instead he believed they were distinct species with different characteristics. The theory of evolution originated from Darwin's explanation of how these different species came to be. This explanation focused on the idea that at some point in time, species from the mainland had migrated to and became isolated on the Galapagos Islands. This isolation led to a different series of changes than those that occurred to the species on the mainland. As a result of the different conditions on the Islands, the original species gave rise to new species with characteristics better adapted for the conditions on the Islands. Since this time, the details have been elaborated upon and specific concepts have been refined, but the theory is still based on the fundamental concepts established by Darwin. These fundamental concepts are variation, selection, and replication, which will be the focus of the next two subsections.

Variation and Selection

The survival of species depends on their abilities to *reproduce*. As species reproduce, various genetic combinations, which may include random mutations, are subjected to selection. In this case, *selection* is a process that determines whether the offspring survive and carry on the new variation. Natural selection involves processes that determine whether a new variation in structure or process is *advantageous* to the survival of the species. In other words, *does the new structure or process enhance the survival of the species in its particular habitat and its niche or function in the habitat?* (See Section 3 for discussions of habitat, niche, and other ecological concepts.) When working on biological inquiry with children, one of the important questions you can ask, and encourage them to ask each other, is: "*What is the advantage of a particular structure?*"

The concept of *survival of the fittest* refers to the ability of a species to reproduce offspring that stay alive. In everyday conversation, the term "fitness" is often associated with characteristics, of strength, competitiveness, and endurance, like going to a fitness center. Although such characteristics may contribute to species survival, in a biological framework, "fitness" is entirely focused on reproduction. Individuals of a particular variety are reproductively fit if they are able to produce enough viable offspring that in turn can produce viable offspring that reproduce. For example, Atlantic cod live in cool water with a preferred annual water temperature range of 44° to 49° F and a survival range of 31° to 59° F. However, if global warming continues to increase the temperature range beyond 59°, this temperature increase could cause many fish to die off before reaching reproductive age. Let's say that of the entire population of this species, 20% of the individuals have genes that provide for a higher tolerance to temperatures above 59°. The result is that the offspring with a higher temperature tolerance will survive and become the dominant variety.

Adaptation, Homologous and Analogous Structures, Convergent and Divergent Evolution, and Speciation

When teaching, you may find that children misunderstand the biological concept of *adaptation*. In an everyday sense, adaptation involves the ability to adjust to particular circumstances

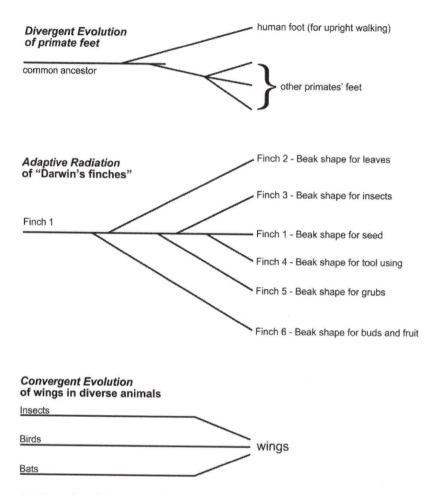

Figure 2.9 Examples of divergent evolution, adaptive radiation, and convergent evolution.

or environments, and this is correct. However, in biology, an individual organism does not adapt. Rather, *an entire species adapts through a genetic change.* As a teacher, you can ask two questions to address the notion of how specific species are suited for survival in their particular environment: *"How is the species adapted to its environment?"* and *"What is the advantage of this structure, process, or behavior for the survival of this species?"*

Over long periods of time, evolution has proceeded in three general patterns: divergent evolution, the related adaptive radiation, and convergent evolution (see Figure 2.9). *Divergent evolution* and *adaptive radiation* occur when new structures and functions, physiological processes, and behaviors are created. This pattern of divergence occurs as one species branches off into different lines. In general, divergent evolution refers to the creation of a new species with one or more new characteristics or structures. Adaptive radiation refers to the creation of several new species with one or more new structures. Such divergence usually occurs relatively rapidly due to *environmental pressures, adaptive opportunities,* such as the development of wings to fly, or *habitat isolation,* such as when a species is stranded on islands. The creation of new species, or *speciation,* occurs through divergent evolutionary processes.

Where divergent evolution and adaptive radiation generate novel traits, *convergent evolution* refers to the generation similar structures and functions in very different lineages (phyla) of organisms. While different types of wings may have been an adaptive radiation for one particular lineage of birds, wings, in general, have arisen in distinctly different lineages, such as in insects and bats. The wings of these organisms have no historical genetic connection. Each one of these groups of animals independently developed wings, which is pretty remarkable!

When we refer to similar structures in different organisms, we label these features as homologous or analogous. *Homologous* structures have a common evolutionary origin. The pectoral fin bones of whales and the shoulder, arm, and hand bones of other mammals are homologous structures, since both sets of structures have common evolutionary origins. In contrast, *analogous* structures may have similar functions, but they do not share common evolutionary origins. The wings of birds and insects are analogous structures with no common evolutionary ancestry.

Extinction

We have talked about adaptations and survival of species, but *extinction* is another important aspect of evolution. As we will see in the next section on ecology, each species lives in one or more habitats and occupies a particular *niche* or function in the ecosystem. Several species may occupy a particular niche, but only one will be dominant with much greater numbers than the other. When environments change, some species may not be able to survive because their adaptations are unable to successfully address the changes. If they all die off over a period of time, they become extinct. If a dominant species has become extinct, one of the surviving less common species may take over that position. If a less common species becomes extinct, it may or may not be replaced by other species. It also is important to think about the "necessity of extinction" for evolutionary processes. If species do not become extinct, then new species may not arise and certainly the Earth would run out of room for new species. *What would have happened if dinosaurs had not become extinct?* Dinosaurs were the dominant animals in many different habitats and ecosystems. If they had survived, human beings may not have appeared, along with many other animal species that exist today. During the history of life on Earth, five mass extinctions occurred. These are described in Section 5.4.

The problem with extinction as a current environmental issue is that the rates of extinction since humans arrived on the scene, and especially since industrialization, are estimated to be 100 to 1,000 times greater than historical rates during the periods between these mass extinctions. The major causes are attributed to:

- over-hunting;
- killing off or removing predators or prey from habitat food webs;
- human destruction of habitats;
- habitat destruction caused by acid rain, pollution, and gaps in the ozone layer;
- global warming;
- invasive species, where non-native species are introduced into new habitats by humans.

While extinction is important for new species to arise as part of the evolutionary processes, extinction that is too rapid may have many effects beyond the loss of species. Living things are not only affected by habitats and the greater global environment, but they also affect habitats and the global environment, as well as other species of life, including humans.

Key Idea 2.11 Replication and Genetics

The two major purposes of *replication* is for growth and repair in multicellular organisms and reproduction in all organisms. These two purposes of replication involve three types of cell division (see Table 2.3): cell fission, mitosis-cytokinesis, and meiosis. The first two are *cloning* processes, which means the cells resulting from such cell divisions are copies of the original cell. *Cell fission* only occurs in cells without nuclei. These simple organisms are referred to as *prokaryotes*, which include all bacteria and *archaea*, which are single-celled organisms that live in extreme conditions, such as in volcanoes. Cell fission is a type of *asexual reproduction*, where the genetic material is duplicated, and separated into two cells.

Mitosis and *cytokinesis* refer to cell division that occurs in tissue growth and repair and in asexual reproduction of cells with nuclei. Mitosis is the duplication of DNA and the subsequent division of a cell's nucleus. The process that divides the rest of the cell's cytoplasm is called cytokinesis. For example, skin cell growth involves both mitosis and cytokinesis. The asexual reproduction of a single-celled organism, such as an amoeba, also involves mitosis and cytokinesis.

Meiosis refers to the cell division involved in sexual reproduction that promotes genetic variation. In meiosis, the genetic make-up of cells from two different individuals (a male and a female) are combined to create offspring. All sexual reproduction cycles are characterized by:

- two parents providing a *gamete*, such as an egg or sperm, with each parent's genetic material;
- each gamete containing a complete set of chromosomes;
- two gametes combining to form a *zygote* or fertilized egg with two sets of matching chromosomes.

Chromosomes are made of DNA and appear microscopically as threadlike strands or as circular strands in bacteria and Archaea. Humans usually have 23 paired chromosomes. In this

Table 2.3 Types of Cell Division, Purposes, Cells, and Organisms

Type of Cell Division	Purpose	Type of Cell	Type of Organism
Fission Mitosis Cytokinesis	• Asexual reproduction • Asexual reproduction • Growth, repair	• Non-nucleated • Nucleated	• Prokaryote* (bacteria, archaea) • Eukaryotes* (all other organisms)
Meiosis	• Sexual reproduction	• Nucleated, sexual reproductive cell (e.g., egg, sperm)	• Eukaryote*

Note: * **Prokaryote** refers to organisms with no cell nucleus for genetic material, such as bacteria and archaea. *Eukaryote* refers to organisms with cell nuclei that contain genetic material, which include protists, fungi, plants, and animals.

scheme, gametes with a complete non-paired set of chromosomes are referred to as being *haploid*. The process of meiosis divides the nucleus in order to reduce the number of chromosomes to half or to the haploid state. These two cells with half of the normal chromosomes then come together to form *zygotes* with sets of paired chromosomes. These zygotes are referred to as *diploid*, because they contain paired sets of chromosomes.

In all animals, from sponges to humans, the adults and offspring are diploid, consisting of paired chromosomes. The eggs and sperm of animals are haploid, consisting of single chromosomes. However, in some single-celled organisms and fungi, the adults are haploid and the fertilized eggs are diploid. Plants, on the other hand, alternate between haploid and diploid from one generation to the next.

Reproduction

Despite the vast variety of organisms, there are only two ways organisms can reproduce: *sexually* and *asexually*. Sexual reproduction occurs when a male, haploid reproductive cell combines with a female, haploid reproductive cell. Once this occurs, the new single, diploid cell, the zygote, goes through rapid cell division and *cell differentiation*. Cell differentiation refers to the points in development where, after cell division, certain cells begin to specialize and become future tissues and organs. *Stem cells* are those cells that have not yet differentiated, but could become any type of specialized cell. This cell specialization, or differentiation, is controlled by DNA. Some of the earliest cells to differentiate in animals are those that will become the mouth at one end of the digestive tract and the anus at the other end. In fact, this early cell differentiation of mouth and anus determine to which of two basic types of animals these cells belong. The *protostomes* are those animals whose mouths develop first before the anus. These animals include most of the invertebrates. The *deuterostomes* are those whose anus develops first. These animals include the echinoderms, such as starfish, and all of the chordates, which are those with central spinal column. Humans are included in this category.

Asexual reproduction involves simple mitotic cell division in a process of cloning where a single-celled organism splits into two separate individuals. Other more complex organisms, such as hydra, create a duplicate "bud." Although there are only two basic ways to reproduce, there are many variations. As discussed previously, hydra reproduce both sexually and asexually, and earthworms contain both sex organs. Some species may start off as one sex then change to the other sex (e.g., most reef fish) either as standard practice or when conditions require it, such as when territory becomes available for a male to take over and mate with a harem. In some wrasses (a type of reef fish), the young are always female. When they grow to a larger size, they change into males. However, some young wrasses will turn into males earlier. These young males look identical to females, which is advantageous for these individuals. When the "alpha" male is not looking, the young males can mate with females.

Sexual reproduction has an evolutionary advantage over asexual reproduction, as the mixing of genetic material from two parents allows for greater genetic variation. Such mixing of genetic material serves as the basis for natural selection, which are the processes that result in the survival of individuals with advantageous traits. Asexual reproduction produces genetic clones of the parent, which results in a genetic constancy from one generation to the next. Any variation in the genetic structure of asexually produced offspring is due primarily to mutation. The lack of genetic variation is not advantageous in the long-term. If the environment undergoes a major change, species that reproduce entirely asexually are at risk of becoming extinct. However, asexual reproduction has two advantages: if no mate is available, organisms that reproduce asexually provide some assurance of species survival; and large numbers of offspring can be produced quickly.

Gene Theory and Genetics

As describe above, cell division involves ways of dividing and transferring DNA. At the same time, the transfer of DNA is of central importance to of the processes of evolution. DNA is the information that:

- controls growth and development;
- determines the characteristics of offspring;
- contributes to the variation within species, as well as the diversity of life in its entirety.

The nature and effects of this information is what *gene theory* describes. *Gregor Mendel* (1822–1884), an Austrian monk, laid out the foundation for this theory, much like his contemporary Charles Darwin did with the theory of evolution. In the 1860s, Mendel's experiments with peas led him to propose the idea of a unit of inheritance, which is now called *gene*, as the determining factor for the inheritance of traits. The term "gene" was coined before we knew about DNA. We originally thought of genes as separate parts of chromosomes. Now, we know that each gene, which determines a specific trait, is a specific section of a DNA strand rather than a separate entity. Mendel's experiments with peas involved cross-breeding peas with different traits, including: wrinkled vs. smooth, spherical seeds; yellow vs. green seeds; purple vs. white flowers; inflated vs. constricted pods; green vs. yellow pods; flowers along the stems vs. flowers at the tips of stems; and tall vs. short stems. From the data he collected from these and other experiments, Mendel was able to demonstrate how inheritance of *characteristics*, such as flowers, seeds, and pods, and their *traits*, such as color and shape, occurred. These findings also showed how certain traits were *dominant*, while others were *recessive*.

Let us return to cell division and chromosomes. Cell division occurs by mitosis or meiosis. These two processes of replication are the basis for genetics or the basis for how information on the structure and characteristics of organisms is organized and replicated. The basic unit of genetics is DNA (deoxyribonucleic acid). DNA can be visualized as two strands of ribbon that wind around one another in what is described as a double helix. These two strands are joined together by a series of molecules that fit together like puzzle pieces. There are only four of these puzzle-piece molecules, and only two pairs (base pairs) are possible:

- *Adenine* (A) connects to *Thymine* (T) as either:

  - A—T or
  - T—A

- *Guanine* (G) connects to *Cytosine* (C) as either:

  - G—C or
  - C—G.

Figure 2.10 Sequence of base pairs (A-T, T-A, G-C, and C-G) in a short segment of DNA.

A DNA molecule is made-up of a sequence of variations of these two pairings (see Figure 2.10).

Your students may be surprised that the complexities of life forms are based on combinations of a *pair of pairs*. However, we can see how such complexity is achieved from simple pairs when we consider that the average length of each strand of DNA is two meters. In order to fit each strand of DNA into the nucleus without getting tangled with other strands, each strand is coiled, then coiled again and again. These multiple twisted strands of DNA comprise what is called *chromatin*. Eventually, these multiple twists form loops, which are coiled again to make up the visible chromosomes.

The information from DNA results in determining the characteristics and traits of all living things. These genetic traits are discussed in terms of *genotypes*, which are the actual genetic codes in the DNA, and of *phenotypes*, which are the appearances of the genetic traits. For instance, if we consider eye color in humans, there are two basic colors: brown, which is pigmented, and blue, which is not pigmented. The blue color of eyes does not have to do with a blue pigment, but rather with the absorption of reds and yellows and the reflection of blue by the retina and liquid in the eye. *What happens when two genotypes come together?* We can predict the possibilities of eye color for a child of brown-eyed and blue-eyed parents. With eye color, brown is a *dominant trait* and blue is a *recessive trait*. We use a capital "B" for brown, which is dominant, and a small "b" for blue, which is recessive. A person with a phenotype for blue eyes has a genotype of b-b, where one blue eye gene was contributed by each parent. However, for a person with a phenotype of brown eyes, there are two possible genotypes: B-B or B-b. In other words, one gene for brown eyes will override a blue eye gene when paired together. Of course, we all know that some people have hazel or green eyes. These other colors are variations in the amount of brown pigment that modifies the phenotype. In such cases, the individual does not have a pure b-b, B-b, or B-B genotype. Instead, some part of the brown eye gene has been fragmented and included in the genotype, so that it is a kind of Bb-Bb mix resulting in a small amount of eye pigmentation. A small amount of brown pigment may give the eyes a greenish or hazel tint. However, simple genotype-phenotype mixing can be predicted using a simple grid (see Figure 2.11).

In this example, two brown-eyed parents, both with a recessive gene for blue eyes, have a one-in-four, or 25%, chance of having a blue-eyed child. It is important to realize that this probability stays the same for each child. If the parents' first child has blue eyes and they are expecting another child, the probability of blue eyes is still one in four. Although many traits can be explored with such a grid, not all genotypes follow these simple rules. Some genetic traits are linked to the sex of the organism, Males have one X- and one Y-chromosome. The Y-chromosome is smaller than the X-chromosome and has less "room" for other traits. Therefore, most sex-lined traits tend to be on the X-chromosome. In addition, in order for a

Parent #1 Genotype

Parent #2 Genotype		B	b
	B	B-B	B-b
	b	B-b	b-b

Possible Offspring Genotypes

Figure 2.11 A grid for predicting the phenotype probability of simple dominant-recessive genotype mixes.

trait to manifest in a male, the gene for this trait has to be on the single X-chromosome. However, for a female to manifest the trait, both X-chromosomes have to have the gene, which means they have to get this gene from both parents. If females have one X-linked gene, they are *carriers* for the trait and can pass it on to offspring. As a result, most sex-linked recessive traits are apparent in males. Examples of sex-linked traits include color blindness, eye color in fruit flies, and calico coloration in cats. Many diseases are also sex-linked, such as hemophilia, diabetes insipidus, and Becker's muscular dystrophy. Other traits result in a blended combination, such as skin pigmentation; dark-skinned and light-skinned parents will have children with a density of pigmentation somewhere in between the two parents.

Key Idea 2.12 Variety of Life

Throughout this section, you have been introduced to the incredible variety of life forms. The classification of living things has been the focus of many scientists for quite some time. One of the major purposes of developing a taxonomy or classification system of living things is to understand the evolutionary relationships among all of these living organisms (both past and present). Up until the 1970s, all life was divided into two kingdoms: plants and animals. As biologists developed their abilities to investigate genetic relationships in much greater depth, they began to rework the traditional classification system. There are still many uncertainties and arguments continuing to this day, and will likely continue well into the future. At this point, most biologists use a five- or six-kingdom system, at least for the time being. In the five-kingdom system, bacteria and archaea are in the same kingdom (see Figure 2.12).

The classification system that is generally used includes a hierarchy of categories. The simple version of these categories involves the following top-down sequence: Kingdom, Phylum, Class, Order, Family, Genus, Species (a good way to remember this sequence is to use a mnemonic device: "**K**ing **P**hillip **C**ame **O**ver **F**or **G**reen **S**oup"). However, the current classification schemes have changed and continue to be modified. There is now a three-domain system on top of kingdoms. These three super-categories or *domains* are *Bacteria, Archaea,* and *Eukaryotes.* Bacteria do not have nuclei to contain DNA. Archaea are bacteria-like microbes that are much simpler than bacteria and live in extreme environments, such as inside volcanoes. In such conditions, they cannot use oxygen or sunlight, so instead thrive on carbon dioxide, nitrogen, and hydrogen sulfide. Eukaryotes are all other living things, whose cells have a "true" nucleus.

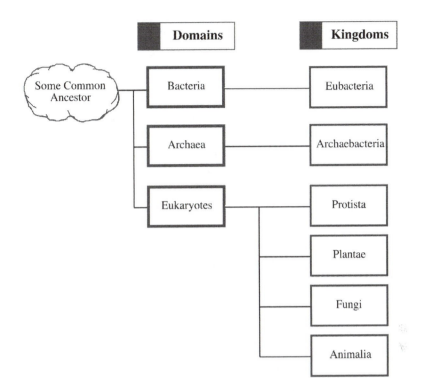

Figure 2.12 The current system of domains and kingdoms of all living things.

The detailed taxonomic or classification system that is currently used is in constant flux, but in general uses additional categories that define the relationships between organisms. Examples of these categories include super-classes, super-orders, sub-orders, and sub-species. For simplicity, the information here will stay pretty close to the system of major categories listed above. The current system of domains and kingdoms appear in Figure 2.12. You will notice that viruses are not included. As discussed previously, biologists do not know whether to classify them as living or not, since they do not fit the characteristics of cells and living things. In some ways, these entities are considered to be at the periphery of life as simple containers of DNA.

Kingdoms Eubacteria and Archaebacteria (Prokaryotes)

The kingdom *Eubacteria* include bacteria, blue-green algae, and spirochaetes. These organisms are all single-celled and do not have nuclei. They have cell walls made of a combination of sugars and amino acids called peptidoglycan. *Blue-green algae* or *cyanobacteria* are photosynthetic and tend to be single-celled, but can grow in colonies. Some blue-green algae produce toxins, so that if they "bloom" in a pond or lake, they can kill off fish and other animals. These organisms have been in existence for about 3.5 billion years and are probably responsible for the Earth's oxygen-rich atmosphere. The *Archaebacteria* also are single-celled and do not have nuclei. Their cells walls are made of a variety of substances that are generally a combination of proteins and sugars, which are resistant to the extreme temperatures and chemical conditions in which they live.

In the remaining kingdoms, all the cells of these groups have nuclei. These kingdoms fall under the domain "Eukaryotes."

Kingdom Protista

Protists are mostly single-celled. In those with multiple cells, the cells are all similar to one another and there is no clear separation of function. These organisms include the amoebas, ciliates, flagellates, all algae except for blue-green algae, dinoflagellates, and plasmodial slime molds. *Amoebas* are single-celled shape-shifters. They extend their cytoplasm as a kind of foot to move along surfaces in fluids. Ciliates have various configurations of tiny hair-like projections extending from their cell membrane. The movement of *cilia* helps these organisms move smoothly through liquids and, in some cases, are also used to move food into their "mouths," such as in parameciums. *Flagellates* have one or a few longer hair-like projections which are used for movement. As opposed to the smooth, wave-like motion of cilia, flagella are moved in a whip-like fashion, which results in a jerkier movement of the organism. *Algae*, including red algae, brown algae, green algae, and kelp, are all photosynthetic. Although they are classified here within the group Protista, biologists have yet to determine exactly how to classify them in terms of their evolutionary relationships to other organisms. They used to be included with plants, since they contain chlorophyll and follow similar patterns in their alternation of diploid and haploid generations. *Dinoflagellates* are single-celled organisms that often are photosynthetic. Some are bioluminescent, which, at night, can give waves breaking on the beach an eerie green glow and leave glowing footprints in the wet sand. Blooms of dinoflagellates are known as "red tides," which can kill other organisms due to the release of toxins. Most of these organisms are surrounded by armored plates made of a cellulose-based substance. The arrangement of these plates gives each species a distinctive symmetrically patterned "home." *Plasmodial slime molds* form a structure from cytoplasm that contains many nuclei without any cell wall or membrane to separate cells. This almost science fiction type "blob" moves slowly over surfaces like an amoeba, while eating other single-celled organisms.

Kingdom Plantae

The classification of plants has changed. The higher, more complex plants are no longer separated into *monocotyledons* with one leaf seeds or embryos and parallel leaf veins and *dicotyledons*, which referred to seeds with two leaves and leaves with radiating veins. These two categories may still be useful in identifying plants. The current classification scheme appears in Figure 2.13. Table 2.2, which appeared earlier, describes the overall increase of complexity of plants from bryophytes with no tubular vascular system to flowering plants with a complex vascular system. However, the major characteristics of plants are that they are multicellular, have cells walls made of cellulose, and contain two types of chlorophyll for the production of food in the form of carbohydrates.

Kingdom Fungi

Fungi used to be included with plants, but have been put into a separate kingdom. The cells of fungi have cell walls made of chitin, which is the same material in the exoskeletons of insects. Fungi do not contain chlorophyll and act as the primary decomposers in ecosystems. The

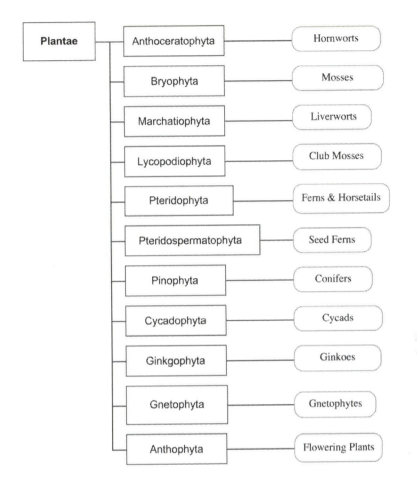

Figure 2.13 The major categories of plants (see Table 2.2 for the development of complexity in plants).

classification of fungi appears in Figure 2.14. The *Chytrid fungi* are primarily aquatic and are the most primitive of the fungi with lineages that extend back to the very first fungi. The category, *Deuteromycota*, is kind of a grab-bag of fungi that have lost all ability to reproduce sexually. The *Zygomycota* are bread molds and other often parasitic fungi. Some of these organisms feed almost exclusively on amoebas, while others reside as parasites in the stomachs of black flies. For those of you who have been "eaten" by black flies, I am sure you are not very sympathetic to their plight. The *Glomeromycota* grow mostly in soil and reproduce asexually. Many of these organisms grow in among plant roots in a symbiotic relationship. The *Ascomycota* include a wide range of economically important fungi. They include yeast, edible mushrooms, fungi used in cheese production, fungi that help with the decay of wood, and fungi and molds that are sources of antibiotics, such as blue mold for penicillin. Other examples are powdery mildews, leaf curl fungus, chestnut blight, Dutch elm disease, green mold, ergot, and morels. The *Basidiomycota* include most of the mushrooms with which we are familiar, as well as bracket fungi, puffballs, rusts, and some less common yeasts. Lichens are often shown as a separate category of fungi, but they actually are fungi and algae in a symbiotic relationship. The fungi in lichens are usually from Basidiomycota or Ascomycota.

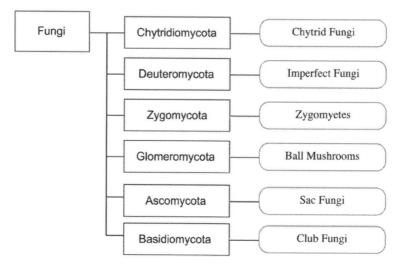

Figure 2.14 The taxonomy of the kingdom Fungi.

Kingdom Animalia

The Animal kingdom is characterized by organisms without a cell wall of any kind. Only a cell membrane surrounds the cells of animals. In addition, animals are capable of movement at least during some stage of development. All animals are multicellular with some degree of cellular specialization. Placozoa and sponges are the two least complex animals and show only the beginnings of cellular specialization, while mammals are the most complex with more highly developed nervous systems and brains. In addition, although some animals can reproduce asexually, they all can reproduce sexually. And as opposed to plants, all adults are diploid and only sperm and eggs are haploid.

Figure 2.15 shows the classification of animals. *Placozoa* are an entirely new category of animals, which were discovered in an aquarium. In fact, these animals have never been observed in their natural habitat. These animals are asymmetrical disks that are two cell layers thick with a liquid filled pocket in between the cell layers. There is a small degree of cellular specialization in these organisms with four distinct cell types:

- ciliated *cylinder cells* on the bottom surface;
- *gland cells* without cilia, which produce digestive enzymes, on the bottom surface;
- ciliated *cover cells* are the only cells on the top surface;
- star-shaped *fiber cells* are distributed through the space in between the two cells layers and are connected to one another by the long star-like extensions.

In contrast, sponges have between 10 and 20 different cells, while we have over 200 different types of cells. The ciliated cells function for movement along surfaces. When a placozoan moves over a protist, it frequently forms a pocket around the organism and then secretes digestive enzymes. The digested material is then absorbed by the cells along the bottom. They generally reproduce asexually, but some observations seem to suggest that sexual reproduction may occur.

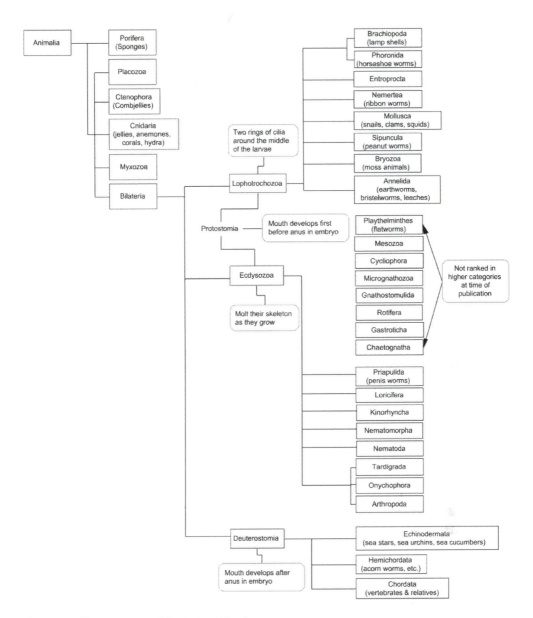

Figure 2.15 The taxonomy of the Animal kingdom.

As discussed earlier in this section, there is a wide range in complexity among animals. From the simplest to the most complex, each group of animals has had to contend with certain issues, such as how to:

- obtain and digest food, then make sure all cells get the nutrients;
- make sure all cells get oxygen and can get rid of carbon dioxide;
- get rid of waste products;
- coordinate various internal functions, as well as movement;
- optimize reproduction.

As various groups developed structures and functions to address these issues, they also had to find ways of coordinating all of these different functions, both in terms of their overall anatomical structure and their coordinated functioning. As a result, we see animals try different formats from asymmetry → radial symmetry → pentagonal symmetry → bilateral symmetry. While asymmetrical animals are rather simple and do not need circulatory systems or body cavities, more complex symmetries have allowed for the development of body cavities and various organs, including those concerned with circulation, respiration, digestion, waste removal, reproduction, and movement (see subsection 2.3 for more details).

Among animals, there is a huge variety of intriguing and sometimes gross and outrageous ways of meeting their survival needs. However, to go through all of these fascinating adaptations would require several other books.

Resources and References

The Tree of Life Web Project: http://tolweb.org/tree/
The Earth Life Web: www.earthlife.net/
Wikispicies: http://species.wikimedia.org/wiki/Main_Page
Micrographia—microphotography of biological organisms: www.micrographia.com
Biology On-Line Dictionary: www.biology-online.org/dictionary/Main_Page
Sponge releasing sperm video: www.youtube.com/watch?v=KOFFzXNYJG0
Encyclopedia of Life: www.eol.org

Section 3
Ecology and the Environment

The National Science Education Standards addressed in this section are:

Content Standard C: Life Science

    K–4:   3 Organisms and environment
    K5–8:   4 Populations and ecosystems

Content Standard F: Science in Personal and Social Perspectives

    K–8:   2 Characteristics and changes in populations
    K–8:   4 Changes in environments
    K5–8:   2 Characteristics and changes in populations
    K5–8:   4 Changes in environments

Ecology is a fairly new science that really did not become an established discipline until midway through the 20th century. Shortly after its establishment another more political movement began called "environmentalism." *Ecology* is the study of how our Earth's geological, physical, chemical, and biological systems work and interact, whereas environmentalism is concerned with making political changes to how we use and relate to the environment. In some cases, environmentalists work from a knowledgebase that is well-grounded in ecological knowledge, while in other cases they operate from tenuous assumptions.

Our challenge as teachers is to help children begin to think about environmental issues from a basis in ecology and to develop the thinking skills necessary to clarify the wide range of claims being made about the environment. In terms of immediate relevance, this section deals with the knowledge behind issues that may well concern the future of life on Earth.

Key Idea 3.1 The Gaia Hypothesis—The Earth System

In ancient Greek mythology, Gaia was the goddess of the Earth and mother of the Titans. In 1979, using the imagery of this Earth goddess, James Lovelock proposed the *Gaia Hypothesis*, which suggests that the entire biosphere of the Earth acts as a single self-regulating, self-maintaining, living system. This hypothesis is based on chaos and complexity theories. In chaos theories, order can be embedded in or can emerge from chaos, much like tornadoes and hurricanes emerge from seemingly chaotic weather patterns. The history of the Earth seems to have followed a similar pattern from chaotic beginnings to a life-sustaining system. The introduction of the Gaia hypothesis has stimulated a great deal of scientific research into this idea of global ecology. As we continue to explore the topic of ecology in this section, you may want to keep in mind a picture of the entire Earth system and how all of the specific concepts play a part in the whole system.

Key Idea 3.2 Levels of Organization

Ecologists have found it useful to divide up the Earth system in terms of organizational levels:

Ecological Hierarchy

- Biosphere
- Biogeographic Region
- Landscape
- Biome
- Ecosystem
- Biotic Community
- Population
- Organism

In this *hierarchy of levels,* each level is dependent upon and affected by other levels. From the perspective of this ecological hierarchy, the higher levels tend to be more stable than those below. An example of this stability occurs in situations where a particular population of fish has been over-harvested to the point where very few members of the species are left in a particular area. While the population of the species has been radically reduced, the biotic community of other species still continues with some degree of effect from the missing population, such as a loss of a specific "predator" or "prey," but the entire marine ecosystem has suffered hardly any effect. The higher up the hierarchy, the less effect you notice. As a result, the functional patterns, such as energy flow pathways (see subsection 3.5), at higher levels tend to stabilize the whole system. As you read through the following descriptions of these levels, it is important to keep in mind that the definitions and descriptions of each level are somewhat tentative or even vague. From one perspective, ecologists are still arguing about how to define many of these levels. From another perspective, the "boundaries" or distinctions are often somewhat fuzzy and dependent upon the specific context.

Organism

The individual organism is the smallest unit of analysis in ecology. The variety of these organisms is described in Section 2. They include bacteria, archaebacteria, protists, fungi, plants, and animals.

Population

The concept of population has to do with all of the individuals of one species that live within the local community of living organisms. Although any particular species may be spread over a larger region, the population of that species refers to only those individuals that live in a specific area.

Community or Biotic Community

A biological or biotic community includes all of the populations of species that live in a particular area. A forest contains a variety of different organisms. All these organisms comprise the forest community. However, the notion of community can be associated with a notion of scale. Even though we may view a forest as a community at a large scale, each individual tree contains its own community of organisms, such as bacteria, fungi, lichens, and certain insects. In fact, we as human beings have our own communities of organisms living all over our internal and external surfaces (e.g., mites, bacteria, fungi).

Communities are characterized by a variety of different species, which interact and affect one another in various ways. Some species are food for others, while others supply various nutrients and chemicals to the community in the form of nitrogen compounds and undigested materials from the excretion and elimination of wastes. Some species provide shelter and habitats for other species, such as trees providing a habitat for birds, squirrels, bacteria, and fungi. In many cases, there are a variety of parasitic and mutually beneficial relationships between certain species. Such interdependencies are a central characteristic of these communities, just as are grocery stores, plumbers, electricians, teachers, doctors, and other people in our own communities.

Ecosystem

An ecosystem or ecological system involves the living organisms in a community and the nonliving materials and energy that are utilized by the community. From the previous level of community, the example of the forest can be seen as an ecosystem when we also consider the geological, physical, and chemical characteristics. The relationships among different aspects of ecosystems become much more complex as the plants, animals, and other organisms affect the geology and chemistry of the area in which they live.

Historically, when bacteria became the first photosynthesizers, they were responsible for adjusting atmospheric oxygen. Now, bacteria function in numerous ways that range from helping to decompose dead material and helping to digest food within the guts of animals to processing nitrogen and numerous other substances in soils and water.

At the same time that organisms are affecting the environment in ecosystems, the geological, chemical, and physical aspects of the environment affect living things. Floods may change habitats and kill some organisms, while they also bring in important nutrients for the plants living in these areas. Fires act in similar ways, especially in the southwest United States, where fires have been necessary providers of nutrients for forests. As a natural occurrence, such fires did not burn hot enough to kill the trees in forests. At the same time, they provided important nutrients from the burning of undergrowth. However, when humans tried to control and prevent fires by removing undergrowth, the fires began to burn hotter. As a result, the fires now destroy the trees that once benefited from fires. In addition to the interactions between the physical and biological environments, we also see how humans have added another dimension of complexity with their abilities to manipulate the environments in ways that other physical and biological components cannot.

There are many ecosystems within the biosphere of the Earth. Although we may have a tendency to think of ecosystems as self-contained systems, they vary considerably in their interactions with other ecosystems. A pond or lake seems to be self-contained, but they are more intricately connected in the following ways:

- Rivers and streams flow into and out of these bodies of water. Water from these bodies eventually flows into the oceans.
- Water also evaporates, which affects atmospheric water content and climate.
- Birds and insects move between ponds and lakes and a variety of terrestrial ecosystems. Some insects lay eggs in the water, which develop into nymphs that live in the water, but then change into adults that leave their aquatic habitat and fly off. Birds may feed, leave their droppings, and nest in lakes and ponds, then fly off to other locations.
- Many animals may move from one ecosystem to another on a regular basis.

In general, all ecosystems interact with one another in a variety of chemical, physical, geological, and biological ways.

Biome

Biomes are smaller divisions of biogeographic regions (see below). They tend to be defined more by the types of environments that define adaptive boundaries for many of its inhabitants. Examples include grasslands, deserts, forests, oceans, and tundra. Although some animals may live in more than one biome, the general pattern is that each of these environmental divisions have their own sets of organisms that are adapted to survive in these areas. While gulls, which are adapted to survive in a variety of environments, may be found in marine environments, they are also found in forests, especially if humans have built dumps in these forests! On the other hand, you're not going to find a shark living in the desert or a palm tree living in the tundra.

Landscape

Within biomes, landscapes are collections of ecosystems along with artifacts of humans. The central and southern area of Arizona is desert. Within this desert ecosystem, there are rivers, artificial canals, artificial lakes, towns, cities, and urban sprawl. This landscape is composed of the desert and aquatic ecosystems, as well as the urban environments that interact with these ecosystems.

Biogeographic Region

Biogeographic regions are the geographic entities that have their own varieties of living organisms. These entities include continents, islands, oceans, and other land forms and bodies of water. Although some species can be found across different continents and bodies of water, each of these regions has its unique characteristics.

Biosphere

There is one biosphere, at least on this planet. The biosphere is Earth and all of its life forms, as well as all of its components, properties, and processes that support life. The biosphere is comprised of multiple interacting systems that are involved in the other hierarchical layers described previously.

Key Idea 3.3 Types of Ecosystems

Some of the major types of ecosystems on Earth are described below.

Marine Ecosystems

1. **Open Ocean**

   - This is the deep ocean beyond the continental shelves. Extends from the abyssal plains and trenches to ridges and the continental rises. The deepest parts of the oceans are in the Marianna Trench in the Pacific Ocean east of the Philippines near Guam. This trench is about 35,840 ft (10,9234 m) or over 6.75 miles (17.5 km) deep.

   The biological communities in the oceans are affected by variations in waves, tides, currents, salinity, temperature, pressure, and light intensity, which in turn affect the composition of the bottom sediments, dissolved gases, and the gases that are released into the atmosphere. The oceans are the *major source of atmospheric oxygen*, which is produced by algae and phytoplankton that live in the zone that gets adequate sunlight along the surface, called the photic zone (see Figure 3.1 later in this section).

2. **Continental Shelf or Inshore Oceans**

   - These shallower areas of the ocean extend out from around the continents.
   - Depths are variable, but extend from the coastline down to just less than 500 ft deep. During glacial periods, the continental shelves were above sea level.
   - The distances continental shelves extend out from dry land vary from almost no shelf at all—where oceanic plates (see Section 5) push underneath the continental plates, such as along parts of the northern California coast—up to about 930 miles for the Siberian Shelf.

3. **Upwelling Regions of Oceans**

   - Upwelling occurs where currents bring nutrients from the depths of the oceans up to the photic zones, where sunlight penetrates the surface. These areas are among the most biologically productive areas with large populations of living organisms, including commercial fish. The coast of Peru has one of the most productive upwelling ecosystems in the world.

- Strong upwelling generally occurs along the west coasts of continents, which also tend to have narrow continental shelves.

4. *Seashores, Estuaries, and Saltwater Marshes*

- These areas are between the land and ocean. They are not just transitional borders, but are unique ecosystems.
- The waters have highly variable temperatures and salinities. Wave and tidal actions have dramatic effects on the physical environment.
- These are extremely fertile areas that are rich in life.
- Estuaries and marshes are incredibly important ecosystems, where they are:

  - *breeding* and *nursery grounds* for many fish and other marine and terrestrial organisms;
  - *nutrient sources* for oceanic and other surrounding ecosystems;
  - *nutrient traps* that filter and recycle wastes, which have been used as sewage systems for cities that in turn have resulted in overuse and the destruction of marshlands;
  - *buffer zones* for terrestrial areas from heavy storms, such as hurricanes; the destruction of the estuarine areas around New Orleans added to the severity of Hurricane Katrina.

5. *Mangroves*

- Mangroves are woody plants that are able to tolerate high salinity. Most mangroves have extensive root systems called *prop roots* that help to support the trees above the water the line and also penetrate deep into the mud underneath the water's surface. The mud is so dense that oxygen does not penetrate and only *anaerobic bacteria,* which do not require oxygen, can survive. However, the root systems of mangroves allow oxygen to penetrate allowing other organisms to survive in these areas. These *aerobic* organisms, which do require oxygen, include clams, oysters, barnacles, shrimp, and other creatures that can attach to or live in and among the roots.
- In subtropical and tropical areas where mangroves occur, they function in many of the same ways as saltwater marshes and may even replace them in these areas. As with marshes, mangroves can help to build land by capturing materials and sediments.
- In the United States, mangroves occur along both coasts of the southern half of Florida. However, a number of Florida's mangrove forests have been destroyed and others are threatened.

6. *Coral Reefs*

- Coral reefs occur in warm and relatively shallow waters of continental shelves and around underwater volcanic mountains, some of which penetrate the surface of the ocean forming islands, such as the Hawaiian Islands. Other coral reefs form atolls, which are semi-circular islands. *Atolls* have been built up from underlying coral reefs that have grown around the top of extinct underwater volcanoes. Some coral reefs occur as *barrier reefs* off the coasts of continents, such as the Great Barrier Reef of Australia.

- Coral reefs are extremely productive ecosystems with rich and diverse varieties of life. Although coral reefs can be well established ecosystems, they are somewhat delicate and are easily destroyed by pollutants, temperature increases, and "over-grazing" by humans.
- As with mangroves and marshes, coral reefs also build land, such as the atolls mentioned above and other barrier islands.
- In the United States coral reefs occur around Florida, off the coast of Freeport, Texas, further out into the Gulf of Mexico, off of the central Georgia coast, and Hawaii. No coral reefs occur along the west coast of the United States, because of the cool waters.

Freshwater Aquatic Ecosystems

1. *Streams and Rivers*

- Streams and rivers are extensive freshwater systems that change in their nature as they flow downstream, which is referred to as a *river continuum*. As streams or tributaries join, the water volume and flow increases. At the same time, the number and variety of species change, which in turn change the overall community metabolism or energy production and use.
- Streams and rivers carry sediments, nutrients, and whatever else they pick up, including fertilizers, wastes, and pollutants, down to the estuaries and saltwater marshes, discussed above. As water flows downstream, the physical and biological make-up of streams act to filter and process much of the material being carried in the water. However, human use of rivers as disposal systems has added so much to the load that the health of river systems has been severely impacted. In addition, the increased waste and pollutant loads are affecting saltwater marshes and oceans to increasing degrees. Almost all of the rivers of the world are severely overloaded with human wastes and pollution.
- As rivers flow downstream, they typically reach maximum biological diversity and productivity somewhere in the middle of their lengths. As they reach the ends near their estuaries, they usually become so heavily loaded in sediments that light does not penetrate far enough to support plant life. From the source to the end of rivers, there is a pattern that moves from a low ratio of plants-to-animals near the beginning of the river, to a higher ratio in the middle of the length, to a return to a low ratio near the end of the river.
- The life in a stream varies as the nature of stream changes along its course. When water is flowing rapidly, there is less sedimentation, more erosion, and rockier bottoms. In such areas, certain types of fish may thrive, while others cannot. Other life forms are those that are adapted to live on and underneath the rocks. Planaria (flatworms) and caddisfly larvae that build little tubular homes out of sand and other materials are

common in these areas. Typically, very few *phytoplankton*—photosynthetic organisms that float in the water—are present along with reduced algae growth. Oxygen is plentiful from the mixing of air and water in the rapids. As the downhill slope of rivers and streams decrease, their width generally increases. As a result, the speed of the water flow slows down, and calm pools and recesses appear along the banks. The slower flow allows for sediments to settle to the bottom, thus changing from rocky to softer and muddier bottoms. Algae, aquatic plants, and phytoplankton growth are more prominent. In these areas of the stream, fish, other aquatic organisms, and amphibians that are adapted to live in calm waters and in the softer and muddier bottoms are common.

- Although sediments are normally created from erosion and carried by rivers, there has been a huge increase in the sedimentation load due to poor agricultural practices, destruction of forestlands, and other human developments. As a result, there has been a huge increase in sediments being deposited into the oceans.

2. *Ponds and Lakes*

- Ponds and lakes occur as both natural and human-made bodies of water. The damming of rivers and streams has created ponds and lakes along almost all river systems. However, dams are also built by beavers and may be created by the build up of dead vegetation and rocks carried by streams.

- The definition of "ponds" varies with location. A pond in Maine may be a couple of miles long, while a body of water only a few hundred yards wide in the arid southwest is referred to as a lake. From the perspective of ecology, *ponds* tend to be smaller and shallower bodies of water that range in age from several weeks as temporary, seasonal ponds to a few hundred years. Most naturally occurring *lakes* were formed during and since the Pleistocene Ice Age or from about 10,000 to 1,800,000 years ago.

- The ecosystems of standing bodies of water, such as ponds and lakes, tend to change at rates that are inversely proportional to their size and depth. The larger and deeper a lake, the slower it may tend to change over longer periods of time. A small pond may undergo rapid algae growth, especially with runoff from agricultural fertilizers, to the point where as the algae dies and decays oxygen begins to deplete. As a result, other organisms in the pond that depend on oxygen die. Over a period of years, the pond may begin to fill in with decayed algae and sediments, and eventually disappear entirely. Such a process is referred to as *eutrophication*. Such eutrophication is a natural process of *succession*, or stages of change in the life of ponds and lakes. However, from the human perspective, as ponds and lakes eutrophicate, their recreational uses are hindered. In addition, their use as a source of drinking water is eliminated due to odor and taste changes that even filters cannot alter.

- Lakes tend to have more distinct zonations, as shown in Figure 3.1. During the warmer parts of the year, the upper layer of water in lakes warms and becomes a distinct layer separated from the cooler water below. This separation is referred to as a *thermocline*. The thermocline acts as a barrier to the flow and exchange of nutrients and oxygen between the lower layer, *hypolimnion*, and the upper layer, *epilimnion*. In the summer, oxygen tends to deplete in the hypolimnion and nutrient shortages for plants occur in the epilimnion. In the winter, this division disappears. In fact, as water cools at the surface to temperatures in the range of 39° F (4° C), where water is most dense, it will move to the bottom setting up *inversion currents*. This process of inversion is important to revitalizing lake ecosystems in most of North America.

3. Freshwater Marshes

- Freshwater marshes function in similar ways to saltwater marshes. They are great sources of food and nutrients for aquatic ecosystems. They also serve as breeding and nursery grounds for a wide variety of aquatic and terrestrial organisms.
- Freshwater marshes often act as ecotones or transitional zones between aquatic and terrestrial ecosystems (see "ecotones" in subsection 3.3).
- Some freshwater marshes have variations in water levels due to their location near the mouths of rivers where they are affected by tidal fluctuations. Others vary with seasonal weather changes and droughts.
- As opposed to saltwater marshes, where fewer plants are able to contend with the stress of high salinity, freshwater marshes can have a wide variety of plants including trees.

  - The *stress of salinity* has to do with osmosis or the transfer of materials across membranes. In *osmosis*, the concentration of dissolved materials in the water on either side of the membrane determines in which direction water will flow to equalize the concentrations. Typically, *terrestrial* and *aquatic* plants have higher concentrations of dissolved materials inside their cells, so water flows into the cells. The cell walls of these cells exert pressure on the cells, which stops osmosis when too much water is taken into the cells. However, if they are exposed to *high saline* water, the water inside of the plant cells will flow out. As a result, the plants die. Only plants that are adapted to contend with this reverse flow can survive in high saline environments, such as saltwater marshes.

- Freshwater marshes help to maintain water tables that are essential as sources of drinking water.
- Many freshwater marshes occur along the rivers where they run into lakes or just before they reach the ocean. One of the largest freshwater marshes in the United States is the Florida Everglades.

4. Forested Wetlands or Swamps

- Swamps and forests that occur in the flood plain are often located near rivers and streams. As opposed to marshes that are inhabited by grasses and shrubs, swamps are inhabited by trees that are adapted to live in very moist to water-covered soils, such as cypress and gum trees. Floodplain forests, on the other hand, cycle between relatively dry to submerged. Winter and spring flooding with dry summers tends to provide for the best growth. The trees that thrive in these environments include maples, elms, ashes, and oaks.

- The Okefenokee Swamp of southern Georgia and northern Florida is the largest swamp in the United States. The Great Dismal Swamp extends from southwest of Norfolk, Virginia into northeastern North Carolina, with Lake Drummond situated in the middle. The bayous in southern Louisiana and other parts of the Gulf coast are swamps.
- As with marshes, swamps are fertile and highly productive areas with a diversity of aquatic and terrestrial organisms.

Terrestrial Ecosystems

1. General Notes On Terrestrial Biomes and Ecosystems

- In each of the following ecosystems, the climax (see subsection 3.4 for information on this term) vegetation is uniform across the particular environment. Exceptions to this uniformity of climax vegetation occur where this vegetation has been destroyed by fire or by human destruction, such as clear-cutting and acid rain.

2. Temperate Deciduous Forests

- Temperate deciduous forests occur north of where tropical forests occur and south of coniferous forests. In North America these forests extend from the Gulf Coast up into Canada through southern Ontario, Quebec, New Brunswick, and Nova Scotia.
- The average year-round temperature is about 50° F (10° C) with a range of –20° F to 84° F (–30° C to 30° C). They receive about 30–60 in (70–150 cm) of rainfall per year, which generally includes snowfall. Temperate forests experience four distinct seasons.
- Temperate forest zonation:

  - *Tree Layer or Canopy* (Overstory)—includes oak, maple, beech, hickory, elm, walnut, basswood, linden, gum, and other deciduous trees. These trees reach heights of 60–100 ft (18–30 meters).
  - *Small Tree and Sapling Layer* (Understory)—includes saplings of the larger trees, as well as smaller trees, such as dogwoods, sassafras trees, and sourwoods. Early blossoms occur before the leaves in the tree layer appear.
  - *Shrub Layer*—includes rhododendrons, azaleas, mountain laurel, and huckleberries. This layer thrives in shaded areas.
  - *Herb Layer*—ferns, certain grasses, wildflowers, and berries. This layer grows quickly in the spring while a lot of sunlight is available, before the leaves appear on the trees.
  - *Ground Layer*—includes mosses, club mosses, lichens, fungi, and leaf litter. Mosses, lichens, and bracket fungi live also live on tree trunks.

- Some forest animals hibernate during the winter, while others continue to forage for food or migrate elsewhere. These animals may include large herbivores, such as deer, moose, and elk, and large omnivores and carnivores, such as bears, wolves, bobcats, and cougars. Other smaller herbivores include skunks, a variety of birds (e.g., sparrows, nuthatches), squirrels, chipmunks, mice and rats, beavers, rabbits, and hedgehogs (porcupines). Other smaller omnivores and carnivores include raccoons, foxes, weasels, voles and moles, coyotes, crows, ravens, hawks, opossums, eagles, owls, salamanders, lizards, frogs, toads, and snakes. A wide variety of invertebrates reside in all layers of these forests, including a variety of worms, insects, spiders, and other arthropods.

- The trees' leaves change color and drop off in the fall. This loss of leaves by the trees and shrubs help to build up fertile soils. The soil layer is deeper than in coniferous forests and provides for the deeper root systems necessary for the larger deciduous trees.

3. Boreal Coniferous Forests or Taiga

- Boreal coniferous forests extend across the northern latitudes of North America, Europe, and Asia—generally between latitudes 45° N and 65° N.
- The average annual temperatures range from 23° F to 41° F (−5° C to +5° C) with long, very cold winters and short summers. Precipitation averages 15–20 in (37.5–50 cm), which is mostly in the form of snow. There may only be 50 to 100 frost-free days per year in these forests.
- As mentioned in Section 2, coniferous trees are adapted for sun angles that are low in the sky, as well as for dropping heavy loads of snow in the winter. The dark colored bark and needles also provide for heat absorption from sunlight. In addition, the root systems do not need deep soil. They do not have taproots, but rely on extensive shallow roots to provide stability.
- Pine, fir, and spruce trees tend to be dominant, with a few deciduous shrubs and trees, such as birch, aspen, and alder. The soils and bodies of water in these forests tend to be acidic due to the tannic acid in the needles that fall.
- A variety of mosses, lichens, ferns, and small shrubs characterize the plant growth near the ground. Wetlands in low-lying areas tend to be bogs covered with sphagnum moss.
- The herbivorous animals in these forests include elk, moose, deer, beavers, hares, squirrels, porcupines, lemmings, and voles. The carnivores include Amur tigers (Siberian tigers in Asia), lynxes, bobcats, wolverines, martins, minks, ermines, and sables. The most recognizable omnivore is the grizzly bear. Among the birds, seed-eaters, such as sparrows and finches, and omnivores, such as ravens, tend to take up year-round residence. Insect-eaters, such as warblers, migrate south after breeding season. Other birds that tend to migrate south in the winter include owls, woodpeckers, sparrows, finches, ravens, and grosbeaks. Some of the seedeaters may stay over winters if a lot of cones are produced during the preceding summer. Many insects and other invertebrates live in these forests. For people, early springs are most uncomfortable, with huge populations of biting black flies, no-see-ums, and mosquitoes. However, many other insects thrive during the short spring, summer, and fall seasons. There are also a variety of reptiles and amphibians.

4. *Alpine and Temperate Coniferous Forests*

- Alpine coniferous forests resemble the boreal coniferous forests except that they tend to have very different undergrowth. While the boreal forests are rich with mosses, lichens, and ferns, alpine forests tend to have very few of these plants and lichens. The soil in alpine forests tends to be much shallower. In fact, much of the landscape is very rocky. In lower altitude temperate coniferous forests, the landscapes can be rocky or sandy. The "Sand Barrens" of central New Jersey and the rocky, shallow soil pine forests of Maine and Nova Scotia are examples of low altitude temperate coniferous forests.
- These forests also occur at higher altitudes in mountainous regions south of the boreal forests.
- Climatic conditions in these forests range from cold winters to hot summers with variable amounts of precipitation. Some of these forests may have large amount of snowfall while others get very little snow. Many of these forests may have to withstand periods of drought and periods of greater than normal precipitation. In some regions, these forests have historically needed periods of fire, which are now suppressed by human efforts.
- Many of these forests may have mixes of deciduous trees, including birches, aspens, and oaks.

5. *Semi-Evergreen Tropical Forests*

- Located in tropical and subtropical regions, these forests have a mix of evergreen and broadleaf trees and experience alternations of rainy and dry seasons. In these forests, the deciduous trees may lose their leaves in order to prevent water loss through their leaves during the dry seasons.
- These forests are often on thin rocky and/or sandy soils. Examples of these forests include those in southern Florida and through the Florida Keys, many Caribbean Islands, and throughout Mexico, Central America, and South America.

6. *Temperate Rainforests*

- Temperate rainforests occur along the west coast of North America, from southeastern Alaska to mid-California, and a few other temperate locations around the world along coastal mountains where temperatures are moderated, rain occurs regularly, and the air is always humid. There are a few interior continental locations that get enough rain to provide for temperate rain forests, such as in the Rocky Mountains of British Columbia, northern Idaho, northwestern Montana, and the southern Appalachian Mountains in North Carolina, Georgia, and Tennessee.
- The average annual precipitation is about 57 in (140 cm) with average annual temperature between 39° and 54° F (4° C and 12° C).

7. *Evergreen Tropical Rainforests*

- When we think of the typical rainforest, we usually think of evergreen tropical rainforests. These rainforests occur around the equator in southern Mexico, Central

American, northern and eastern South America, central west Africa and Madagascar, and southeast Asia and the South Pacific islands.

- Yearly rainfall averages between 69 and 79 in (175–200 cm) with maximum rainfall amounts reaching 263 in (660 cm) or almost 22 ft (6.7 m)! Throughout the year, the temperatures are above 64° F (18° C) with maximums reaching 122° F (50° C).
- Tropical rainforests are rich in plant life that has provided sources for modern medicines. Over 80% of the world's biodiversity occurs in rainforests. Banana, coffee, chocolate, mango, papaya, avocado, and many other fruits and hardwoods were first found in rainforests. Most of these products are now cultivated in other areas (some of which were once rainforests but are now agricultural lands).
- There are typically five layers in tropical rainforests:

  - *Emergent Layer*—includes a few very tall trees that emerge above the dominant canopy layer. These trees can reach heights of 146 ft (45 m) to 260 ft (80 m). Eagles, bats, insects, and monkeys live in this layer.
  - *Canopy Layer*—a dense layer that prevents a lot of plant growth near the ground level due to the blocking of sunlight. If this canopy is destroyed for some reason, an undergrowth of vines, shrubs, and small trees takes over, creating what we typically call a *jungle*. Snakes, toucans, and tree frogs are among the animals that live in this layer.
  - *Understory*—a layer of trees with very large leaves that maximize their surface area to capture what little sunlight penetrates the canopy. These trees are generally less than 12 ft (3 m) tall. Huge numbers of insects live in this layer along with tree frogs and cats, such as leopards and jaguars.
  - *Shrub Layer*—includes very few plants due to the general lack of sunlight.
  - *Floor Layer*—is a very dark layer with almost no plant growth. This layer is primarily a decomposition layer. When leaves fall they decay quickly—within weeks. Insects, decomposing bacteria, invertebrates—including giant anteaters—reside here. In contrast to temperate forests and their fertile, humus rich soils, the floor layer of tropical rainforests are quite infertile. The rapid decay prevents humus build-up and much of the nutrients are leached out of the soils and washed away.

- Rainforests are being destroyed rapidly for use as agricultural land. Most of this destruction is by burning, which just adds to the carbon load in the atmosphere. You can use the Google Earth tool to explore the inland areas of Brazil, where most of the area was once covered by rainforests. You can see that vast expanses of this land are now mostly used for cattle, destined for fast food restaurants.

8. *Temperate Grasslands*

- Temperate grasslands occur in the interior of continents. The soils are rich in nutrients from decaying vegetation, which also helps to hold the soil together. The plants of these grasslands include grasses, wildflowers, and other herbs. Very few, if any, shrubs and trees are found naturally.

- Most of the rain in grasslands occurs during the late spring and early summer with an average annual accumulation of rain between 20 and 35 inches (50–89 cm).
- The temperatures during the winter can drop to –40° F (–40° C). During the summer, temperatures can exceed 100° F (38° C). The lack of rainfall during the summers along with the high temperatures can lead to destructive wildfires caused by lightning or human carelessness.
- The mammals that inhabit grasslands include: gazelles, zebras, rhinoceroses, and lions in Africa; wild horses, wolves, prairie dogs, deer, rabbits, mice, coyotes, foxes, skunks, and badgers in North America. A variety of quails, sparrows, hawks, and owls are also found in grasslands, along with a large variety of insects and other invertebrates.
- In North America, the grasslands are prairies known as the *Great Plains* with tall grasses. In Asia, the grasslands are known as *steppes* with short grasses. These grasslands have been used for grazing and farming. Overuse combined with dry summers has led to dust storms in these areas.

9. *Tropical Grasslands and Savannahs*

- Savannahs are grasslands with scattered trees. They occur in areas with hot climates, such as in central Africa, Australia, South America, and India.
- These areas have six to eight months of heavy rainfall followed by very dry conditions, where wildfires keep these areas from growing into rainforests. Most savannahs receive between 20 and 50 inches (50–127 cm) of rain during the wet season, but some receive less.
- The mammals found in savannahs include lions, giraffes, zebras, elephants, and hyenas in Africa; kangaroos in Australia; and various gophers, ground squirrels, mice, and moles in most savannahs.

10. *Chaparrals*

- Chaparrals are arid locations with mild winters and hot, very dry summers. These occur in southwest United States, western South America, western Australia, South Africa, and along the Mediterranean coast.
- Temperatures range from about 50° F (10° C) in the winter to over 104° F (40° C) in the summer. Conditions can be so hot and dry in the summers that wildfires are common. These fires tend to burn and move quickly.
- These areas tend to be sandy and rocky and can be relatively flat to mountainous.
- Vegetation is characterized by tough, low shrubs, with leathery leaves that hold moisture.
- Animals include coyotes, jack rabbits, mule deer, as well as various rodents, reptiles, and insects.

11. *Deserts*

Deserts cover about 20% of the surface of the Earth. There are two basic types, hot deserts and cold deserts.

- *Hot Deserts*

  - Average temperatures range from about 68° F to over 122° F (10° C to 50° C). Rainfall is generally less than 6 in (15 cm) per year. Much of this rainfall is not absorbed and runs off. Heavy rains may result in flooding, because of the lack of absorption.
  - Vegetation varies from none or very sparse to fairly dense coverage. The types of vegetation range from scrubby brushes to cacti, succulents, and larger shrubs and trees adapted for hot, arid conditions.
  - Animals include snakes and lizards, rodents, and coyotes.
  - These deserts usually occur between the Tropics of Cancer and Capricorn, but can extend further towards the poles as with the deserts in the southwest United States.

- *Cold Deserts*

  - Average temperatures range from well below freezing in the winter to 77° F (25° C) in the summer. Precipitation varies from snow in the winter to rain in the summer. The average annual precipitation amounts to between 6 and 10 inches (67–107 cm).
  - Vegetation tends to be limited to grasses and small shrubs.
  - Animals include antelope, rabbits, rodents, and insects.
  - These deserts usually occur in northern areas of North America, Europe, and Asia.

12. *Arctic and Alpine Tundra*

- These ecosystems occur in arctic and high altitude alpine areas, where snow and ice melts during the summer.
- The average annual temperatures are around −18° F (−28° C). The winters are characterized by long nights, which can last 24 hours, and temperatures less than −90° F (−70° C). Summers have long, up to 24 hour, days and temperatures as high as 60° F (16° C).
- Precipitation is mostly in the form of snow, with annual averages between 6 and 10 inches (67–107 cm) (in liquid form).
- Permafrost or permanently frozen soils are covered by shallow soils that thaw and support the growth of vegetation during the short summers.
- Vegetation includes grasses, wildflowers, low shrubs, mosses, lichens, and sedges.
- Animals include bears, wolves, wolverines, foxes, bears, caribou, deer, rodents, hares, and many different types of insects.

Domesticated Ecosystems

1. *Agro-Ecosystems*

- These ecosystems are those that have been cultivated for farming and ranching. The soils tend to be tilled with varying degrees of chemical treatment depending on the farming techniques used.

- Animals include birds, reptiles, wolves, coyotes, deer, and various insects. Some of these inhabitants or visitors to farmlands are considered to be pests. Insects may be killed using insecticides.

2. *Urban, Techno-Industrial Ecosystems*

- These ecosystems include cities and other areas of industrial development.
- City ecosystems include varieties of plants. Many of the trees may be transplants from other locations and not native to the area. However, many grasses and flowering plants grow in various locations where there is any soil in which to send out roots, including cracks in concrete pavement. Parks and small backyard and rooftop gardens also support various types of plants.
- Animals include birds that take up residence in cities, such as pigeons and sparrows; rodents; raccoons; skunks; lizards; amphibians; insects; and feral cats and dogs.

3. *Rural Techno-Ecosystems*

- These ecosystems occur around smaller towns and villages in rural settings, along highways and railroads, along power and utility line easements, and natural resources extraction.
- Vegetation includes those species that have grown back after initial disturbances. These plant species may have to tolerate continued stresses, such as increased salt content from winter run-off, as well as pollutant effects from petrochemicals and other chemicals. Other vegetation may be introduced through landscaping efforts.
- Animals include those that pass through and are able to survive with the additional stresses placed on them by living close to human activity. However, construction interferes with natural patterns of movement.

Key Idea 3.4 Features of the Biosphere and Its Ecosystems

There are other features of the biosphere that are important to understanding the dynamics of and relationships within the environment. These features, discussed below, include time, space, gradients, zonation, ecotones, habitat, niche, and ecological succession.

Time

When thinking about ecology, we need to realize that change over time is a fundamental characteristic of our world. Interactions among organisms, linear and cyclical change in environments and environmental conditions, the cycling of materials, and flow of energy all take place over various periods of time. As you sit reading this, there is a continuous flow of materials and energy taking place all around us. During this same period of time, organisms are interacting with each other and with their environments. They are eating, reproducing, respiring, digesting, eliminating and excreting waste materials, which in turn contribute to the flow of energy and cycling of materials. Everything that is happening is occurring over various scales of time, ranging from very rapid changes to very slow. Even though global warming is occurring much more rapidly than predicted, these changes are fairly slow compared to those changes involved with the reproduction of bacteria. Other changes, like the extinction of species and the erosion of landforms, may be occurring over even longer periods of time than what appears to be happening with global warming.

Space

The levels of organization discussed previously all relate to various scales of space. The study of ecology focuses on these scales of space and the interactions between spaces, such as those between ecosystems and how ecosystems affect the biosphere. Changes in spaces occur over time. Some changes are cyclical, while others are linear. Examples of cyclical changes to spaces include:

- the periodic flooding of specific environments, such as those in some areas of the rainforests along the Amazon River and in the lowlands of the central United States;
- annual snow and ice coverage in the northern latitudes of North America;
- tidal areas along the coastal regions, where high and low tides move in and out over land in a twice daily cycle;
- periodic fires across areas of the western United States.

All of these cyclical changes are natural occurrences, which are integral parts of the ecology of these areas. However, from a human-centric point of view, each of these cyclical changes is "problematic." People move into flood plains and then suffer the consequences. While the floods help to fertilize the soil in flood plains, they destroy people's properties. Snow and ice are problematic for people in a number of ways, yet this frozen precipitation helps to provide moisture for spring and summer growth, shelter for animals that live in these environments during the winter, and may be needed for seeds to grow the following spring. Tides circulate nutrients and waste materials, as well as eggs and larvae and planktonic organisms. At the same time, they can create problems for buildings and other structures when they are exaggerated during storms.

Examples of more linear changes to spaces include:

- developers filling in a marshland areas to build homes and businesses;
- volcanic activity creating a new island;
- building a dam for hydro-electric power generation, while changing a primarily terrestrial ecosystem in to an aquatic ecosystem.

Many changes that appear to be linear may in fact be cyclical at a very large scale. Even the volcanic building of a new terrestrial ecosystem or island may be cyclical over a very long period of time. The same cyclical scale view may apply to changes to environments that are made by people. Filling in a marshland or building a dam are changes that are long-term in comparison to what would naturally occur if these human-made changes did not take place. However, if left unmaintained, the dam will likely fall apart and return the area to how it was before.

Gradients

Environments and environmental conditions are not consistent across space and time. We can look at these conditions as gradients in temperature, moisture, humidity, amounts of sunlight, and other factors. These condition gradients may vary depending upon the location. The temperature gradients in the mountains of the west may show a daily change in temperature of 40 degrees or more between day and night whereas the daily temperature gradient along the southeastern coast of the United States may vary by only a few degrees. Yearly gradations in temperature vary as well, with more pronounced variations in the northern latitudes.

In addition to variations and gradients in conditions, environments themselves can be characterized by gradients. The gradients of terrains can affect the nature of communities and habitats. Sharp gradations in the terrain, such as cliffs and canyons, are going to limit the types of organisms that can live there. Certain birds and plants can thrive in such conditions, but other animals and plants cannot live in these areas. Gradations in the terrain also can affect the erosion in these areas, as well as the dynamics of water absorption.

Gradations between ecosystems also create different dynamics in the interactions between them (see "Ecotones," below). Where ecotones are sharper borders, gradient borders may extend some distance. Shallow coastlines with an intertidal area that may extend hundreds of yards will alternate between submersion in water and exposure to air. In other areas, there may be a rather steep slope but very high tides, such as in the Bay of Fundi, located between Nova Scotia and New Brunswick (Canada) just north of Maine (US), where high and low tides fluctuate by about 50 ft (15 m). At this location, you could drive by a dock and see a boat gently floating next to the dock at one moment, then return a few hours later and see the boat tilted on the ground 50 ft (15 m) below the dock.

Rivers and streams generally have two basic gradients. One is the gradient down which the streams flow. The steeper the gradient, the faster the water flows. The second gradient is the transition from the surrounding land to the stream environment. These transition gradients can vary in steepness, in composition, and in vegetation. Different organisms live in these transitional gradients than those in the midst of the stream. In addition, the types of organisms vary depending on the transitional gradients in which they live. Banks of streams with lots of aquatic vegetation will have very different organism living among the vegetation than the banks that are rocky and exposed to the rapid currents of the stream.

Zonations

Zonations are more distinct changes along a gradient that may occur either within an ecosystem or between ecosystems. Some examples of what we may call macro-zonations are depicted in Figure 3.1. The top example shows the zones of a lake ecosystem. The middle example depicts the zones in an oceanic biome. The bottom example in the figure shows the zonation of various terrestrial ecosystems across the landscape of Arizona. Other terrestrial macro-zonations include those that appear as you move inland from the coast of an ocean (see Figure 3.2) and from riverbanks and lakeshores.

What we can call micro-zonations are those that occur within the bigger macro-zonations. Figure 3.3 provides an example of how the transitional area between land and the ocean is divided into smaller zones.

Lake Ecosystem Zonation

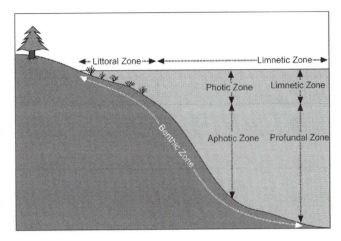

Ocean Biome Zonation

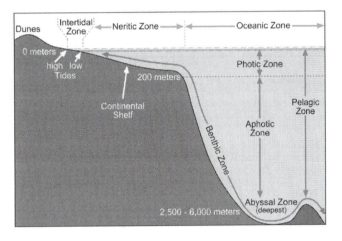

Terrestrial Landscape Zonation – Arizona Example

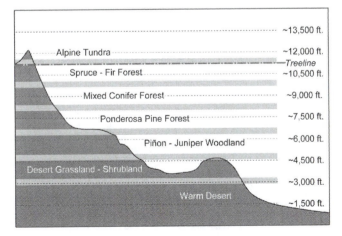

Figure 3.1 Examples of ecological zonation in an ecosystem, biome, and landscape.

Coastal Zonation

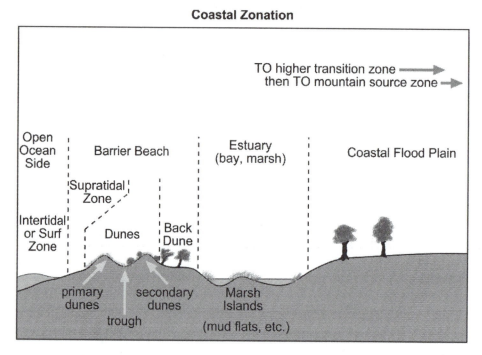

Figure 3.2 Coastal zonation typical of the east coast of the United States.

Intertidal (Micro) Zonation

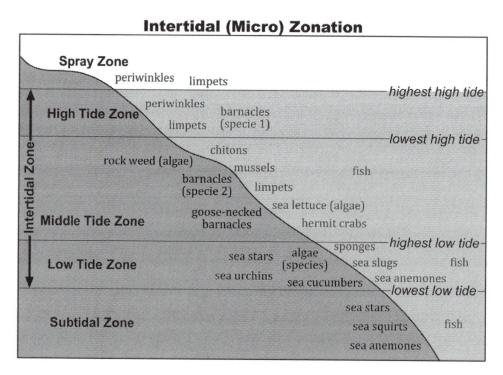

Figure 3.3 An example of micro-zonation in the intertidal zone.

In general, zonations are transitions from one habitat or ecosystem to another. In addition to differences in the organisms, zones also play important functional roles. Some examples of these *functions* include the following:

- *Physical features* can provide *protection for habitats* and communities on other sides of these transitional areas.
  Example: dunes provide protection from storm tides and other storm effects for terrestrial and marshland habitats.

- *Characteristic vegetation* can provide *habitat protection.*
  Example: grasses on dunes provide protection from wind and water erosion.

- A great deal of *food energy is cycled* through these areas, since these transition zones are often areas where different populations of organisms meet and cross-over between zones.
  Example: tidal zones serve as energy source areas, where dead materials wash up and decay, from which the rest of the food webs extend to both the marine and terrestrial ecosystems.

As you may have noticed from Figures 3.1 to 3.2, different organisms live in different zones. This differentiation of organisms is often what defines a particular zone. However, these differences are not just arbitrary. Each zone is characterized by certain environmental conditions, such as climate, temperature, moisture, substrate material (soil, rock, sand), and other features such as waves and tides in ocean shoreline zones. The organisms that live in different zones are adapted for survival in these areas (see Section 2 for a thorough discussion of adaptation). For example, a periwinkle that lives just above and below the high tide zone is adapted to:

- be able to cling to the rocky substrate with its "foot";
- withstand the pounding of waves with its shell;
- breathe both in and out of water;
- lay eggs in ways that they are not destroyed by environmental conditions;
- eat by scraping algae and other material off of the rocks with a rasping structure called a *radula.*

In Figure 3.1, the organisms living in the hot deserts are adapted to survive in arid conditions where temperatures can vary from below freezing to above 115 F (47° C). Typically, the vegetation is characterized by thick and leathery leaves and stalks that prevent evaporative loss of water, such as with cacti, succulents, and certain types of shrubs. Grasses that live in these desert areas can withstand long periods of dormancy. As you move upward through the zones, the arid climate may persist, but the temperatures decrease at about 4 F (15.5° C) per 1,000 ft (305 m) in altitude. At the same time, variations in temperature between night and day average around 40 degrees. Seasonal changes occur with the potential for large amounts of snow, and thus more moisture. Plants in the higher altitude zones are adapted to survive alternating dry and wet periods with large variations in temperature. At the same time, as altitude increases, atmospheric pressure drops along with a corresponding drop in oxygen concentration. The angle of the sun also changes in the same way as it does if we go to higher latitudes. As a result, plants need to "capture" sunlight that varies from low angles to high angles. Pine and other fir trees (see Section 2) are well adapted for both arid conditions and low sun angles. In general, the variations in zones are characterized by variations in environmental features and conditions and by organisms that are adapted to these variations.

Ecotones

Ecotones are somewhat sharp and distinct borders between different ecosystems. We often see them between an open field and a forest. This border is an area where the two ecosystems interact, which results in this area having properties that don't exist in either of the adjacent ecosystems. An example would be a grassy back dune area and the dense shrub growth at the beginning of a coastal forest. Other examples of ecotones include the transition zones between:

- forests and prairies;
- intertidal zones;
- alpine tundra and fir forest;
- river and land;
- school yard and surrounding forest.

Certain animals thrive in these transition zones. For example, dragonflies and many other insects lay eggs in the water and mate on or above dry land. In between intertidal zones, some animals can tolerate more time out of water—for example, barnacles do better than oysters out of water. In such intertidal zones, some animals are limited to particular zones, while others move back and forth. Frogs and salamanders spend their time moving back and forth from the aquatic to the terrestrial ecosystems. Some marine snails that live in marshes move up and down the marsh grasses along with the tides. These snails eat the debris that is brought in with the tides. As a result of such movements of organisms across these boundaries, we find that ecotones are important areas for the movement of energy and materials between ecosystems. In some instances, greater numbers and more kinds of animals are found in ecotones than on either side. Wildlife managers refer to this phenomenon as the *edge effect*. When you have the opportunity to spend a little time along an ecotone, look at how many birds, squirrels, and other animals you see along the edges as opposed to in the interiors of the environments on either side.

Habitat

Habitat is a somewhat confusing term, which tends not to be used all that frequently among ecologists. In general, the term "habitat" refers to just the environment in which specific organisms can be found. We might find an earthworm in our backyard garden, which is its habitat. That same *species* of earthworm can be found in different habitats, but each *individual* organism has its own habitat. On the other hand, some organisms move from one habitat to another, such as some species of birds. Gulls are quite happy living along a specific coastline region, eating whatever they can scavenge from what the tides bring in along the coastline or from the oyster and mussels they snatch and drop on highways to break the shells. At the same time, these same gulls find garbage dumps to be extraordinary food sources. In fact, gulls are quite adept at living in a variety of habitats.

Niche

Where habitat refers to the *place* where a particular organism is found, *niche* (pronounced as [1] "*nitch*" or [2] "*neesh*") refers to what the particular organism *does* in the ecosystem. We can think of niche as the organism's occupation or function in the ecosystem, just as your job or function may be to help children learn and develop. There are basically two ways to think of niche:

1. From the perspective of the organism → as the *function or "job" of that organism* in the ecosystem.

    – We can examine a number of organisms and talk about their niches.
    – In this instance, we link an organism to its niche.

2. From the perspective of the ecosystem → as the *functional position that is occupied by one or more species of organisms.*

    – We can look at the ecosystem and list the niches necessary for the ecosystem to function.
    – In this instance, we can find organisms that fill particular niches.

Some of the more generalized niches can be those associated with food webs, such as producers, consumers, and decomposers. However, many more niches exist, such as changing certain chemical compounds into others that are more useful—an example is *nitrogen fixation*, where the inert form of nitrogen (N_2) is converted into nitrates, ammonia, and other forms of useable nitrogen. Other niches include:

- photosynthesizing;
- absorbing water and releasing water vapor into the atmosphere;
- providing soil stability;
- providing shelter for certain other organisms;
- aerating the soil.

Although some niches can be occupied by only one species in a specific environment, some niches can be occupied by multiple species. In addition, some organisms may occupy more than one niche. For example an earthworm:

- functions as a *decomposer* by eating material in the soil and producing nutrient materials for plants and other organisms;
- helps to *loosen and aerate* the soils in ways that benefit plant growth;
- helps to *increase the amount of moisture soils can hold*;
- *increases the rate at which water is absorbed* in the soil.

These functions benefit plant and fungal growth. In addition, soil that absorbs more water at faster rates prevents some degree of flooding and erosion.

One of the current problems we have involves "*invasive species.*" These species of organisms have been brought from one environment to another. The problem arises when these new species out-compete the local residents for the same niche. A common example is the *zebra mussel* that has replaced other organisms and clogs water pipes and other structures in freshwater lakes and streams across North America.

Invasive species take over niches and can even change the nature and chemistry of environments.

Ecological Succession

Ecological succession refers to a sequence of changes that occurs when new environments are created or when an existing habitat is destroyed by fire or some other means. In coastal regions, the local habitats are undergoing constant change, most often occurring after major storms. In some circumstances, a new "beach pond" may be created above the tidal level. At first, there may be very little evidence of plant and animal life anywhere in the vicinity of this new pond. Over time, two basic changes start to take place:

- new species start to grow and inhabit the pond and its surroundings;
- there is an increase in the diversity of species.

Depending upon the particular habitat, these two changes usually occur in a specific sequence. As new species move in and take up residence, there is an increase in the amount of dead and waste material that begins to build up. In the pond context, the muddy bottom and surrounding areas begin to build up a richer sediment and soil base that provides habitats for other organisms.

With each successive change in the soils and sediments, comes a greater variety of organisms. However, the succession stops when a *climax* community is achieved. These climax communities are characteristic of certain regions and represent a relatively stable ecosystem. In the mountains of the northeast United States, the climax community is a mixed hardwood or deciduous forest. A typical succession to climax community often starts with rocky outcroppings. The first species to arrive may be lichens, then mosses. Each of these "capture" soil in the wind and help to break up the surfaces of the rocks. The next ones to arrive are grasses and wildflowers, then small shrubs. As the soil builds up, fir trees begin to grow in the shallow soils. Eventually, hardwoods take up root and out-compete the firs and many shrubs. This ecological succession follows a sequence of changes that eventually result in the establishment of a stable ecosystem. The time it takes to reach this point depends on the location, conditions, and the climax community for that area.

The same sort of succession takes place after devastating fires or other major changes. However, in such cases, the soil has already been built up. The beginning of such *secondary successions* usually start with different species from those that had been part of the original succession. In the beginning, these species are often hardy weeds and briars, followed by the types of species that were part of the original succession.

Key Idea 3.5 Dynamics of Ecological Systems or Ecosystems

As we have seen so far from the previous discussion, an ecosystem is composed of complex sets of relationships between the physical and chemical environment, including the sun, atmosphere, and biological make-up. Many of these relationships are composed of functional interactions, such as earthworms aerating and fertilizing the soils so that certain plants can grow, which in turn provide stability to the soil, and oxygen and food for herbivores. All of these functional relationships create the vast web of ecosystems. These webs or networks of relationships create stability at each level of organization, whether this is at the level of community, ecosystem, landscape, biome, or biosphere. However, if one tree's photosynthesis changes, at the organism level, it is certainly dramatic and probably a sign of impending doom for the tree, but it makes little difference to the forest, at the ecosystem level, and even less of a difference at the biome or biosphere levels. Such diminishing effects have to do with the stability of hierarchically nested systems. Minor changes at one level have little effect at higher levels. However, a major change at a lower level can have escalating effects at higher levels. We are just now seeing how changes at lower levels of organization are affecting multiple biomes and the biosphere, such as with global warming.

When we look at the level of ecosystem, in particular, we should pay attention to the interactions and relationships among the five basic parts of these systems listed below.

1. *Properties*

   • Properties are the physical objects, states, features, or substances in ecosystems. Such objects, states, and substances can vary over time and location.
   Examples include a specific species of organism, the geological features, or chemical make-up of the soil or water.

2. *Forces*

   • In the context of ecology, force is not the same as the force discussed in physics (see Section 4). In ecology, force has to do with some "thing" or quality that affects properties of the ecosystem.
   Examples include energy from the sun, human encroachment on a particular environment, rising water levels, and long-term droughts.

3. *Flow Pathways*

   • Flow pathways describe how:

     – particular forces enter and flow through the system;
     – particular properties interact to form new properties;
     – and where the outputs of this system travel.

   Example of a flow pathway involves:

     – the energy of the sun entering the leaf of a plant;
     – this energy is used to produce sugar as stored energy;

    – this stored energy is transferred when the plant is eaten by a herbivore;

    – the energy is stored in various ways after digestion;

    – the herbivore is eaten by a carnivore;

    – this carnivore may be eaten by yet another carnivore;

    – eventually the carnivore dies and decomposes by the actions of bacteria and other organisms.

4. *Interactions*

- The dynamics of how two or more properties *interact* in a specific location can result in the production of a new property.
  Example of this interaction can involve the introduction of an invasive species like the *Tamarix* or salt cedar (property #1) along a specific river in New Mexico:

  – The light from the sun (force) plus the water (property #2) along the river lead to the salt cedar's rapid growth and spread.
  – These interactions result in the new property (#3) of high saline soils along the river.

5. *Feedback Loops*

- If we continue with the previous example of the *Tamarix,* the increase in the salinity of the soils acts as a feedback loop to the overall property of soils, which in turn interacts with other plants (properties #4 and higher). The results can be death and disappearance of those plants along the entire area. This disappearance of plants can in turn affect (as a feedback loop) the habitats of certain animals. Some animal populations may increase due to the change, while other populations decrease. Such feedback loops are paths through which some sort of information travels backwards through the system. The resulting feedback can produce new effects or it can change or modulate the particular process—a *modulation effect*—that has been taking place.
  Example of a modulation effect involves a pigeon population. The pigeons lay their eggs, but find that too many survive due to a low predation rate (a force). As a result, they abandon enough eggs to modulate the population. If too many eggs are eaten by predators, then they lay more eggs.

Another key concept that is related to these five components ecosystems involves homeostasis. This concept is discussed below.

Homeostasis

At the beginning of Section 3.5, we looked at how the death of a single tree in a forest ecosystem has little effect on the forest or the biosphere as a whole. This sense of "balancing" the effects has to do with sets of processes and feedback loops that make adjustments to changes at lower levels of the hierarchy in order to maintain a particular balance in the ongoing systems at higher levels. These sets of processes and feedback loops result in what is called *homeostasis.* At a "micro" level, homeostatic systems keep each of our bodies alive. We contract an infection and our bodies start sending out defensive cells and raise body temperature. Our body temperature gets too high and we sweat to try to maintain a constant body temperature. All of our bodies' systems operate together to maintain a reasonably constant internal environment. At a "macro" level, the biosphere and the level of systems below it operate to try to maintain a reasonably constant environment. From the early history of life on Earth, bacterial photosynthesis helped to create and maintain a homeostatic environment within which other life forms arose. Even today, bacteria are essential components of every ecosystem on Earth; and they continue to function in the regulation of systems at all levels of the ecological hierarchy.

Key Idea 3.6 Sequences and Cycles—Life, Energy, and Materials

Almost everything that happens in the biosphere is part of a cycle. Cycles serve to maintain life-supporting systems in the biosphere. They cycle materials throughout all parts of ecosystems, from "storage" to "usage" and back again. As these materials move through the cycles, they are changed from one form or state to another. Before we discuss the specific cycles, let's look at their general characteristics and features. These *biogeochemical cycles* move materials from some form and location for storage to some form and location for use by organisms either in fairly distinct sequences or through a variety of pathways. Certain cycles tend primarily to use one or the other of these *storage* or *reservoir* locations, which are: *atmosphere— gaseous reservoirs* or *soil—sediment reservoirs.*

Nitrogen Cycle—Primarily an Atmospheric Reservoir

Nitrogen is an extremely important element for all forms of life. Every protein and all nucleic acids, such as DNA and RNA, are constructed with nitrogen as a basic building block. At the same time, nitrogen is the largest elemental compound in the atmosphere and appears as N_2. However, organisms cannot use nitrogen in this form. We breathe in nitrogen with every breath, but it is only the oxygen that we utilize. Atmospheric nitrogen must be changed into usable forms through a process called *nitrogen fixation.* As atmospheric nitrogen gets into the soil and water mostly through rainfall, certain bacteria and algae use a specialized enzyme to split apart the N_2 and combine each nitrogen atom with four hydrogen atoms to form ammonia (NH_4^+). Another mechanism for nitrogen fixation involves lightning, which converts atmospheric nitrogen into ammonia and nitrates (NO_3^-). Although some plants can use ammonia, ammonia tends to be toxic to most organisms.

However, bacteria come to the rescue again with processes called *nitrification.* In nitrification, bacteria convert ammonia into nitrites (NO_2^-) and then into nitrates, which are taken up by plants. As plants, animals, and other organisms die, bacteria come into play as the primary decomposers. During the process of decomposition, these bacteria produce ammonia, through a process called *ammonification,* which links back to the nitrification phase of this cycle. The last phase of the nitrogen cycle involves nitrogen making its way back into the atmosphere through a process called *denitrification.* If you haven't guessed, the key players in this process are, once again, bacteria. These denitrifying bacteria are mostly found in wet soils, especially in wetlands and areas that have been flooded, where oxygen is difficult to get. In order to produce the needed oxygen, these bacteria break down nitrates (NO_3^-) into oxygen

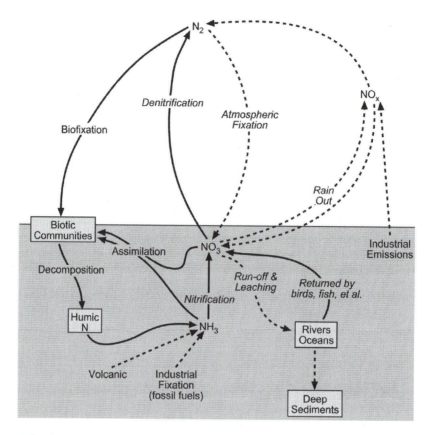

Figure 3.4 The nitrogen cycle with a primary atmospheric reservoir.

and nitrogen ($2 NO_3^- \rightarrow N_2 + 3 O_2$). The nitrogen returns to the atmosphere and the oxygen is made available to a variety of microorganisms in the soil. A representation of the nitrogen cycle appears in Figure 3.4.

Carbon Cycle—Primarily an Atmospheric Reservoir

As with the other material cycles described here—nitrogen, sulfur, and phosphorus cycles—the carbon cycle involves a substance that is a critical building block of all life. Everything in our bodies and in all living things is made of carbon. Carbon as the fundamental structural component of life has some incredibly flexible attributes. Because carbon has four bonds, it can form all kinds of attachments, from a single carbon atom with four hydrogen atoms to complex strings, rings, lattices, and spheres. The structures of all living things are based on carbon's ability to create all kinds of forms. At the same time, carbon has been implicated in a number of environment issues, including global warming.

If you notice in Figure 3.5, there are two types of intersecting carbon cycles. One part dips down towards the bottom of the figure, where it says "peat, coal, oil, and sedimentary rocks." This cycle is the *geological carbon cycle* that operates very slowly over very long periods of time—in the hundreds of millions of years. As dead organisms decay and become part of the soil, this soil in turn is covered by new soil. As you will see in Section 4, these soils are eventually built up so that lower layers are compressed and form sedimentary rocks. Some of this

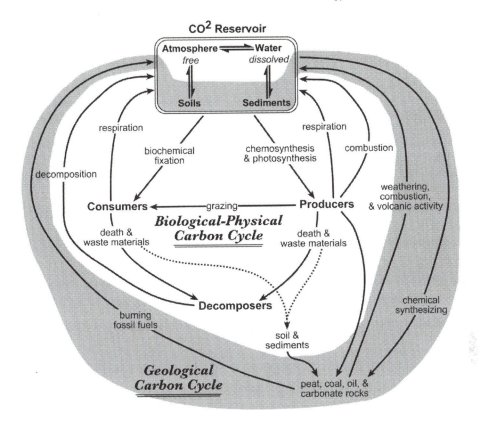

Figure 3.5 The carbon cycle with a primary atmospheric reservoir.

material turns into peat, coal, oil, and gas, while others turn into carbonate rocks, like lime-stone. The reservoir for this cycle is in the rocks and other sedimentary materials.

The second cycle, the *biological and physical carbon cycle,* operates much more quickly, over periods that range from days to years. We're an intimate part of this cycle with every breath and nearly every action we take. The major reservoir of carbon in this cycle is in the atmos-phere as carbon dioxide (CO_2). In this form, carbon is not particularly useful to organisms. In fact, in too great a quantity, carbon dioxide is poisonous. We are now finding more problems with excessive carbon dioxide, which we will discuss shortly.

In the biological and physical carbon cycle, the first issue has to do with how to convert atmospheric CO_2 to a form that is useful to organisms. In this case, rather than bacteria as the primary "fixers" of the nitrogen problem, plants and other photosynthetic and chemosyn-thetic organisms become the carbon "fixers." Through photosynthesis they absorb CO_2 and use water and energy from sunlight to convert the CO_2 into sugar (a carbon-based substance) and oxygen. The formula for this *photosynthetic* process is: *energy* $+ 6 H_2O + 6 CO_2 \rightarrow 6 O_2 + C_6H_{12}O_6$ *(or sucrose).* The sugar is then used as food for the plants and any animals that eat them. This food is used for energy production and storage and for building and repairing structures in organisms. After digestion, some of this carbon returns to the soils through waste products and to the air during respiration.

At the cellular level, respiration is a chemical process that creates energy in the form of ATP (see Section 2 for more details). The formula for this process is generally the reverse of the photosynthesis formula (see above). Within respiration, the production or conversion of energy involves the addition of a phosphorus ion to ADP forming ATP. As plants and animals die and decompose, the carbon in their structures is also returned to the soil. Throughout the decomposition process, some carbon is released into the air as CO_2 and some remains in the soil. In the oceans, much of the carbon settles to the bottom. The carbon that remains in the soils and that sinks to the bottom of the ocean leaves the biological—physical carbon cycle and enters the geological carbon cycle.

Human interference with the geological carbon cycle has been an escalating problem. The geological carbon cycle is a very slow moving cycle. However, as humans have extracted and burned oil, coal, and natural gas, we have escalated the speed of this cycle. A result of burning these hydrocarbon fuels is the release of CO_2. Ever since the Industrial Revolution during the late 1700s to early 1800s, we have been pumping increasingly huge amounts of CO_2 into the atmosphere. We also have been altering the biological-physical carbon cycle through deforestation and a variety of land uses. Over 50,000 sq miles (129,490 sq km) of forests are destroyed each year. Over half of deforestation is from cutting and burning, while about 20% is from logging. Removal of trees for building, farming, and ranching accounts for the remainder.

- When we burn forests, large amounts of carbon are released directly back into the atmosphere.
- Any kind of removal of trees eliminates a primary means of extracting CO_2 from the atmosphere through photosynthesis.
- The large-scale removal of trees destroys the habitats of many organisms.
- Large-scale removal of trees changes the entire dynamic within the biosphere and between ecosystems.

Excessive CO_2 in the atmosphere contributes to increases in *greenhouse gases*. These gases create a kind of envelope that absorbs and emits heat radiation. About half of the radiation from the Sun passes through this envelope, while the remainder is reflected away from the Earth or absorbed by the greenhouse gases. The heat that reaches the Earth's surface is reflected back into the atmosphere, which in turn is reflected back to Earth. As the amount of greenhouse gases increases, the overall temperature at the Earth's surface increases as well. Such increases not only raise the temperature in the oceans, but also set up cascading effects on climate patterns. While the overall average temperature increases, we also experience extremes of hot and cold along with different and less predictable weather patterns. These changes then affect glacier and icecap melting, which affect sea levels and ocean currents. These changes also start cascades of effects on ecosystems, economic systems, and so forth (see Section 5 for more information on climate).

Sulfur Cycle—Primarily a Soil–Sediment Reservoir

Sulfur is a common element on Earth that we don't often consider to be particularly important to living organisms. However, this element is a critical component of many proteins, vitamins, amino acids, and hormones. The reservoir for sulfur in the biosphere is in rocks and sediments. The sulfur in these rocks and sediments makes its way into the atmosphere through a several avenues, including through:

- *volcanic activity*;
- *erosion*;
- a process called *gasification*, where sulfates enter the atmosphere from the ocean and surface soil.

Sulfates are the form most easily used by living organisms. As you can see in Figure 3.6, sulfates make their way through the food web in the aerobic phase of the sulfur cycle. Sulfur is returned to the soils and sediments in waste materials and when organisms die. In water and shallow soils and sediments, sulfur cycles rapidly through various forms including hydrogen sulfide and sulfites, and then back into sulfates. In deep sediments and rocks, the cycling, as with the geological carbon cycle, is very slow. In this part of the sulfur cycle, sulfur is combined with iron in various forms.

Phosphorus Cycle—Primarily a Soil–Sediment Reservoir

If you recall from Section 2, phosphorus is the key component of the energy carrying compound in living things: Adenosine di- and tri-phosphate (ADP and ATP). Phosphorus also is a key building block in the structure of DNA and RNA, as well as a key structural component in bones, teeth, and other biological structures. The *phosphorus cycle* (see Figure 3.7) is critical to the survival of all living things. The main features of this cycle are the processes by which

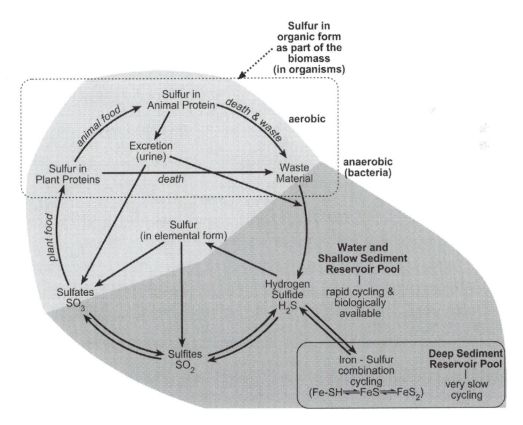

Figure 3.6 The sulfur cycle with a primary soil–sediment reservoir.

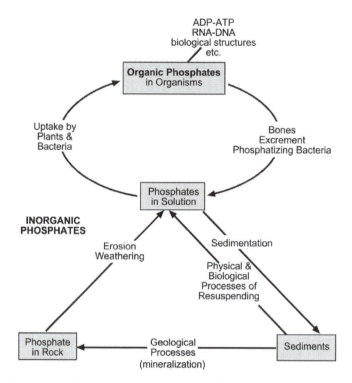

Figure 3.7 The phosphorus cycle with a primary soil-sediment reservoir.

phosphates in sediments and rocks—the major reservoir of phosphorus—make their way into solution and then into plants, which in turn are eaten by animals. As animals and plants die, phosphorus either makes it way back into solution or back into the sediments. Notice that the phosphorus cycle is the only one of the biogeochemical cycles in which there is no gaseous phase. The only time phosphorus is found in the atmosphere is in the form of phosphoric acid, which contributes to *acid rain*. Excesses of phosphorus in aquatic ecosystems are considered a pollutant, since it stimulates the growth of plankton, algae, and other plants. Excessive growth can lead to ponds and streams being over-run by algae and plants. Most of the oxygen produced by these plants does not stay in the water, but bubbles to the surface. However, the plants utilize oxygen as they respire. As a result, the oxygen in these waters is depleted, which results in the deaths of other forms of life, such as fish.

Water Cycle

The water cycle is probably the most familiar of the Earth system cycles. A simplified version of the cycle appears in Figure 3.8. Basically, there are *five reservoirs*:

1. The oceans
2. Ground-water
3. Ice and snow in mountains, glaciers, and polar regions
4. Freshwater ponds and lakes
5. The atmosphere.

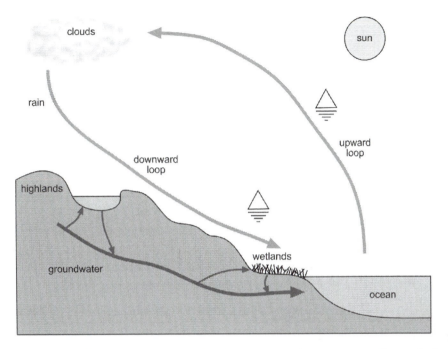

Figure 3.8 A simplified model of the water cycle with reservoirs in the oceans, groundwater, freshwater, atmosphere, and ice and snow. The triangles indicate energy in both the downward and upward loops.

The water cycle is in constant movement as water molecules move from one reservoir to another. If we start with the atmosphere, water molecules are most visible in the form of clouds, but water molecules are distributed throughout the air as well. We measure this quantity as *relative humidity* or the percentage of the atmosphere's water-carrying capacity. In some locations, relative humidity—or atmosphere's water content—is very low. In the southwest United States, average relative humidity is about 30%, while in other locations, the average humidity may hover around 85%. The atmospheric water content regularly precipitates in the form of rain and snow. Some of the rain is absorbed in soils and some runs off into lakes, streams, and oceans. A portion of this absorbed rain is taken up by plants and some works its way into the ground-water systems. Frozen water as snow and ice melts and then follows similar patterns of absorption and run-off.

The major avenue for water returning to the atmosphere is through evaporation. The lower the humidity, the faster water *evaporates*. On the other hand, ice and snow in dry climates will sublimate, such as those in the mountains in the southwest United States and in very cold high-altitude locations. *Sublimation* occurs when ice and snow skip the melting phase and evaporate directly. Water also returns to the atmosphere through animal respiration and transpiration from plants.

Although the total water of the biosphere remains relatively constant, access to water for human and animal consumption, including for agriculture, can vary. As demands for water increase, both local ground-water stores and freshwater surface stores become depleted. Although the global water stores remain relatively constant, the water available for consumption decreases as water moves into the atmosphere and oceans. Most of the water—in the range of 97%—is in the oceans. Only about 1% of the global water supply is available as usable freshwater. According to the Environmental Protection Agency, agriculture uses the largest percentage of water in the United States at about 42%. Another 39% of our water is used in the production of electricity, including the cooling of nuclear reactors. Home and office usage is about 11%, and manufacturing and mining uses about 8%. The water that is used for home and office consumption comes from local or regional lakes and reservoirs and occasionally from ground-water wells. When the water is used, such as with bathing, cleaning, cooking, and flushing toilets, the water enters a sewage system, which eventually dumps the water into the oceans, not back into the reservoirs.

In addition to human use, water obviously is important for life in a variety of ecosystems. A concept that is important in understanding terrestrial (land) ecosystems is the notion of watershed. *Watersheds* are the land areas where water from rain infiltrates the ground-water system and runs off into ponds, lakes, and streams. The ground-water and surface streams eventually make their way into the ocean. The result of this system is that any material that makes its way into the run-off will end up in marshlands and marine ecosystems. If a farmer uses pesticides and fertilizers and a factory dumps toxic chemicals upstream near the source of the watershed, these chemicals will make their way into the streams that feed into the marine environments. Watersheds also contain the sources of usable water for people in their homes. The reservoirs are part of the watershed for the particular area where people live. In some locations where water is scarce, such as in the deserts of Arizona and California, water is taken from one watershed and used in another. Even if the locations that use the water return it to the local watershed, the water they used has been extracted entirely from the original watershed.

Energy Flow

The way energy works in the biosphere is described in the same way as energy from the perspective of physics (see Section 4). In other words, two laws of thermodynamics govern the way energy behaves. The first law deals with the fact that energy is conserved and can't be destroyed. It can, however, be transformed from one form to another, such as from light to chemical energy, as in photosynthesis. The second law involves *entropy*. Entropy involves the tendency of systems to lose energy to forms that are not available for use by the particular system. For instance, a mountain lion chases its prey by contracting its muscles. The muscle contractions are "fueled" by converting ATP to ADP. In the process, the muscles contract and heat is produced. *The heat energy is lost to the entire ecosystem.* The conversion from ATP to ADP cannot be reversed without an input of new energy from food, which enters the cellular respiration process where phosphates are added back to ADP to form ATP.

The most important energy source for the biosphere comes from the Sun. As we discussed previously in terms of the carbon cycle, the greenhouse gases in the atmosphere absorb and reflect a great deal of the Sun's radiation. The approximate amount of energy covering 1 square meter of the atmosphere over the period of one year is 5 million kilocalories. The sunlight that makes it to the Earth's surface is about 1,000,000 kcal/m²/year (or 20% of what hit the atmosphere). About half the amount of this light energy is absorbed and reflected by soils, sands, water, and so forth, leaving 500,000 kcal/m²/year. The amount of light that is stored in plants and available as food is about 2,000 kcal/m²/year. After the herbivore eats the plant, the energy remaining is 200 kcal/m^2/year. After the next carnivore, the energy left is about 40 kcal/m^2/year.

Another way of looking at these energy relationships is as a *trophic or energy pyramid*. The most available energy is from plants, followed by herbivores and saprovores, such as fungi, then omnivores, and finally carnivores.

Energy drives everything in the biosphere. From the evaporation of water to the cycles of materials discussed above to the ongoing cycles of life and death, energy is what drives the whole biosphere. As discussed previously, solar energy is transformed into chemical (food) energy, which in turn is transformed into ATP as a widely used energy source in biological organisms. Solar energy also drives evaporation and numerous weather systems, which in turn drive ocean currents, which move energy and materials in marine ecosystems. All of these sequences of energy transformations stem mostly from solar energy. Volcanic energy is the only other primary source of energy in the biosphere. A few archaea-bacteria (see Section 2) utilize this source of energy. Otherwise, all other life forms are dependent upon the Sun.

As discussed above, energy is a one-way trip for usable energy. This basic understanding of how energy works is critical to our understanding of current conservation efforts. Although we try to "recycle" materials, such as water, paper, metals, and glass, we cannot recycle energy. It takes energy to extract and make or use these items, but that energy is gone once it's used. It takes even more energy to recycle these items. From an ecological point of view we can think of everything that happens as costing "energy dollars." When we add human usage to the equation, we use both energy dollars and real dollars. The only sources of energy that are "renewable," or at least in a relatively endless supply, are solar, wind, and possibly geothermal. Beyond these sources, we can either run out of them, such as coal and oil, or use energy sources that are very costly in both ecological-energy "dollars" and real dollars, such as with ethanol production and use.

As energy goes through sequences of transformations, the quantities available decrease, as discussed at the beginning of this subsection. These dramatic decreases may seem a bit overwhelming when we think about how to get the most energy out of food. However, the interesting part of the ecological energy transformations is that as the quantities decrease the "quality" of usable energy increases. This energy "quality" has to do with the ability to use this energy to do something or to perform some sort of "work," such as the mountain lion running after its prey.

It takes about 10,000 kcals of sunlight to produce 1 kcal of "predator." The important point here isn't so much the actual number as the ratio of 10,000:1. On the other hand, the "cost" of producing a herbivore has a ratio of 100:1. The predator is much more "expensive." We may want to think of this as the difference between buying an expensive and very fast sports car versus buying an inexpensive and more fuel-efficient car. The sports cars cost $100,000 and gets 10 miles per gallon, which is a 10,000:1 ratio for dollars to mileage. The cheaper car costs $10,000 and gets 40 miles per gallon for a ratio of 250:1. We get more speed or higher performance with the sports car or predator, but at a much higher cost. However, just as higher performance may be important to buying a car, predators are important to ecosystems. They help to maintain a healthy balance in the populations of other animals. However, too many predators could be problematic and much too costly in ecological dollars, which is why there are far more plants than herbivores and far more herbivores than carnivores. The energy pyramid, discussed previously, illustrates how this also applies to the number of organisms at each level.

Resources and References

Callenbach, E. (2008). *Ecology: A Pocket Guide (Revised and Expanded)*. Berkeley, CA: University of California Press.

Climate Change.Net: www.climatechange.net

Ecology and Society: A Journal of Integrative Science for Resilience and Sustainability: www.ecologyandsociety.org

Ecology Global Network: http://ecology.com

Gotelli, N. J. (2008). *A Primer of Ecology (4th ed.)*. Sunderland, MA: Sinauer Associates.

Karban, R. (2006). *How to Do Ecology: A Concise Handbook*. Princeton, NJ: Princeton University Press.

NOAA's Coral Reef Information System: http://coris.noaa.gov

Odum, E. P. (1993). *Ecology and Our Endangered Life-Support Systems*. Sunderland, MA: Sinauer Associates.

Terrestrial Ecology at the Environmental Science Division of the Oak Ridge National Laboratory: www.esd.ornl.gov/research/terrestrial_ecology/index.shtml

Volk, T. (2008). *CO_2 Rising: The World's Greatest Environmental Challenge*. Cambridge, MA: MIT Press.

Section 4
The Physical Sciences

The National Science Education Standards addressed in this section are:

Content Standard B: Physical Science

K–4:	1 Properties of objects and materials
K–4:	2 Position and motion of objects
K–4:	3 Light, heat, electricity, and magnetism
K5–8:	1 Properties of objects and materials
K5–8:	2 Motions and forces
K5–8:	3 Transfer of energy

Content Standard G: History and Nature of Science

K–4:	1 Science as a human endeavor
K5–8:	1 Science as a human endeavor
K5–8:	2 Nature of science
K5–8:	3 History of science

This section discusses some of the basic concepts involved in our everyday experiences with the physical world. These concepts include mass and weight; forces and motion, energy, work, mechanics, simple machines; the nature and composition of matter, natural resources and their uses; waves, sound, light, and optics; temperature, heat, and thermodynamics; and electrical phenomena.

Key Idea 4.1 Mass and Weight

One of the basic concepts in physics and chemistry is "mass." However, the concept of mass is often confused with the concept of weight. *Mass* describes the actual substance of matter as it would be when not affected by any kind of force, such as gravity. *Weight* describes the mass under the influence of *gravity*. The confusion begins with the measurement of mass and weight, since their units of measurement are the same. Let's say a particular object has a mass of 20 kg. (1 kilogram = 2.2 pounds). On Earth, that same object weighs 20 kg. However, if this object were taken to the Moon, where the gravity is 1/6th of Earth's gravity, the object would weigh 3.33 kg, even though the mass has not changed.

As the above example demonstrates, weight equals mass times gravity (w = m × g). In everyday usage, we use the American Standard System to express weight in ounces or pounds. Scientists all over the world use the metric system to express mass as grams or kilograms, and Newtons to express the effects of force on mass.

> One *Newton* is the amount of force needed to accelerate a 1 kg mass at 1 meter per second squared
> N = mass × 1 m / sec².

This expression of acceleration, as well as the topics of force and Newtons are discussed in more detail below.

Key Idea 4.2 Force and Motion

Velocity and Acceleration

In our everyday lives we use "speed" to describe how fast something is moving. However, in science, the term "velocity" is used instead of "speed."

- *Velocity* describes how fast something is going and in what direction it's moving
  - velocity is speed plus direction.
    Example: "we drive our car on the interstate highway at 62 miles per hour or 100 kilometers per hour to the east, then change *velocity* to the east-southeast after traveling one mile."

When we drive on a highway and set the cruise control, our speed remains relatively constant, but our velocity changes every time we turn the steering wheel or when we change our speed.

We commonly use the term *acceleration* in referring to what we do when we step on the accelerator or gas pedal in our cars. Consider a driver entering a freeway. When she's stopped, she's at point 0. Shortly after she steps on the gas pedal, she is travelling at 10 mph. After 1 more second, she is travelling at 20 mph, and after 2 seconds she is travelling 30 mph, and she will keep accelerating the car until she has reached a desired velocity. This change of velocity over time is called "acceleration" We think of this as increasing speed. However, in science, acceleration refers to:

- increasing the velocity at a specific rate
  - *speed* is distance covered per unit time → *Example:* meters per second
  - *direction* plus speed is velocity, as we've seen
  - when we say that acceleration is an increase in velocity, we are saying, for example:

Example: "the object is accelerating at a rate of 2 meters per second (velocity) every second" → or 2 meters per second squared → 2 m/s^2

Negative acceleration or deceleration has to do with decreasing velocity over time. When we apply the brakes in our cars, we decelerate. For example, this rate can be expressed as "-2 m/s^2" or as "we are decelerating at a rate of 2 m/s^2."

We will return to velocity and acceleration throughout the next few subsections, but this brief introduction will help as an orientation to Newton and his laws of motion.

Force

Force is often misunderstood because of its multiple usages and meanings in everyday life, such as someone delivering a "forceful speech," the *Star Wars* notion of "the force be with you," and I'm going to "force this door open." However, in physics, "force" has a very specific definition. Force is a pull or a push that causes a mass of some sort to accelerate. It can be expressed as:

force = mass times *acceleration*
f = m × a

This relationship or equation is Newton's 2nd Law of Motion, which will be discussed shortly. Meanwhile, here is a brief example:

- We throw a ball in an arc to someone else.
- The ball is always being affected by the force of *gravity* at all points in the arc.
- The *initial force* of throwing only exists while the ball is in contact with the accelerating hand.
- After leaving the hand, the ball is affected by gravity and a small force from friction with the air.
- The final force that is applied is the force applied by the hands catching the ball (see Figure 4.1).

Momentum

An object traveling at a constant velocity is said to have *momentum*. Momentum can be described by the formula:

momentum = mass times *velocity*
M = m × v

If either the mass or the velocity of the object increases, the momentum increases. The following example illustrates this concept:

- You and your car weigh 2,500 lb.
  You are driving your car north on a road at 35 mph.
    Momentum = 2,500 lb × 35 mph
    Momentum = 87,500 lb-mph

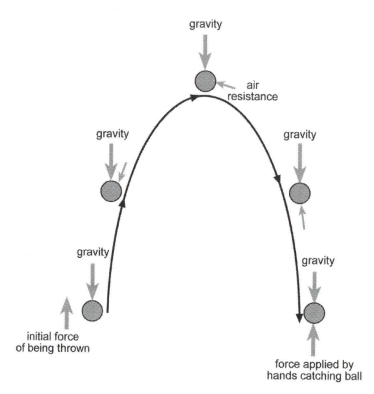

Figure 4.1 The forces acting on a ball that has been thrown into the air.

- You are carrying passengers and baggage—the total weight is 3,500 lb.
    You are driving your car north on a road at 35 mph. Momentum = 3,500 lb × 35 mph
    Momentum = 122,500 lb-mph
- You and your car weigh 2,500 lb.
    You are driving your car north on a road at 45 mph.
    Momentum = 2,500 lb × 45 mph
    Momentum = 112,500 lb-mph

These examples show how changes in the mass, such as extra passengers and baggage, can dramatically change your car's momentum. You can imagine how collisions between cars and tractor trailers are not favorable to the cars.

Conservation of momentum is a concept that states that no momentum can be lost or gained in a system, but only transferred.

- Two cars are heading towards each other and both are going 60 mph.
    Both cars weigh 3,000 lb.
        The momentum of one car is 180,000 lb-mph.
        The momentum of the other car is -180,000 lb-mph, since it's traveling in the opposite direction and has a negative momentum.
        When the two cars collide, the resulting momentum is 0 because the two momentums cancel out each other.

Newton's Laws of Motion

Isaac Newton's (1642–1727, born the year Galileo died) investigations of the movements of astronomical bodies and objects on Earth revolutionized our understandings of the physical universe. Although quantum mechanics and the theories of relativity overthrew the applications of Newton's laws to very large (expansive astronomical) and very small (sub-atomic) scale phenomena, Newton's laws still apply to most of the phenomena we encounter in our everyday lives. The laws of motion he formulated are listed below:

1st Law of Motion: Inertia

- *Every object that is stationary will remain stationary unless acted upon by a force. Every object that is in motion will continue at the same velocity unless acted upon by a force.*

    – An object that is not moving will not move unless some force affects it.
    Example: If a soccer ball is lying on the ground, it is not going to move until someone comes up and kicks it by applying a force with his or her foot.
    – An object that is moving at a particular velocity will only change its speed or direction if some force affects it.
    Example: If the soccer ball has been kicked and is traveling down the field, it will not change its speed or direction (velocity) until some force affects it, such as someone's foot kicking it in a different direction or the friction of the grass slowing it down.

2nd Law of Motion: Force

- *When a force acts on an object, the object will accelerate in the direction of the force and in direct proportion to the amount of force. The acceleration also will be inversely proportional to the mass of the object so that as the mass increases, the acceleration decreases.*

    – We can understand acceleration in terms of our previous formula for force.
    If *force* equals *mass* times *acceleration*: $f = m \times a$, then:
    acceleration equals *force* divided by *mass*: $a = f / m$.
    – When we think about acceleration as a relationship between force and mass, we see that as we increase the mass of an object (m) and the force (f) stays constant, the mass will accelerate more slowly. This result is apparent when you use some specific numbers:
    If force starts out at 1 and mass starts out at 1, the formula begins as:
    $a = \frac{1}{1}$
    then as we *increase* mass the formula changes to:
    $a = \frac{1}{2}$, then
    $a = \frac{1}{3}$, and so forth.

    – Conversely, if a mass is kept constant and the force increases, then the rate of acceleration will increase:
    If force starts out at 1 and mass starts out at 1, the formula begins as:
    $a = \frac{1}{1}$

then as we *increase* force the formula changes to:

$a = \frac{2}{1}$, then

$a = \frac{3}{1}$, and so forth).

Example: If you are driving a compact car, your acceleration depends on the mass of your car and the force your engine can produce. If you load your car with 500 lb of bricks, the car will accelerate more slowly, because the mass of your car has increased. If you replace your engine with one that is more powerful, your car will accelerate more rapidly because force has now increased.

3rd Law of Motion: Equal and Opposite Reactions

- *Every action has an equal and opposite reaction.*

  – This law states that every action is balanced by an equal and opposition reaction. If you hit a wall, the wall hits back. That's why it hurts. This law involves what was discussed previously about momentum and collisions.
  Example: If you cut a length of pipe insulation in half lengthwise, you can make a marble ramp. Bend this insulation into a curve and let two marbles roll down from opposite sides. The two marbles collide and bounce back the same way they came down the ramp. Try this again, but leave one marble at the bottom of the curve and roll the other marble down the ramp. When they collide, the marble at the bottom will move off in the opposite direction from where it was hit. The marble that was rolling will remain motionless at the bottom.

Natural Forces

There are four forces that occur naturally in our physical world:

- Gravitational
- Electromagnetic
- Strong nuclear
- Weak nuclear.

Gravity is the attraction between two masses, which in the scheme of things is a rather weak "pulling" force. Gravity is a function of the masses of object and the distance between them, where the greater the mass, the greater the gravitational attraction, and the greater the distance between the objects, the less the gravitational attraction. Every object has a gravitational field that interacts with other objects' gravitational fields. All of the planets are held in orbit around the sun by this mutual attraction between them. People also have gravitational fields, as do our pens, computers, and cars. However, the force of these objects is so weak that we really do not notice the effects of these gravitational attractions. Earth also has a gravitational force, which every object on this planet is affected by. Because Earth has such a great mass and we are so close to it, we and all objects are pulled toward the Earth at the same rate of 9.8 meters per second squared or 9.8 m/s^2. The following example shows gravity in action:

- *If both a marble and a bowling ball are dropped at exactly the same time, which one hits the ground first?* The answer is that they both hit the ground at the same time. You may argue that acceleration equals force divided by mass, so the mass of the objects must affect the acceleration. Mass does affect acceleration, except in the presence of gravity. Gravity exerts a different amount of force depending on the mass. Since gravity is based on "mass," when we replace "force" with "gravity" in:

$a = f / m$ so that it is $a = g / m$
the "mass" that is embedded in "gravity" cancels out the "masses"
as a result, we are left with:
$a = $ distance $/$ second^2 on Earth, this is $a = 9.8$ m $/$ s^2

Consequently, both objects hit the ground at the same time. *Gravity is* the force responsible for acceleration during free fall.

Electro-magnetic force, the second type of natural force, involves attraction and repulsion. This force is situated in the structure of matter. The electrons that circle the nucleus of protons and neutrons provide the basis for attractive and repulsive forces between atoms and molecules. Molecules arrange themselves based on these types of attractions and repulsions.

- A water molecule is triangular, with hydrogen and positive charges at two points and oxygen with a negative charge at the other point. When water freezes, the arrangement of water molecules is based on the arrangement of positives and negatives into a crystalline pattern.

The electromagnetic forces that repel and attract molecules are most apparent in solid mass, where the molecules are more tightly arranged. In some metals, the molecular orientations can change to create magnets, which will be discussed later in this section.

The other two natural forces are strong nuclear and weak nuclear forces. The *strong nuclear* force is the one that holds the nucleus of atoms together. The nuclei of atoms are comprised of neutrons (no charge) and protons (positive charge). The *weak nuclear* force is the one involved with the dynamics of subatomic particles, such as neutrinos and quarks.

Other Common, Everyday Forces

Some of the common forces that we encounter in everyday life are described below.

Pressure

Pressure is a force applied to a surface area. It is expressed as Newtons per square meter (N/m^2), which is the same as Pascals (Pa) in the science community. We also use pounds per square inch (PSI) in everyday settings, as when we fill a car or bicycle tire. Pressure in fluids, such as air and water, does not occur in one direction. Rather, it is omni-directional; the arrows of force point in multiple directions. *Applied pressure*, on the other hand, can be discussed as multiple arrows pointing in one direction upon a surface area.

In the past, *atmospheric* pressure was referred to in terms of inches of mercury, but Kilopascals are used now. If we live at sea level, we experience on average 101.325 kPa, 29.92 inches of Mercury, or 14.696 PSI. These numbers refer to the pressure of "1 atmosphere." If you travel to a higher elevation, the atmospheric pressure is reduced:

- at 18,000 ft we experience ½ an atmosphere;
- at 27,480 ft it's ⅓ of an atmosphere.

If you are a scuba diver, whale, or diving bird, you will experience an additional atmosphere of pressure for every 10 m (33 ft) of descent into the ocean:

- 10 m = 2 atmospheres
- 20 m = 3 atmospheres
- 30 m = 4 atmospheres

If a diver without a scuba tank, or a bird, descends to 10 meters, they experience 2 atmospheres of pressure, which reduces the volume of air in their lungs by 50 %. At 20 m (66 ft or 3 atmospheres), their original lung volume is reduced to ⅓ of its original volume. At a certain point, you might expect that these animals would be crushed by the pressure. This would be true for a sealed container, which is a problem that has to be contended with in the design and operation of submarines. However, as animals dive down to points where they would be crushed, the body adjusts: body fluids seep into the lungs and prevent crushing by filling in the residual volume of the lungs, which is the volume of air that is left in the lungs after we breathe out as much as we can. We can begin to see the effects of water pressure if we submerse a balloon in swimming pool:

- at 1 ft (0.3 m) of depth, the balloon is experiencing 3 % of an additional atmosphere of pressure;
- at 10 ft (almost 3 m), the balloon is affected by 30 % of an additional atmosphere of pressure → the balloon should be 30 % smaller.

Friction

Friction is a contact force, where an object moves in contact with another object or substance resulting in *resistance* (or negative acceleration). For example, a skier experiences friction with the air and between the skis and the snow.

Although we may talk about friction as "resistance," which has a somewhat negative connotation, friction is an important force in our everyday lives. Without friction, we could not walk, ride a bicycle, or drive a car. For example, in situations where there is reduced friction, such as after an ice storm, it is very difficult and dangerous to walk, drive a car, or ride a bicycle. Without friction, we would also have difficulty drinking coffee, holding a pen, eating, holding hands, and doing just about everything that requires moving or holding.

Tension

Tension, *stress*, and *strain* refer to forces that stretch or pull.

• **Stress** is a stretching (or pulling) force, which is expressed as force (or a load = F) per area (A), so: stress = F/A.

> As discussed, "pressure" has the same formula of F/A, but refers to the force applied at a 90-degree angle to a surface. This force of pressure usually refers to a fluid; however, "stress" refers to the force that is applied to specific materials, whose shapes can be changed.

> *Example*: When hanging a plant from the ceiling by a wire, the weight of the plant applies a force to the wire (and ceiling). The amount of stretch (or stress) is a function of the length, diameter, and material of the wire. The longer the wire, the more it will stretch. The thicker the wire, the less it will stretch.

• **Strain** refers to the amount a material can stretch or extend per unit of length: strain = extension length ÷ original length. Where "stress" refers to the force applied to stretch some material, "strain" has to do with a material's ability to stretch. You may see this referred to as *tensile* strain, which is expressed as a ratio or percentage.

• **Tension** refers to the amount of force applied to stretch some material, such as a wire. We increase the tension force when we tighten a guitar string.

Spring

Spring force operates by either stretching or compressing. If we take a coiled spring and compress it together, the spring acts to supply a force in the opposite direction (e.g., against our hands as we compress it). If we pulled the spring apart, it would supply an opposite force of pulling against our hands. The force it takes to compress or stretch a spring is directly proportional to the distance stretched or compressed. In other words, if we stretch a spring by 1 cm, then it will take twice as much force to stretch it to 2 cm.

Torque

Torque is a rotational force that produces a movement around a central axis. This force is involved when a car's engine turns the axles. The transmission that sits between the engine and the axle adjusts the amount of torque when gears are changed. Lower gears have more torque than higher gears. Torque is a critical force when a golfer hits a ball and when a baseball hitter swings at a ball. Many other activities require torque whenever a twisting motion is involved, such as opening a jar and using a wrench or screwdriver.

Applied forces

Applied forces are those forces that are applied to an object, such as pushing or pulling an object across the floor, throwing a ball, and hammering a nail.

Thrust

Thrust is the force that accelerates an object is one direction. It is expressed in the same way as that of the general sense of force: force (thrust) = mass × acceleration.

Buoyancy

Buoyancy describes an upward force. Physicists do not consider buoyancy a force, but rather the resulting force of object *displacement.*

Displacement

Displacement occurs when an object is placed in a fluid. When you climb into a bathtub, you displace a volume of water equal to the volume of your body that is submersed in the water. The water that has been displaced in turn pushes back, as in Newton's third law. For example:

- If a toy boat that has a volume of 1,000 cm³ and weighs 500 g is placed in the water, it displaces 500 cm³ of water, which is equivalent to 500 g of water pushing back on the toy boat. If you weighed this boat in the water, its weight = 0.
- An object that sinks in water undergoes the same effect of displacement. If this object weighs 500 g and takes up a volume of 200 cm³, it weighs 300 g underwater. This reduction in weight is due to the displacement of 200 cc of water, which pushes back with 200 g of force.

The difference in the weight of the boat and the sinkable object is equivalent to the amount of water displaced. The water that has been displaced pushes back on the mass. As was discussed previously in relation to "pressure," as you go deeper in the water, the pressure increases. Even though pressure acts in all directions when an object is lowered into the water, the bottom portion of the object is lower in the water and therefore has more pressure being exerted on this bottom part of the object. Less pressure is being exerted at the top of the object. As a result, buoyancy is really this difference in pressure. More pressure is exerted against the bottom of an object, which pushes upward against gravity.

Magnetism

Magnets, of course, are examples of how the molecules in certain metals can be re-arranged in a positive-negative orientation. The positive end of one magnet attracts the negative end of another magnet. Likewise negative-to-negative ends and positive-to-positive ends repel one another. In metals that can become magnets, each molecule of the metal has a positive side and a negative side. Ordinarily in its non-magnetic state, these molecules point in different directions somewhat randomly. However, when this particular piece of metal is magnetized, all of the molecules line up in the same direction so that all of the negative sides point in one direction. You can see how this works by pushing a magnet down a large nail. Start at the head and brush the magnet down to the tip. Lift up the magnet and repeat this a number of times. Then, try picking up something with the nail. Try positioning the nail in a different way near the magnet. *Do they attract and repel?* You can scatter the molecules to de-magnetize the nail by hitting the nail with a hammer a few times.

There are three basic types of magnets: permanent, temporary, and electromagnets. Only a few metals can be used to make permanent magnets. The characteristic of these metals is that their molecules can align along a north (positive)—south (negative) orientation. The most common material for magnets is iron.

- *Permanent Magnet:* these magnets retain their polarity.

    - The most common magnets we see and use, such as bar magnets, refrigerator magnets, and the magnets of audio speakers, are permanent magnets.
    - The Earth acts as a huge permanent magnet, even though it will occasionally reverse its polarity. Its metallic core is the permanent magnet.

- *Temporary Magnet:* this type of magnet takes on the properties of a magnet when in contact with another magnet.

    - If you have ever played with fairly strong magnets and a bunch of paper clips or pins, you probably have noticed that you can pick up one paper clip with the magnet, then another paper clip will attach to the first paper clip and so on until the force becomes so weak that they no longer hold onto each other. If you remove the magnet, all of the paper clips return to their original non-magnetic state.

- *Electromagnets:* this type of magnet is created by an electrical current. Figure 4.2 shows how a simple electromagnet is constructed with a battery, wire, and nail. Objects that cannot be magnetized, such as a cardboard tube or pencil, also can be used in electromagnets, but they are far weaker. As an electrical current passes through the coil of wire around the nail, it creates a magnetic field that is transferred to the nail. In fact, every time an electric current flows through any wire, an electromagnetic field surrounds the wire as a circle that is perpendicular to the direction of the wire (see Figure 4.3). If you change the direction in which the electricity is flowing through the wire by flipping a battery around, the magnetic field will reverse.

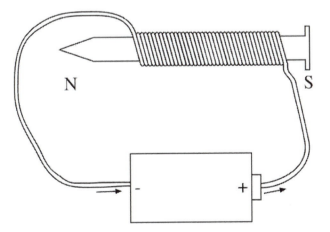

Figure 4.2 A simple electromagnet.

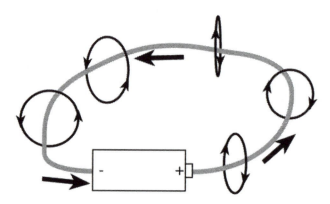

Figure 4.3 The orientation of the electromagnetic field around a wire.

Key Idea 4.3 Energy, Work, Simple Machines, and Other Mechanical Concepts

Energy

In physics, *energy* is defined in a number of related ways depending upon the particular context.

- In general terms, energy is the *ability to move matter.*
- It also means the ability to *bring about a chemical change* of some sort.
- And, within the field of mechanics, energy means the *ability to do work* ("work" will be explained shortly).

Within this very general notion of energy, there are two basic types of energy:

1. *Potential energy* is stored energy. "Stored" energy can be positional, such as a rock tenuously balanced on a ledge. Seeing that the rock could fall, the rock is considered to contain potential energy. In living things, the potential or stored energy is mostly in the form of ATP (adenosine triphosphate), which is a molecule with a very high-energy bond holding onto one of the three phosphate molecules. When that phosphate is released, it releases a great deal of energy. Batteries that are not being used have potential energy, as do stretched rubber bands, the gunpowder in a bullet, and the gasoline in a car's gas tank.
2. *Kinetic energy* is the active form of energy. When the rock falls, the rubber band snaps, the gasoline burns, and the battery lights a bulb, the stored energy is released and becomes kinetic energy.

The basic forms of energy are: *mechanical energy, electrical energy, thermal energy, wave energy* (including solar or light energy, x-rays, ultraviolet waves, and sound waves), *chemical energy*, and *nuclear energy*. These are described below:

- Many of the machines we see and use are examples of *mechanical energy*. Some examples include a bicycle, a mechanical can opener, and an old mechanical grandfather clock. Any kind of moving object has mechanical energy.

- *Electrical energy* involves electrons transferring energy through some sort of material, such as, a copper wire, a filament in an incandescent light bulb, the gas in a fluorescent light bulb, or our bodies when we get an electrical shock. Electrical energy is needed for televisions, cell phones, computers, cars, most watches, and many more devices.
- *Thermal energy* involves the movement of molecules in a substance. The faster these molecules move, the more energy is present. As the air, water, or any substance is heated, its molecules start moving faster. In flames, the molecules are moving very rapidly and are generating a lot of heat. When the elements in an electric stove start to heat up and then glow, the molecules in the metal are moving quite rapidly and are generating a lot of heat as well.
- *Wave energy*, such as from the Sun (which involves a wide spectrum of light waves, including ultraviolet) can burn skin, heat the atmosphere, heat objects, drive photosynthesis, and can be captured with solar panels and turned into electrical energy. Wave energy also includes sound (vibrating matter), which is used when animals produce a variety of sounds or speakers "play" music. Certain frequencies of sounds can vibrate objects, such as the blaring bass speakers in cars driving by and rattling objects in nearby houses. Sound does not occur in a vacuum; it requires a medium in order to vibrate, which can be a solid, liquid, or gas. Forms of radiant wave energy, such as light, ultraviolet, and X-rays, do not need a medium through which to travel.
- *Chemical energy*, such as the potential energy of ATP discussed above, is released when a chemical reaction occurs. One common chemical reaction involves burning a candle. The flame burns the melted and then vaporized "wax" (a carbon compound) by using oxygen to produce carbon in one or more forms (including carbon dioxide) and water, while releasing heat and light energy. Rust is a similar "oxidation" reaction that occurs much more slowly, during which the release of energy is not as noticeable. Another example of chemical energy occurs when you place a chicken bone or egg into a glass of vinegar, which is acetic acid, or other household acid. The acid with its hydrogen ions reacts with the calcium carbonate in the shell or bone. The result is the creation of a new calcium compound plus water and carbon dioxide, which is seen in the form of bubbles coming from the eggshell or bone.
- *Nuclear energy* involves the energy released from the nuclei of atoms splitting during nuclear fission or fusing during nuclear fusion. Some of these nuclear reactions are slow and release a steady stream of radiation, while others occur rapidly, as in nuclear bombs.

The *law of conservation of energy* states that there is a fixed amount of energy in the universe and that this energy cannot be lost or gained, but only transformed into other types of potential or kinetic energy. Such *transformations of energy* are constantly occurring around us. When we turn on an electric stove, the historical and current transformational events may have followed this path:

Nuclear energy → heat energy → boiling water to create steam → mechanical energy to drive a turbine → electrical energy → heat energy on our stove burner (and hopefully not burn our food).

In this example, you can substitute the "nuclear" with chemical energy in the burning of coal. With hydroelectrical sources, the "nuclear to heat to boiling water" is replaced with moving water as kinetic energy. In many chemical energy reactions that go from potential to kinetic to potential also gives off heat. We can notice this type of heat transformation more when we exercise. We expend a lot of chemical energy in a short period of time. As a result, we generate more heat, which raises our body temperature. When light energy hits a plant leaf, the light energy is transformed to chemical energy. When we drive, our car's engine runs on a chemical reaction, which is the controlled explosion of gasoline vapor and oxygen. This chemical reaction is transformed into heat as a loss to the system of the engine and mechanical energy that turns the camshaft and then the axles. We could actually calculate the *efficiency of the system* by determining what percentage of the chemical energy is transformed into mechanical energy. Our stoves transfer electric energy into heat or thermal energy. Light bulbs result from the transformation of electrical energy into light and heat energy. Again, the efficiency of light bulbs can be calculated by finding out what percentage of electrical energy is transferred into light energy. This loss of energy to systems is important in our understandings of energy in ecological systems, which was discussed in Section 3.

Work and Power

Work, from a physics perspective, involves using *energy* to apply a *force* to move some object a specific *distance.* Work equals force times distance:

$$(W = f \times d).$$

The most common unit that is used for work is a *joule,* named after James Joule (1818–1889), a British physicist:

1 joule = the force of 1 Newton applied over a distance of 1 meter.

Work is involved in our walking and running, in driving, moving furniture, lifting weights, and all kinds of activities that require moving some sort of object a distance in some direction.

- *Example:* You push a box 5 m across the floor using a 20 Newton force:
  REMEMBER: 1 Newton = mass $\times$ 1 m/sec^2
  20 N $\times$ 5 m = 100 joules

Let's say this took you 6 seconds to complete. If you repeated this task in 3 seconds, it will still be the same amount of work, but you will have used twice as much power, which brings us to the next concept.

Power has to do with increasing the speed at which work is done. The term *watt* (named after James Watt, a Scottish inventor 1736–1819) is used as the unit for power that has to do with the speed with which work is done. Although we commonly associate the term "watt" with the power of light bulbs, it is the scientific term used for power in general. The other term commonly used to describe power, especially in cars and tools with motors, is *horsepower.* Interestingly, the term "horsepower" was also coined by James Watt. He found that when experimenting with horses, his horses were able to pull 22,000 lb of coal the distance of 1 ft in 1 minute, but later changed it to 33,000 ft-pounds per minute. One horsepower is equivalent to the electrical horsepower of 746 watts. Most subcompact cars have horsepower ratings between 105 and 115.

Machines

A variety of machines have been invented to decrease the amount of force needed to do work or to increase the power or speed at which work is done. Ancient people invented these machines as ways to reduce the effort needed to do work. These machines are now referred to as *simple machines*. There are four basic simple machines: the inclined plane, the lever, the wheel and axle, and the pulley. Two other types of simple machines are often included in the list, which are the wedge (a version of an inclined plane) and the screw (also a version of an incline plane). All of these machines were designed to reduce the amount of effort or force to move something. The amount of "work" stays the same, but the force is reduced. In other words, in the equation:

$$W = f \times d,$$

if force is reduced, distance is increased to compensate.

The intriguing aspect of investigating machines with children involves how they think of "machine" and "work." Children will think that all kinds of things are machines, from computers to video games to light bulbs. They may say that computers help us do work, which is true in our *everyday* contexts and meanings of machine and work, but not in terms of moving something across a distance. As mentioned in the discussions of "force," our everyday meanings and uses of words, like "work," differ from the scientific meanings.

The use of a machine to reduce the effort needed for a particular task is referred to as *mechanical advantage*. The easiest way to think of mechanical advantage is in terms of the amount of force needed with and without the machine. The numerical value used for mechanical advantage is the ratio of the forced needed without the machine to the force needed with the machine. Two ways of expressing this relationship are:

- MA = force without machine / force with machine;
- MA = resistance force / effort force.

In other words, if the force needed by the machine is ½ of what it would be without the machine, then the mechanical advantage (MA) is 2. If the force needed is ¼ of what would be without the machine, the MA is 4. However, if you see that the MA = 0.5, then the use of the machine requires more force than it would need without the machine. When the mechanical advantage is less than 1, the use of the machine generally reduces the distance to move an object, but requires more force. For example:

- Place a book on a table as in Figure 4.4.
- First, place a pencil under the book with another pencil underneath, as shown on the left side of the figure.

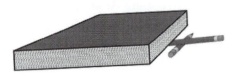

Figure 4.4 Example of mechanical advantage.

- Push down on the end of the pencil to lift the book.
- Now, try the set-up as shown on the right side of the figure and push down on the pencil to lift the book.

The set-up on the left side required much less effort on your part to lift the book. However, the set-up on the right side raised the book further. Although the mechanical advantage was higher with the left side set-up, it did not raise the book as far. As we'll see soon, there are times when a lower mechanical advantage is better.

The following list provides more information about each of the simple machines.

1. An ***inclined plane***, such as a ramp, allows one to apply less force to an object over a greater distance than lifting the object vertically. The smaller the angle of the inclined plane, the less force is needed to move an object up the inclined plane. In Figure 4.5, an example of two inclined planes are shown. The ramp is the classic example, while the steps are less obvious, but they function as a "bumpy" ramp.

2. A ***lever***, such as a crow bar, bottle opener, shovel, or seesaw, is some sort of "arm" or extension that pivots or rotates around some point, which is called a *fulcrum*. Our arms and legs are levers with the fulcrums at the joints. If we want to move a huge rock on our lawn, we may not be able to move it with our bodies. However, if we put one end of a long steel pipe under the rock and then placed a brick or a smaller rock under the pipe near the huge rock we are trying to move, we can then push down on the other end of the pipe and lift the huge rock. The distance on each side of the fulcrum of the lever determines how much force is needed to push down on the lever. Figure 4.4 shows a simple example of the difference in the force needed to raise the book. The fulcrum is close to the object or book on the left side of this figure and further away on the right side.

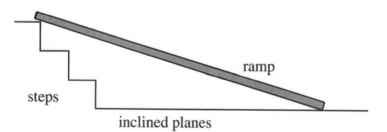

Figure 4.5 Inclined plane.

Examples of different classes of levers (see Figure 4.6) include:

- *Class 1*—crow bar for a pushing force, prying can opener for a pulling force, scissors that are two class 1 levers, bolt cutters that are two class 1 levers, pliers that are two class 1 levers, single hole punch, hand trucks for lifting a load, and oars.
- *Class 2*—wheelbarrow, hand dolly in motion, hinged doors, ratchet and simple wrenches, nutcracker, multiple hole-multiple page hole punch, and doing a push-up exercise.
- *Class 3*—arms and legs, fishing rod, tweezers or forceps, nail clippers, and chopsticks.

The mechanical advantage of various types of levers in each class can be calculated from the differences in distances between fulcrum and weight or resistance and fulcrum and force or effort.

3. **Wheels and axles**, such as a wheel barrow, wagon, car, rolling pin, door knob, pencil sharpener, steering wheel, gyroscopes and spinning tops, and ceiling fans, work like a

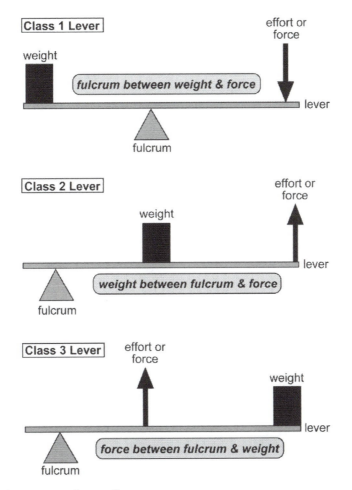

Figure 4.6 The three types or classes of levers.

lever that rotates. One of the circular pieces, the axle, is like the *effort arm* of a lever. The other circular piece, the wheel, is like the *resistance* or *weight arm* of the lever. The point where the two join is like the *fulcrum.* You can determine the mechanical advantage by dividing the radius of the resistance circle, such as the wheel of a bicycle (R-r), by the radius of the effort circle, such as the axle of a bicycle (R-e): R-r/R-e → the inverse of this ratio = mechanical advantage. For example, if the radius of a car's axle is 1 inch and the radius of the wheel is 14 inches, we have the inverse or 1 / 14, which is a mechanical advantage of approximately 0.071. If we consider that the thinner axle is providing the force to move a much bigger wheel, more force or effort is going to be required to move the wheel. However, if we use a steering wheel for a car, the effort part is the wheel and the resistant part is the axle. In this case a wheel with a radius of 8 and an axle with a radius of 1, we get a mechanical advantage of 8 (inverse of 1/8 = 8). As a steering wheel gets bigger, the mechanical advantage increases. In older cars without power steering, the steering wheels were bigger to provide a greater mechanical advantage. Old sailing ships had huge wheels at the helms.

4. **Pulleys**, such as winches, cables on many elevator systems, blocks and tackles, are adaptations of a combination of the lever and wheel and axle. However, pulleys use a rope to transfer the force or effort. Figure 4.7 shows eight different pulley arrangements. In example 1, the pulley is attached above with a weight on one end of the rope, which is looped up through the pulley and down to where someone is pulling on it.

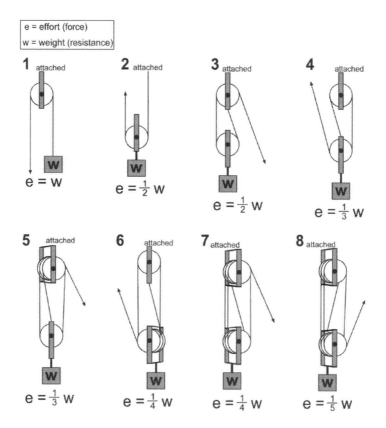

Figure 4.7 Various pulley arrangements with the amount of effort needed for each.

The force that is needed is equal to the weight. In example 2, the rope is attached above, which is looped through a pulley and back up again to where someone is pulling up on the pulley. Since one end of the rope is attached to an upper structure and the other end of the rope is held by someone (while the weight is attached to the pulley), each end of the rope supports half the weight. So, the amount of effort or force needed to raise the object is half of its weight. The mechanical advantage of these examples is the inverse of each fraction shown in Figure 4.7. So, in the first example, the MA equals 1; in the second example, the MA equals 2.

5. A *wedge*, which is a moving inclined plane like an axe, chisel, or doorstop, can raise a mass with less force than by lifting the mass directly. As the angle of the wedge decreases, the force it can exert increases. Wedges can be used to lift, hold, separate or divide, or stop objects.

6. **Screws**, such as wood and metal screws, bolts, drill bits, screw-based car jacks, jar tops, corkscrews, monkey wrench adjustments, are a combination of an inclined plane and wheel and axle. The wheel of the screw is the inclined plane that winds or spirals upward around the axle (central axis) of the screw. A screw works by moving its inclined plane through some resistance, such as wood or the weight of a car. The distance between each spiral, which is referred to as its "pitch," determines the mechanical advantage. In other words, when the spirals are farther apart, the slope of the inclined plane is steeper than when the spirals are close together. For each complete turn of the screw, the object is lifted or the screw goes into the material the distance between the threads. When this distance is small you lengthen the inclined plane and increase the mechanical advantage, thus making it easier (requiring less force) to turn the screw.

Dynamics of Objects

Another set of concepts in mechanics that comes into play when working with children's explorations is the *center of mass* and the *center of gravity*. In most cases, the center of an object's mass is the same as its center of gravity. For a baseball or basketball, the center of mass should be at the exact center of the ball. For all practical purposes, the center of gravity also is at the exact center of the ball. For large objects, such as a planet like the Earth, the center of mass is at the exact center, but its center of gravity changes as the gravitational pulls from the Sun and Moon vary.

For the objects children can explore in the classroom, the centers of mass and gravity will be the same. When a baseball is thrown into the air, it follows a smooth curve upwards and then downwards, which is called a *parabolic curve*. The ball also spins around its center of gravity in one way or another, while maintaining a smooth motion through the air. If we were to throw another object that did not have its center of gravity or mass at its physical center, such as a hammer or lollypop, it would appear to wobble as the handle or stem rotates around the center of mass as it goes through the air. At one moment the handle is pointing up, which makes the object's physical center appear to be higher than when the handle is pointing down. However, if you were to mark the hammer's or lollypop's center of gravity and then throw it through the air, you would see that the center of gravity moves through the air in a smooth arc, even though the whole object seems to move up and down. Jugglers who toss flaming torches and bowling pins into the air count on this smooth motion and stable center of gravity.

The center of gravity is also important in all kinds of moving objects, static structures, and large biological organisms. With paper airplanes, you can find the approximate center of gravity or mass by turning the plane upside down and finding the point at which it balances on the tip of your finger. You'll notice this center of gravity is forward of the plane's longitudinal center point. You can adjust this center of gravity by adding paper clips to the front or rear of the plane.

In ships and boats, the center of gravity needs to be not only in the center from right (starboard) or left (port), but also near or slightly to the rear (aft) of its longitudinal center. The center of gravity has implications for all kinds of moving objects, including cars, trucks, bicycles, skateboards, and rockets. Skateboards and surfers adjust the center of gravity to make turns and perform various maneuvers. A car with too much weight in its trunk lifts the weight off the front tires, making steering more dangerous. Pickup trucks have to place more weight in the back during the winter so that they can get more friction in the snow. Another problem for vehicles involves the height of the center of gravity off the ground, such as with jacked-up pickup trucks and some SUVs. When the center of gravity is higher off of the ground, the vehicle becomes much more unstable during turns. A turn that could be handled easily by a car with a low center of gravity could flip a vehicle with a high center of gravity.

Another interesting aspect of the centers of gravity and mass has to do with circular motion. Spinning tops and gyroscopes are basically wheels and axles, which spin around a vertical axis. In essence, the spinning wheel focuses the distributed mass towards the center axis. In other words, all parts of the disk of the gyroscope or spinning top are acted upon by gravity. When the disk spins rapidly, each point around the rim of the disk is acted upon equally by the downward force of gravity. The mass of the disk is equally distributed around the edge as is the force of gravity on each point. The spinning points, according to Newton's 1st Law of Motion, will keep moving in the same direction (around the axis). When the gyroscope or top is not spinning it falls over on its side, because each point around the edge is subject to the force of gravity. The spinning distributes the forces on each point. Another variation on spinning masses has to do with the speed of the rotation. If you have a spinning stool, sit and spin yourself. If you keep your arms tucked in, you spin more rapidly than if you extend your arms out. By moving your arms in and out, you can vary the speed of the spin. Figure skaters do these kinds of spins as part of their routines. This sort of motion has to do with *angular momentum* and the *conservation of angular momentum*, which are similar to linear momentum. Objects in motion want to keep moving in the same direction. When the mass is changed from near the axis to away from the axis, the angular momentum is changed and slowed down. When the mass is brought towards the axis, the angular momentum is increased.

For buildings and other structures, the centers of mass have to be as close as possible to the centers of their foundations or support areas. If you are standing, your center of gravity is positioned over your support area, which is the area around and between your feet. If you lean too far backward or forward, your center of gravity moves outside of this support area and you fall over. For tall structures, the larger the support area or foundation, the more stable the structure.

If we return to the topic of airplanes, the flight of airplanes is affected not only by the center of its mass or gravity, but also by the position of its wings in relation to its center of gravity. However, the primary issue with airplanes concerns how they can fly. The fundamental principle of flight for birds, bats, and airplanes is known as *Bernoulli's Principle*, named after Daniel

Bernoulli (1700–1782), a Swiss mathematician born in The Netherlands. He worked not with flight, since airplanes had not yet been invented, but with fluids and pressure. His principle of fluid pressure states that:

as the speed of a fluid increases, its pressure decreases.

If you look at the bottom of Figure 4.8, you see how air moves around an airplane's wing. The air that goes underneath remains relatively stable in terms of its speed in relation to the wing. However, the air that goes above the wing has to move faster to "keep up with" the slower air below the wing. The air *above* the wing moves faster and lowers the pressure. The higher pressure below the wing provides the *lift* that is responsible for airplane flight. In jet planes the basic parts of the wings include the ailerons near the tips on the rear of the wings, the flaps that are closer to the fuselage, and the elevators on the smaller tail wings. These parts help to change

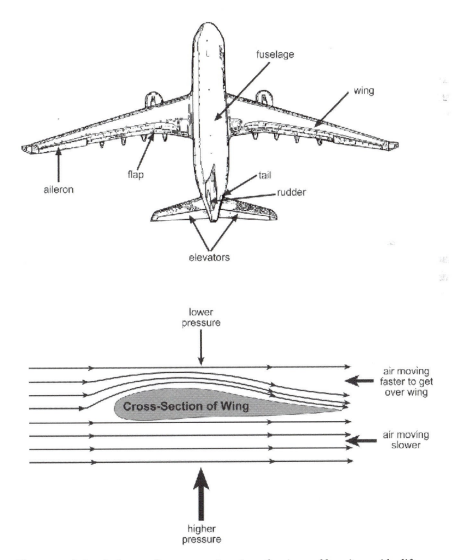

Figure 4.8 The parts of a jet airplane and a cross-section view of a wing and how it provides lift.

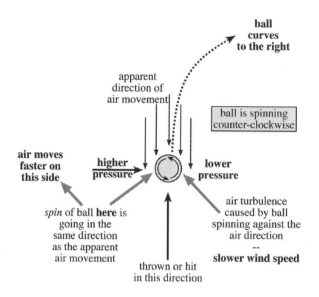

Figure 4.9 Bernoulli's Principle explains ball flight.

the wind speed and therefore the lift on various sections of the wing and tail. On helicopters, the blades of the rotor are actually moving wings. Each blade moves, providing lift.

The same principle of fluid speed and pressure is involved in a variety of other phenomena. In golf and baseball, a ball curves in the air based on the direction of its spin. In Figure 4.9, a ball is shown with a clockwise spin as it is hit or thrown forward. The apparent wind direction as the ball moves through the air is the opposite of the direction the ball is moving. On the right side, the ball spins into the wind, which causes turbulence due to the friction between the air and the ball. On the left side of the ball, its spin is going in the same direction as the wind so that the wind is moving faster on this side. As a result, the higher pressure is on the left side where the wind is moving more quickly. This pressure pushes the ball to the right as it moves forward. In golf, this curve is a slice for a right-handed golfer and, in baseball, it's a curve ball for a left-handed pitcher. A right-handed pitcher can't put a right curve on the ball without risking severe damage to his or her arm.

Key Idea 4.4 Matter: Atoms, Molecules, Solids, Liquids, and Gases

Matter is comprised of *elements*, which are the most basic and simplest types of matter. The simplest element is hydrogen. The hydrogen atom is composed of one proton in its nucleus and one electron. At the next step of greater complexity, the element is helium with two protons, two neutrons, and two electrons. These two naturally occurring gases—hydrogen and helium—are the two most common elements in the universe. Elements such as these are defined as individual atoms. Each atom has a nucleus composed of a specific number of *protons* with a positive charge and *neutrons* with no charge. The only element without neutrons is hydrogen. In addition, each atom has a specific number of electrons, which are very tiny particles with a negative charge. Strangely enough, at this point, the number of naturally occurring elements is not certain. We know of 90 naturally occurring elements. Others that have been "made" in the laboratory may exist naturally, but we haven't yet found evidence of their existence on Earth. Uranium with its 92 protons is the largest element found naturally on Earth or in space. Other elements with up to 118 protons have been created in the laboratory, but most decay very rapidly—in less than a second.

In terms of scale, if you placed a nickel at the middle of the 50-yard line in a football stadium, the nickel would be the nucleus of the hydrogen atom and the electron would be at the very last row at the top of the stadium. For larger elements, you can add nickels and then after two electrons you would have to move out beyond the stadium for additional electrons.

Atomic Structure

Although quantum physics describes a different model of atomic structure, it is easier to think of an atom as a nucleus with protons and neutrons surrounded by *shells* at various distances from the nucleus where electrons orbit. The following list shows each shell and the maximum number of electrons it can hold:

- Shell #1 (innermost)   2 electrons
- Shell #2   8 electrons
- Shell #3   18 electrons
- Shell #4   32 electrons
- Shell #5   50 electrons

For hydrogen, only one electron occupies the first shell, while for helium, two electrons occupy the first shell. The rest of the elements add electrons to outer shells. The maximum number of electrons that can occupy each shell is determined by the formula that each electron shell can contain 2 times the shell number squared (electrons $= 2n^2$).

An element, such as hydrogen, oxygen, or iron, is defined by its number of protons. In most cases, each element has the same number of electrons as it has protons in the nucleus. The *periodic table*, in Figure 4.10, is an organizational layout of the elements according to their *atomic numbers*. Atomic numbers refer to the number of protons in an element. The arrangement of the periodic table is such that certain similar types of elements align in columns or blocks of columns. The "similarities" have to do with the number of electrons that are available for bonding. These "bond" electrons are referred to as *valence electrons*. The "magic" number of valance electrons is eight. Elements with a full complement of eight electrons, such as the "Nobel gases" in the far right column, are not reactive and are chemically inert. The elements in the first column on the left have one electron available in the outer shell that can be used to bond with other elements. Elements in the second column have two electrons available for bonding. These first two columns with one or two valence electrons tend to "give up" their electrons in chemical reactions and form positive ions, such as the sodium ion, Na^+. The middle columns, labeled as "transition metals," including the "rare earth metals" inserted at the bottom, have a more complicated arrangement with their electrons. The elements in the right-hand columns, labeled as having 3 through 7 valence electrons, *tend* to take on or accept, rather than give up, electrons. As a result, these elements tend to form negative ions.

When elements combine, they form what are called *compounds* with new characteristics and features. All naturally occurring elements have the ability to attach or bond to other atoms

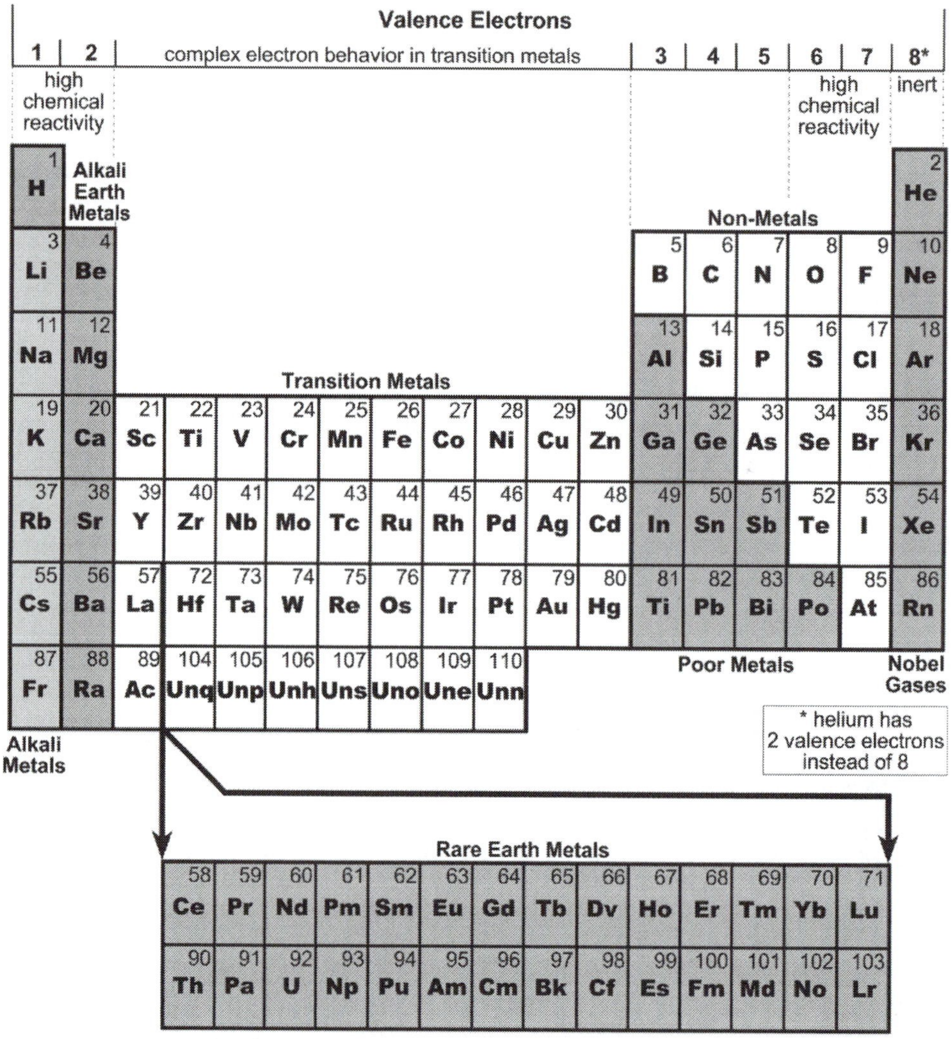

Figure 4.10 The periodic table of the elements.

of the same or different elements. The electrons in the outer shell are those that are involved in various types of bonds between atoms. Each element has a specific number of possible bonds. These bonds are one of four types:

- *covalent bonds*—a sharing of electrons between two atoms;
- *ionic bond*—the giving of electrons to another atom, which in turn creates a negative-to-positive ion attraction;
- *metallic bonding*–involves a tightly compacted lattice of positively charged ions, where these ions are atoms that have given up or lost one or more electrons from their outer shells, and held in place by a "sea" of "free" electrons—this is the common form of bonding in the transition metals in the middle of the periodic table as discussed above;
- *hydrogen bonding*—involves an "intermolecular" force of attraction between one atom's negative charge and the positive hydrogen nucleus.

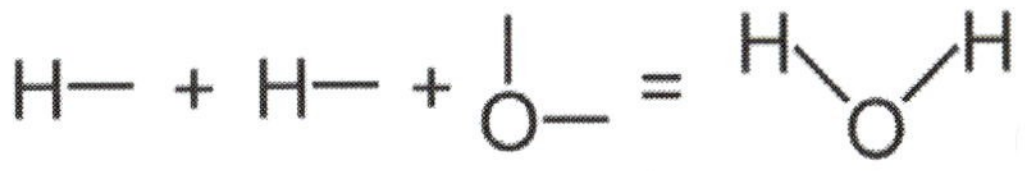

$$H- + H- + \overset{|}{\underset{O}{O}}- = \overset{H}{\underset{O}{\diagdown}} \overset{H}{\diagup}$$

Figure 4.11 Two hydrogen atoms and one oxygen atom combine to form water.

When the two gases of hydrogen and oxygen combine, they form the liquid water (H_2O) in a bonding arrangement depicted in Figure 4.11. The bonds between the oxygen atom and the two hydrogen atoms are strong covalent bonds, but each water molecule is held together by the weaker hydrogen bonds. The characteristics of these bonds provide water with its unique properties.

The basic pattern is somewhat like a set of Lego-type blocks. Some blocks have one or two projections to link with other blocks that have up to five holes in which the projections fit. For instance, hydrogen has one projection or electron. Oxygen has two holes. Oxygen has six valence electrons, which leaves an opening of two in order to have a complete set of eight. As a result, oxygen can share the two electrons available from two hydrogens: H—O—H. Carbon has four available holes or slots for electrons. As a result, carbon can create complex chains and rings with a variety of electrons that share their electrons, which also includes other carbon atoms. Figure 4.12 shows a simple example of a carbon-based molecule, ethyl alcohol, which is the kind of alcohol one can drink.

Carbon is the major element of all of life. Carbon makes up proteins, carbohydrates, fats, and DNA itself. Carbon has two electrons in the first shell and four electrons in its outer shell. These four electrons, as mentioned, provide carbon with four bonds. And these four bonds provide for a large number of possible arrangements, including rings and zigzag strings of carbon atoms with room for bonds with other atoms, such as oxygen, hydrogen, chlorine, and so forth. Carbon bonds provide for the construction of very complex compounds that make up our cells, cells parts, enzymes, and hormones.

While elements are defined by the number of protons, some elements have different forms based on varying numbers of neutrons. These variations are called *isotopes*. Some but not all isotopes are radioactive. For example, Oxygen 16 has 16 protons, 16 neutrons, and 16 electrons—this is the standard form of oxygen as listed in the periodic table. However, it has two isotopes: oxygen 17 and oxygen 18. Oxygen 17 and oxygen 18 have 17 and 18 neutrons, respectively. Neither of these two isotopes of oxygen (17 and 18) is radioactive.

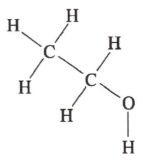

Figure 4.12 A simple carbon molecule of ethyl alcohol showing the bonding or sharing of electrons with other atoms.

Carbon has 6 protons, 6 neutrons, and 6 electrons. In the periodic table it is listed as number 6 (for its 6 protons) with an atomic weight of about 12 (6 protons + 6 neutrons). The carbon-13 isotope is not radioactive. However, there is an isotope of carbon referred to as *carbon-14*, which has its 6 protons, plus 8 neutrons, rather than 6. It occurs in trace amounts throughout the Earth system. This isotope radioactively decays at a rate that is predictable and measurable with a half-life of about 5,730 years, which makes it an important "tool" in *carbon dating* for determining the age of organic material such as bones, wood, and archaeological artifacts that are up to 50,000 years old. About one in a trillion carbon atoms is carbon-14. While organisms are alive, the carbon-14 atoms that decay and change into nitrogen-14 are replaced by new carbon-14 atoms. The ratio remains constant. However, once an organism dies, the carbon-14 atoms decay at their normal rate and are not replaced. By finding the ratio of carbon-14 to carbon-12 in artifacts, we can determine the age of the artifact based on how much carbon-14 is left.

Radioactive decay is a spontaneous and random process that cannot be predicted absolutely. As with most of quantum physics, radioactive decay is viewed in terms of statistical probabilities. *Half-life* is the amount of time for half of the elemental material to decay and change into a different element. As mentioned above, carbon-14 changes into nitrogen-14. When carbon-14 decays, it loses one electron and an antineutrino. An *antineutrino* is what is emitted from the carbon-14 neutron when it changes into a proton. For carbon-14 with 6 protons and 8 neutrons, one of the neutrons changes into a proton forming nitrogen with 7 protons and 7 neutrons. All radioactive decay involves atoms that are unstable and lose some part of their make-up over time and change into a more stable element. The rate of decay varies. While carbon-14's half-life is about 5,730 years, uranium-235 is 704 million years and uranium-238 is 4.5 billion years. Rubidium-87 has a half-life of 49 billion years.

States of Matter

Matter comes in three common forms or states: as a solid, liquid, or gas (a fourth super-heated state is plasma). Most of the basic elements are solids in normal temperature ranges. A few others are gases (e.g., hydrogen, helium, neon, argon, krypton, xenon, and radon). Bromine and mercury are the only two naturally occurring elements that are liquid at normal temperatures. However, various combinations of the elements create substances that can be solids, liquids, or gases at normal temperature ranges.

The central concept in understanding states of matter has to do with *kinetic theory*.

- *Kinetic theory states that all matter is made of particles and that all particles are in constant motion.*

  - *Solids* are characterized by molecules that are closely arranged in a lattice-like formation. These molecules do not move around, although they do vibrate in place. Solids have a *fixed shape and fixed volume*.
  - In *liquids*, the molecules are moving around one another, but they are still loosely arranged in ways that hold them in fairly close proximity. Liquids have a *fixed volume, but have no fixed shape*.
  - In *gases*, the molecules are moving rapidly and are not arranged in any particular way and can separate from one another. Gases have *neither a fixed shape nor a fixed volume*.

Substances can *change their states* by changing from solids to liquids to gases, and in reverse. Each substance has a *melting point* at which the solid form becomes liquid and a *boiling point* at which the liquid form becomes a gas. For instance, at sea level water in its solid form, ice, becomes a liquid at 0° C (32° F) and becomes a gas at 100° C (212° F).

- *"Sea level"*—when scientists refer to sea level, they are referring to a context where the atmospheric pressure is at the standard "1 atmosphere" of pressure (101.325 kPa, 29.92 in of Mercury, or 14.696 lb per square inch). Melting and boiling points change with variations in atmospheric pressure.

Some substances, such as carbon dioxide, have solid and gas states, but do not have liquid states. "Dry ice," which is solid carbon dioxide, will turn directly to a gas if left out at room temperature. Going directly from a solid to a gas is called *sublimation.* This point for carbon dioxide is –78° C (–108.4° F). In addition to the boiling point as the transition point to a gaseous state, liquids can become a gas through the process of *evaporation.* Molecules near the surface of a liquid can absorb heat energy from the surroundings. As they heat up, they move faster and faster until they escape into the atmosphere.

The Material World

Ever since the beginning of human history, people have been using various materials in their everyday lives. Early humans used rocks as grinding and hammering tools, then as axes, dart-heads, and arrowheads. Some apes and birds use tools, such as sticks for getting at food, but humans have been able to manipulate and combine materials for a variety of uses. From the early tools of humans to the incredibly numerous and diverse materials of today (e.g., computers, cars, cell phones.), humans have continued to refine their knowledge and use of the Earth's natural resources.

Our *natural materials* include:

- rocks; minerals that are naturally occurring elements, some of which are referred to as "ores," such as iron and uranium ores;
- soils, which are comprised of clays, sands, various mixtures of organic materials, and other substances;
- air, including oxygen, nitrogen, and carbon dioxide;
- fresh and salt water;
- various living materials, such as wood;
- natural gas;
- natural petroleum deposits, including oil, coal, and natural gas.

From these natural resources, humans have manufactured a huge variety of other materials. Some of these *manufactured materials* include:

- refined metals and metal alloys that are mixtures of different metals;
- glass;
- ceramics;

- plastics and rubber;
- papers and cardboards;
- fabrics;
- superconductors;
- fuels;
- cleaning products;
- wood products.

In the beginning, humans used clays, rocks, and wood for various constructions. From about 3,300 BCE, humans began melting down and combining copper and tin to form bronze. The Iron Age, during which various tools were made from iron, began about 1,200 BCE. However, it was this ability to manipulate natural resources in various ways that has led to numerous inventions and technological developments.

One form of manipulation of metals involves the making of alloys. Alloys are combinations of metals and/or other substances, which are mixed together when these metals and substances are melted. Some of the common *metal alloys* include:

- *bronze* = copper and tin;
- *steel* = iron and carbon;
- *stainless steel* = iron, carbon, chromium, and nickel;
- *brass* = copper and zinc;
- *sterling silver* = silver and copper;
- *pewter* = tin, lead, and copper;
- *solder* = lead and tin;
- *alnico* = aluminum, nickel, and cobalt (used in some magnets)

There are many other metal alloys as well. Some of the most recently developed alloys are used in heat resistant materials for jet and rocket engines, in stronger cables and supports, and in orthopedic replacement joints.

Other materials and their component substances include:

- *Ceramics*—made from various combinations of clay (aluminum silicate), sand (silica dioxide), and other materials.
- *Glass*—made from melted sand, calcium carbonate, and sodium carbonate; if boron is added it produces heat resistant glass; if lead is added it produces crystal glass.
- *Plastics*—made from refined crude oil.
- *Rubber*—made from the sap of rubber trees, called latex. Adding sulfur hardens and strengthens the rubber through a process called vulcanization. A type of latex can be found in the white sap of dandelion stems. Synthetic rubbers are made from petroleum products and are used to make neoprene for wetsuits and butyl for pools.
- *Paper*—made primarily from wood pulp, along with other materials such as cotton and plastics.
- *Fabrics*—made from cotton, wool, and other natural plant and animal fibers. Synthetic fibers are used alone or in combination with natural fibers for clothing, furniture coverings, carpeting, and so forth.

Some sensory properties and characteristics include:

- *Texture*—smooth or rough?
- *Hardness*—soft or hard?
- *Reflectivity*—shiny or dull?
- *Flexibility*—stiff or flexible?
- *Shape*—regularities, crystalline, etc?
- *Size*—large or small, which can be useful in conjunction with weight?
- *Feeling of temperature*—does it feel cool or warm?
- *Buoyancy*—does it float or sink?
- *State of matter*—is it a solid, liquid, or gas?
- *Taste and smell*—does it have a taste or smell?

Some of the major properties and characteristics of materials will be discussed in detail below. These properties and characteristics are important concepts not only for specific natural materials, but also for a wide variety of other materials and objects, such as boats and building structures.

1. ***Density:*** Children and many adults often confuse density with weight. Although weight, or more accurately *mass*, is a factor in density, it is not the determining factor.
    - Density has to do with how much mass is contained in a particular volume. The formula for calculating density is:

Density = Mass / Volume

When using this formula it is best to use the metric system for mass and volume, since this system provides a simple equivalency. For instance, since water is often the baseline for density, the density of water in its pure form (not saltwater) is 1.0. The density of water is calculated based on 1 cm^3 or 1 ml of water that weighs 1 g: a density of $1.0 = 1$ g $/ 1$ cm^3.

   You can calculate the densities for all kinds of objects using this formula. However, an interesting example has to do with floating objects, such as boats. You can calculate how much cargo (mass or weight) a simple aluminum foil boat can carry without sinking. If you make a square shaped boat, you can measure the dimensions (length × width × depth) to calculate the volume, then weigh the empty boat. These calculations can give you the density of the empty boat (weight ÷ volume). Let's assume the mass of the boat is 10 g and the volume is 40 ml, which results in a density of 0.25. *How much weight can we add before sinking the boat?* If we added 30 g, the total weight would be 40 with a density of 1.0. So, to safely load up the boat we would want to add less than 30 g. You also can determine just how much of the boat will be underwater. For instance, if you determine that the density of the boat and its cargo is 0.70, the boat will be 70 % submersed in freshwater.

   - All substances, with the exception of water, become more dense as the temperature decreases and less dense as the temperature increases. Water is unique in that as the water temperature decreases, the density increases until it reaches its maximum density at 4° C (about 39° F). As the temperature continues to drop from 4° C to 0° C, the density of water starts to decrease. Once frozen, water as ice has reached its lowest density. If this did not occur, ice would sink and be on the bottom of bodies of water. If ice was at the bottom of lakes and oceans, it would have a significant impact on life. Lakes circulate water and its nutrients annually from the bottom to the top as temperature inversions occur. At the same time, fish and other creatures live at the bottom or at least below the ice on lakes.

2. **Hardness:** The hardness of a material is the measure of its resistance to permanent or temporary changes by scratching or denting.

   Example: Moving parts in machinery need to resist wear. Brake pads on cars need to be hard enough to resist wear.

   • Hardness is measured on a relative scale from 1 to 10 (Moh's Scale):

   1 = talc, which you can scratch with your fingernail
   2.5 = fingernail
   4.0 = iron nail
   6.0 = steel nail
   7.0 = quartz
   10 = diamond.

3. **Strength:** The strength of a material has to do with the extent to which it can withstand a force, load, or stress without breaking.
   • The *load* is measured as force per unit area or Newtons per square meter (N/m^2).
   • Materials and structures need to withstand four basic types of forces:

     – compression force, which is a downward force as with the walls that support the roof of a house or the piers supporting a bridge;
     – tensile force, which is a stretching force as with guitar strings, towing or crane cable, suspension bridge cables, etc.;
     – shear force, which is an oppositional or tearing force as with scissors or shears;
     – torsion force (torque), which is a twisting force as in the crankshafts of cars.

     Example: The Tacoma Narrows Bridge succumbed to the torsion or twisting force of the wind in the now classic video of its collapse.

   • Materials and objects are often described as having compression strength, tensile strength, shear strength, and torsion strength.

4. **Elasticity:** Elasticity has to do with a material's ability to return to its original size and shape after it has been stretched or compressed.
   • Most materials will stretch or compress at least a little when a force is applied to them.

     Example: Rubber bands can stretch, then return to their original size and shape. However, if enough force is applied to a rubber band, it will break.

   • When an object or material reaches the breaking point, it has reached its *ultimate tensile strength.*
   • When an object or material stretches or compresses so much that it does not return to its original size and shape, it has reached its *elastic limit* or *yield stress.*

Example: Rubber bands and metal springs have high elastic limits, while cast iron, which is quite brittle, has a very small elastic limit.

5. ***Flexibility and Rigidity:*** Flexibility and rigidity have to do with the degrees to which materials can be bent or stretched out of shape. In general, the greater the rigidity, the more brittle the material.

   Example: Drinking glasses are highly rigid and brittle.

   - However, a drinking glass's rigidity is useful in holding liquids and in not bending out of shape when held in the hand.
   - Buildings in earthquake zones, such as along the San Andreas Fault in California, are more likely to survive an earthquake if they are flexible. Rigid buildings break and fall apart, while flexible buildings sway with the shaking of the ground.
   - Newer cars have crumple zones and unibody construction that act as springs in collisions. Even in small collisions, the unibody can be compressed. To repair this compression, body shops will pull the unibody back into its original position.

6. ***Toughness:*** The concept of the toughness of materials has to do with their ability to change shape under load without breaking. There are two related aspects of toughness:
   - *Ductile*—the ability to stretch and elongate.

     Example: metals that are drawn out into wires or blowing heated glass into various shapes.

   - *Malleability*—materials that can be bent or beaten into shape.

     Example: paperclips can be bent; lead can be pounded into different shapes; modeling clay can be molded, pounded, and stretched into all kinds of shapes.

7. ***Compressibility:*** Some materials can be compressed into smaller spaces or volumes. For the most part, solid and liquids cannot be compressed to any significant extent. However, gases can be compressed.

   Example: We compress gas, such as air, when we use a hand pump to fill a bicycle or car tire.

8. ***Thermal Conductivity:*** Different materials can conduct heat to varying degrees.
   - Houses are constructed with wood, brick, stone, hay bales, or a variety of other materials. Each of these materials has a different degree of thermal conductivity. Houses built with most of these materials need additional insulation. However, more recently, hay bales and tires and cement are used to build houses and serve as both structural support and insulation. In terms of house construction, lower thermal conductivity is better for insulating by either keeping most of the heat in during the winter or out during the summer.
   - Since metals are very good thermal conductors, windows with metal frames are not as good as those made with wood or some form of synthetic material.

     Example: If you leave a teaspoon in a hot cup of coffee or tea for a few minutes, you can burn yourself when you return to remove the spoon. If you had used a plastic spoon or a spoon with a plastic handle, you would not feel any significant heat after leaving the spoon in a hot liquid.

- Thermal conductivity is measured in watts, which is the power or the amount of work that can be done per meter per degree Celsius (see the subsection 4.7 on electricity for more information on these concepts). With thermal conductivity, the higher the number, the greater the efficiency in conducting heat.

    Example: Aluminum, copper, and gold are very good conductors of heat, while argon gas, cotton, kapok, nitrogen and oxygen (air), Styrofoam and urethane foam are the best insulators with the lowest thermal conductivity.

Key Idea 4.5 Waves, Sound, and Light

Waves occur as two basic types: mechanical and light. The most common mechanical waves are those of sound, water, and earthquakes. Other mechanical waves and wave-like motions occur in phenomena, such as jumping rope, slinkies, waving hands, sports stadium waves, radio waves, microwaves, pendulum motion, swinging on a swing, various swimming strokes (e.g., butterfly), and the motion of fields of tall grasses in the wind. In general, mechanical waves are cycles of some sort of disturbance in a physical medium, such as in gases, fluids, and solids.

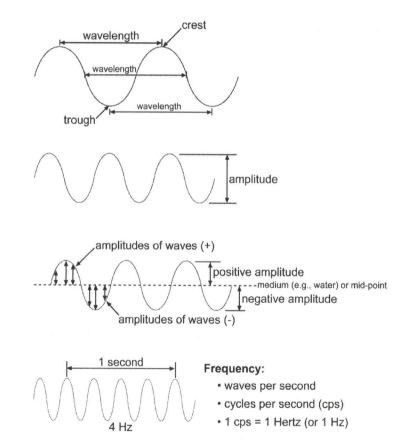

Figure 4.13 Parts and nature of waves.

Figure 4.13 describes some basic parts of waves and related concepts. As we can see in this figure, *wavelength* can be measured from any point in one wave to the same point in the next wave. However, it is probably easier to make these measurements from either the tops of crests or bottoms of troughs.

Amplitude is the term used to describe the size of waves. The waves crashing along the coasts on normal days have smaller amplitudes than larger storm created waves that can be quite large. *Tsunamis* are waves that result from earthquakes. Although we hear about the big, destructive ones, they can range in size from less than a meter in amplitude to over 25 m (80 ft) high. The amplitude of sea waves is measured from sea level.

Types of Waves

One way of categorizing waves is by the materials through which they travel, such as gases, liquids, or solids. In these cases, waves are categorized in terms of how the particles in the medium or material move in comparison to the waves.

- *Transverse waves*: The particles of the medium move in a direction that is perpendicular (at 90 degrees) to the direction of the waves.

    Example: This behavior can be seen when a rope is held fixed at one end, and the other end is moved up and down rapidly. The particles in the rope move up and down while the waves move from one end to the other.

- *Longitudinal waves*: In these waves the direction of the particle movement is parallel to the direction of the waves.

    Example: If you can take the outside cover off a bass speaker while listening to music, you can see the center of the speaker moving in and out. You also can see these kinds of longitudinal compression waves in a tub of water. Tap on the side of the tub and you will see these longitudinal waves move from one side to the other.

- *Surface waves* are the third basic type of wave.

    Example: The waves we encounter on ocean beaches and along the shores of lakes are called surface waves.

    – These waves occur as circular movements of water, as opposed to longitudinal or transverse waves. In a way, these waves are a combination of transverse and longitudinal, where the particles move both parallel and perpendicular to the direction of the waves. Under the surface of these types of waves, the water molecules are moving in a circular pattern. When the bottoms of these waves hit the solid surface of the beach, they "break." The circular pattern is interrupted and the water crashes down. This interrupted circular pattern is most notable in the large waves where surfers ride in and out of the tubular cavities of the breaking waves.

Waves can *reflect* off hard surfaces as well as off other waves. Echoes are reflected sound waves. On beaches, where waves hit a seawall, the waves reflect off at an equal angle to the angle at which they hit the wall. *Standing waves* occur when two waves hit one another from opposite directions. You can slosh in a bath tub or a smaller plastic tub so that the waves reflecting off the sides come back and hit each other with such a rhythm that the waves do not appear to go any where, but just move up and down. You can create transverse and longitudinal standing waves with slinkies. Two people can move each end of a slinky towards each other with the same rhythm so that you can see a compression (longitudinal) wave in the middle. If moved up and down in the same rhythm, you can create a standing transverse wave.

The *energy* of waves moves in the direction of the wave movement, whether they are transverse, longitudinal, or surface. Wave energy can move sand, rocks, and other objects. Bigger waves with large amplitudes have greater energy. Large tsunamis and large storm-related waves can cause a great deal of damage to beaches, shorelines, and any structures in their paths. Other examples of wave energy include:

- feeling the vibrations of sound, even inside buildings, by cars driving by with their bass speakers cranked up;
- earthquakes where the bigger the waves, the greater the damage;
- larger tides carry more energy, as at the end of the Bay of Fundy in Nova Scotia, where the tides are the largest in the world at over 50 ft.

With mechanical waves (such as, ocean waves, earthquakes, and sound), the energy of the waves involves not only the amplitude, but also the frequency. Higher frequency waves and larger amplitude waves carry more energy than lower frequency and smaller waves. In contrast, the energy carried by electromagnetic (including light) waves is purely a function of the frequency. Higher frequency and shorter wavelength light and other electromagnetic waves have more energy, such as in the violet ultraviolet range rather than the infrared and red ranges.

All mechanical waves need some sort of medium. They cannot occur in a *vacuum*, which means sound needs a gas, liquid, or solid through which to travel. Slinky waves need the material of the slinky. Earthquakes need the earth. In vacuums, there is no substance for waves to occur. However, in science fiction movies with sounds of spaceships blowing up, the sounds are purely a function of the movie director's imagination. If a spaceship explodes in outer space, there is no sound. Although outer space is not a pure vacuum, the density of particles is so small that there is no medium for sound waves. The only waves that can travel in a vacuum are electromagnetic waves, including those in the light spectrum; radio waves, TV signals, microwaves, ultraviolet rays, X-rays, and other radiation waves can all travel through vacuums, as well as through gases, liquids, and solids to varying degrees. For example, radio waves can penetrate a certain amount of solid material to enter into houses, but cannot penetrate through a lot of water or earth. This is illustrated when you drive through a tunnel, as the radio no longer works. X-rays are quite good at penetrating through certain solid materials. They easily penetrate soft tissues, but to lesser degrees through bones and other denser tissues, such as tumors.

Sound

As we have seen, sound travels in waves and is a form of *energy* that, unlike light, is created by some sort of *mechanical vibration*. In some cases where we can create sound, we can see and even feel the vibrations. You can see sound vibrations of those made by the strings of various

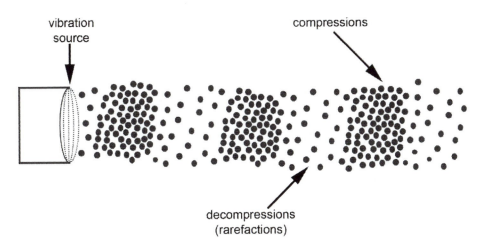

Figure 4.14 Sound waves as pulsations of the compression of air particles.

instruments, such as violins, guitars, and dulcimers. As you have probably experienced, you can feel the vibrations of our voices by feeling our voice boxes (larynxes) or chests, especially when making a low-pitched sound. Young children often love to have their backs drummed while they hum; they not only seem to be intrigued by the feeling and sound combination, but also by the feeling of the vibrating air escaping through their throats.

When we see representations of sound waves in books and on our computers' music players, they appear as waves like those of the ocean. However, sound waves occur as longitudinal compression waves. These are waves of oscillations in the compression of particles in the particular medium through which the sound is traveling. Figure 4.14 shows how sound waves are pulsations of compressions of air particles.

You can explore the question of what actually vibrates in various objects that make sound. Some examples of objects you can use include a variety of musical instruments, such as a guitar, piano, drum, flute, and saxophone; hands clapping; whistles; rattle; and rubbing sandpaper. One way we can *classify musical instruments* is by how the sound is made:

- blowing with or without vibrating lips;
- strumming or plucking;
- rubbing as with a bow or hands;
- shaking;
- beating;
- hammering.

When we think of musical instruments, we generally think of the traditional ones, such as guitars, pianos, or saxophone. However, almost anything that can make a sound can be a used for making music. Bobby McFerrin, the American vocalist and conductor, has the amazing ability to use his voice to create the sounds of a wide variety of musical instruments. In some of his concerts, he will recruit the audience with groups of people making different sounds with their voices, then orchestrates the audience as he performs. The musical performing group, Stomp, is known for using anything they can find, like brooms, knives, forks, and trash cans, to make music as they move through different settings, such as restaurant kitchens and alleys.

When investigating sound and music, the terms you encounter appear below, along with explanations of the concepts they describe.

- *Beat*—refers to the pulsation or repetitive sequence of tones. See also "Rhythm."
- *Chord*—usually three or four notes played at the same time, as when a guitar is strummed with different strings held against different *frets*, which are the ridges along the neck of the guitar. See "Octave," below.
- *Interval*—the gap, distance, or time between two notes.
- *Loudness*—each sound wave has *amplitude*, which refers to the amount of air, water, or other substance that is moved by the sound. It is often visualized as the height of the wave, but sounds are compressions not waves like in the ocean. Increasing the amplitude increases the *loudness/volume*.
- *Measure*—the somewhat arbitrary measurement that is divided into two, three or four beats.
- *Note*—the duration of a specific sound with a particular pitch.
- *Octave*—the musical scale is divided into eight notes or full tones. An octave refers to moving eight full tones higher than the initial note. Think of each note as a particular frequency. Middle C is about 256 Hz. If we go one octave higher to high C, the frequency is 512 Hz. Since sound involves compression waves, each cycle is comprised of an area of high pressure followed by a pocket of low pressure. When we hear middle C, there are 256 areas of high pressure hitting our eardrums every second. Every other high pressure area of high C occurs at the same time as every high pressure area of middle C. This is why playing two notes an octave apart sound like the same tone, only one is higher in pitch. When a chord is played, such as with middle C, middle E, and middle G, the compression areas line up every $1/64$ th of a second or so. There is a separation, as well as a correspondence, which seems to make chords so interesting and pleasing to hear.
- *Pitch*—is the *frequency* of a sound wave, which is the number of pulsations or waves that move past a particular point, like your eardrum, during a particular period of time. We measure frequency in *Hertz* or the number of waves or cycles per second. What happens to the wavelengths of sounds as the frequencies increase? Since higher frequencies are more cycles per second, this means that the wavelengths must get shorter. In other words, the wavelengths of sound are inversely proportional to their frequencies (see Figure 4.15). Normal human hearing is sensitive to frequencies between 20 Hz and 20,000 Hz (20 kHz). As we age, we tend to lose hearing at the upper range.
- *Resonance*—refers to the transference of sound waves from one medium to another medium or object, which often amplifies the sound. If you stretch a guitar string between two posts and pluck it, you hear the sound, but not as loudly as when the guitar string is attached to the guitar. The guitar "box" amplifies the sound by transferring the sound vibration from the string to the air in the box. Resonance also can be explored with tuning forks. If you hit a tuning fork on your shoe then hold it up in the air, you may not hear anything. However, if you place the bottom part on a table, the larger surface area of the table amplifies the sound so that you can hear it. You can experiment by placing tuning forks on different objects, such as different size cardboard and wooden boxes, metal tables, glass windows, and drinking glasses.

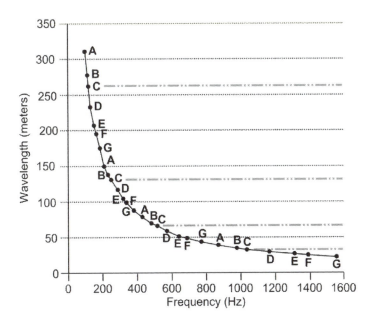

Figure 4.15 A graph showing the inverse relationship between sound frequency and wavelength, along with the notes of the western musical scale ("C" is a thick broken line).

For example, you can build a box with dimensions that are multiples of the wavelength of a specific sound frequency or musical note. When that note is played, the sound waves will act to reinforce each other and increase the volume even further.

• *Rhythm*—refers to a repeated pattern of unaccented and accented beats within a unit of time.

• *Scale*—the notes of an octave. Although there are eight notes in the scale of the octave, this scale is made up of ratios between five notes, as shown in Figure 4.16.

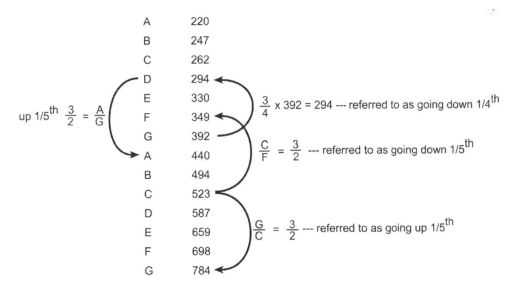

Figure 4.16 The ratios of the five-note scale.

Tempo—the *speed* at which the rhythm occurs or the number of beats per minute. A very fast tempo is 200–208 beats per minute. The slowest tempo is 40–60 beats per minute. The speed of sound varies with the medium through which it travels. In general, the denser the medium the faster sound will travel. Sound travels faster through solids than through liquids, and faster through liquids than through gases. Light, on the other hand, travels over 1 million times faster than sound in air. If you have watched baseball from high up in the stadium, you may have noticed that you hear the bat hit the ball sometime after the batter makes contact. The same thing occurs in golf. If you hit a long drive into the trees and get lucky, you see the ball bounce into the fairway about when your hear the sound of the ball hitting the tree. At 68° F, sound travels at 343.6 m/s (1,127.3 ft/s) through air and at 1,482 m/s (4,862 ft/s) through water. In old cowboy movies, people would put their ears on railroad tracks to find out if a train was coming. This technique allowed them to hear the train from the track before they could hear it through air, since sound travels through steel at a rate of 6,100 m/s (20,000 ft/s).

Light and Other Electromagnetic Waves

Of course, just when we think we may understand waves, along comes light. For some peculiar reason, light acts as both a wave and a particle. Let's first examine light as a wave. The term, "light" refers to the visible range of the electromagnetic spectrum of radiation. The *visible light range* extends from red with the longest wavelength of about 0.00007 cm to violet with the shortest wavelength of about 0.00004 cm. As we increase the *brightness* of light, the amplitude or height of the wave increases. As the *frequency or wavelength* changes, the *color* of the light changes, just as the pitch of sound changes with changes in frequency or wavelength. Figure 4.17 shows the wavelengths of the electromagnetic spectrum, including that of visible light.

In this figure, the spectrum is shown in terms of wavelengths extending from 10^{-6} nanometers (a *nanometer* is a billionth of a meter) to 100,000 kilometers in length. However, instead of wavelengths, the electromagnetic spectrum is often referred to in terms of *Hertz* or *cycles per second*, as is done with sound. You can calculate Hertz by dividing the speed of light in meters per second by the wavelength in meters. Some of common electromagnetic items with their frequencies are:

AM radio = 3 KHz
TV signals = 300 KHz
Microwaves = 29 MHz to 29 GHz
Cell phones = 390 MHz to 1.990 GHz
Laptop computer processor speed = 2.4 to 3.2 GHz
[*Note*: K = kilo or thousand; M = mega or million; G = giga or billion.]

There are two basic types of light: incandescence and luminescence.

- *Incandescent* involves the vibration of whole atoms, which includes the light we see from the Sun, fires, and incandescent light bulbs.
- *Luminescent* involves only electrons, which includes fluorescent light bulbs, neon light bulbs, LED lights, television screens and computer monitors, and fireflies.

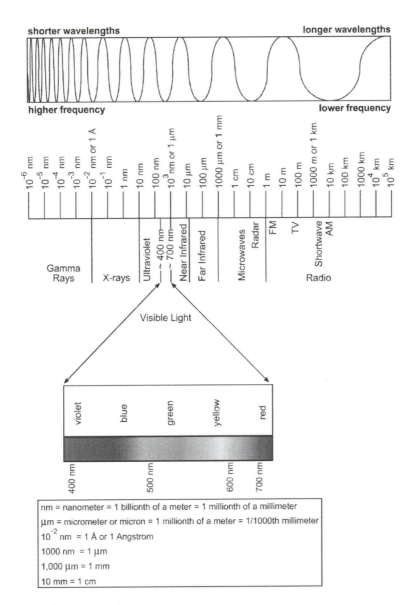

Figure 4.17 The electromagnetic spectrum.

We already know from buying light bulbs that incandescent light requires more energy than luminescent or fluorescent light bulbs.

The *color* of light, which is related to the frequency of the waves, is determined by how fast the particles are vibrating in the material that is emitting light. However, all atoms and molecules vibrate in their normal state, which is due to the amount of energy they contain from electrons spinning, the protons and neutrons vibrating within the nucleus, and the atoms within molecules vibrating. When different substances are heated up, such as burning a candle, filaments in incandescent light bulbs, and stars, each substance emits a unique set of light wavelengths based on the vibrations of the particular molecules in the substance. This set of wavelengths is known as a *spectrum*. We see the spectrum emitted by the sun when we see a rainbow. We can see the spectrums of various light sources by recreating the effect of a rainbow by using a spectrometer, prism, or diffraction grating.

At the same time, molecules of different substances absorb light of specific wavelengths. Opaque materials reflect the wavelengths that are not absorbed. Transparent or translucent materials allow the wavelengths not absorbed to pass through. When we see objects of different colors, we are seeing the wavelengths of light that are reflected and not absorbed. Tinted glass and camera filters absorb specific wavelengths and allow only certain wavelength of light to pass through. We can see the relationships between light and color in a variety of instances. If we use different color light bulbs in a room, the objects in the room will change colors. We can look through different colors of plastic, glass, or cellophane. The objects we see will appear to be different colors. If we Scuba dive, the colors of fish and other objects become more drab the deeper we go. As light passes through water, the deeper the light penetrates, the more different wavelengths are absorbed until there is no light and it is completely dark.

The idea of darkness is sometimes difficult to understand. When young children—and even some adults—are asked to imagine what would happen if they were placed in a *completely* dark cave, they will respond that after their eyes adjust to the dark they will be able to see some things. This is an incorrect assumption, because in order to see anything we need light. Children also have difficulty understanding of how we see objects in daylight. Research shows that when children are asked to draw a picture of the sun with a tree to one side and a person on the other, and then asked to draw arrows illustrating how we see the objects, the common response is to draw an arrow from the sun to the tree. Sometimes they'll draw an arrow from the eyes of the person to the tree. The correct representation would be an arrow coming from the sun to the tree and an arrow from the tree to the person's eyes as light is reflected off of the tree, but children don't easily understand that reflection of light off of objects, which proceeds to our eyes, is the key point in understanding the relationship between light and seeing.

Another characteristic of light is its *speed*, which is 299,792,458 km/second or 186,282 miles per second. To put this into perspective, light can travel around the Earth at the equator—which is a distance of about 40,070 km (24,900 miles)—once in about half the time it takes to start and stop a stopwatch (in less than 14/100th of a second). Another example is when you watch television from 3 m (10 ft) away; an image takes about 10 millionths of a second to reach your eye.

Light and Other Electromagnetic Waves as Particles

If light were only waves, photosynthesis would not occur and radiation treatment for cancer would not work. However, Einstein suggested that light not only acts as if it were a wave, but also as if it were made of particles called *photons*, which move at the speed of light and carry energy and momentum.

The other important characteristic of light as a particle is that *particles*, not waves, can collide and interact with electrons and other atomic particles. This notion of light as both a wave and a particle is part of Einstein's famous equation:

$e = mc^2$
$e = energy; m = mass; c = speed\ of\ light$ (see below).

This equation essentially states that mass and energy are different forms of the same thing. Mass can be transformed into energy and energy can be transformed into mass. The confusing aspect of the c² part of the equation is trying to think of the speed of light squared. What is more helpful is to think of the c² as energy or joules per kilogram, as suggested in the example of the 80-kg person below:

- From this formula, we see that an 80 kg (176 lb) person can be converted to energy by multiplying 80 by the square of the speed of light or 299,792,458 × 299,792,458. The result is 7,190,041,429,890,000,000 joules.
- To get a sense of this amount of energy, if you drop a stack of five copies of this book, you release about 1 joule of energy.

Einstein also developed his *Theories of Relativity*, which in part addresses the behavior of light at very large scales. Although light and other electromagnetic waves travel in straight lines, at such large scales astronomical objects can bend the path of light slightly. He demonstrated that the wavelengths of light coming from objects with strong gravitational fields will lengthen, which is called a *redshift*.

Optics: The Behavior and Technological Applications of Light

Light can be reflected or bounced off of surfaces and refracted or diverted at an angle as it passes through transparent or translucent materials, such as the Earth's atmosphere, water, lenses, prisms, and rain. As we have already seen, light that isn't absorbed by something it hits either reflects off of this material or passes through it. Children do not consider things they see as *reflections* of light. While they do know that mirrors and other shiny surfaces reflect images, they do not consider these images to be reflected light. As we help children make sense of light and optics, we need to pay attention to how these concepts of light, reflection, and refraction are being used as they construct their understandings.

Reflection, as we've seen, involves the bouncing of light off of a surface. Figure 4.18 shows a simple demonstration of reflection using a mirror. The basic idea is that light bouncing off of a flat surface, such as a mirror, will reflect at the same but opposite angle at which it hits the reflective surface. In the figure:

- the *angle of incidence* is the angle at which the approaching light hits the reflective surface;
- the *angle of reflection* is the opposite of and the same number of degrees as the angle of incidence;
- the line labeled *normal* is the line that is perpendicular to the surface and represents the point of the vertex of each angle and the axis between the angles of incidence and reflection.

The reflection of light is important in understanding not only how light reflects off objects and other materials, but also how mirrors work. With mirrors, light reflection has a couple of characteristic behaviors:

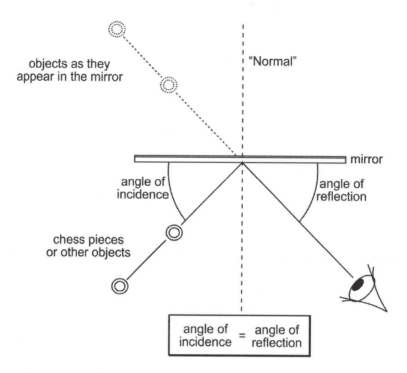

Figure 4.18 The reflection of light as demonstrated with a mirror.

- The image you see in a mirror is horizontally reversed to what someone sees when they look at you directly.

    When you look in the mirror, your image is being reflected back so that you see the left side of your face on the left. When someone else looks at you, they see your left side on the right.

- When you stand far from a mirror that is hanging on the wall, you may see the top of your head at the top of the mirror and the top of your chest at the bottom of the mirror. If you stand closer to the mirror, the amount of "you" that you see doesn't change.

    This is a geometric problem. The angles change with the distance away from the mirror, but image coverage remains the same (see Figure 4.19).

The other basic behavior of light involves *refraction*. Unlike reflection, refraction doesn't follow the same angular equivalence between the angle of incidence and the angle of refraction. If we shine a beam of light into an aquarium full of water, the light bends towards the "normal" angle, which is perpendicular to the surface of the medium. This angle between the normal angle (perpendicular to the surface) and the angle at which the light is traveling towards the surface is called the angle of incidence. The angle of refraction is the angle between the normal angle and the angle of the light traveling through the new medium (such as the aquarium water). There is a relationship between the angles of incidence and refraction, but this relationship is a ratio that depends on the medium through which light is passing. This ratio is expressed as the *refraction index* for a particular substance. Some examples of the refraction indexes of various substances include:

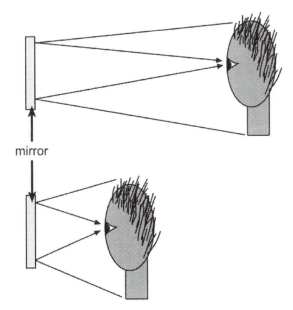

Figure 4.19 The image reflected in the mirror does not change with distance.

air = 1.0003	eye's aqueous humor = 1.33	milk = 1.35
beer = 1.345	eye's cornea = 1.38	vacuum = 1.0000
crystal = 2.000	eye's lens = 1.34	vegetable oil = 1.47
diamond = 2.417	eye's vitreous humor = 1.34	water = 1.3316
ethyl (grain) alcohol = 1.36	ice = 1.309	window glass = 1.5171

We generally assume that light travels at one speed. However, light does slow down in proportion to the density of the medium through which it is traveling. Although the difference in speed between a vacuum and air is very small, even this small difference acts to refract light as it hits the atmosphere from an angle. Then, when light goes from air into water the difference in density again refracts the light. Generally, when light goes from a less dense medium to a denser medium, the light will bend toward the "normal" angle. The light also will bend more as the difference in density increases. If light is traveling from a denser medium into a less dense medium, such as from water into air, the light will bend away from the "normal" angle. This ratio between the angles in either direction is important and well "understood" by archerfish that take aim and spit water at insects sitting above the surface of water. Fishermen who walk through shallow water with spears also need to understand how this ratio of angles works, otherwise they would continually miss the fish they are trying to spear.

Lenses

Refraction is the basis for how lenses work. Figure 4.20 shows how light refracts as it passes through three different types of lenses. Only the double convex in this diagram bends light to a focal point. It is this lens that children like to use to burn things by focusing sunlight on them. As the thickness of the lens increases, the focal point moves closer to the lens.

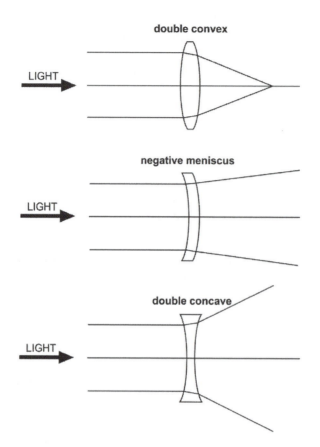

Figure 4.20 Some examples of three common types of lenses and how they refract light.

The ray diagram in Figure 4.21 shows how light refracts as it travels through the lens. When the light traveling through the air hits the curved surface of the lens, it bends towards the normal or perpendicular angle as it enters the denser medium of the glass or plastic lens. When the

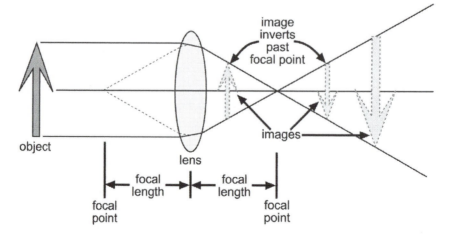

Figure 4.21 Images through a convex lens.

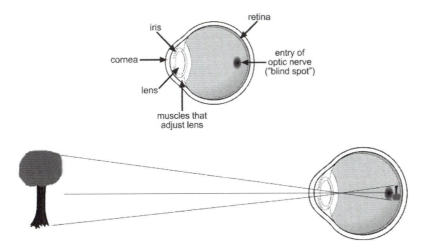

Figure 4.22 The parts of an eye (above) and how the lens of an eye produces an image on the retina.

light moves from the outer curved surface of the lens to the air, it again bends, but this time it bends away from the normal angle as it moves into a less dense medium. With convex lenses the image of the object will invert or turn upside down after the focal point. Lenses have two focal points—one on either side of the lens, since light travels in both directions through lenses.

The lenses in our eyes work in the same way (see Figure 4.22). In the eye, the iris is adjusted to regulate the amount of light entering the eye. In cameras, an iris-like part functions in the same way to adjust the aperture. In low light, the iris is wide open. In bright light, the iris closes to a fairly small point. The width of the lens also can be adjusted by muscles attached around its perimeter. When these muscle contract, the lens flattens allowing us to focus on objects that are at a distance. When these muscles relax, the lens widens allowing us to focus on objects that are close. As we age, the flexibility of the lens thickens, requiring most of us to use reading glasses or to increase the strength of our bifocals.

Lenses are not only used in eyes and cameras, but also in microscopes, telescopes, magnifying lenses, lasers, projectors, CD and DVD players and recorders, eye glasses, and some flashlights. The magnification of microscopes and telescopes is determined by the following formulas:

- Magnification = the apparent size of the object ÷ size of the image.
- Magnification = focal length of the objective mirror or lens ÷ focal length of the eyepiece.

Key Idea 4.6 Temperature, Heat, and Thermodynamics

Temperature, heat, and cold are often misunderstood by children and adults who think of hot and cold as separate entities. "Cold" is a relative term, as are "warm" and "hot." Even though we may say that it is cold outside, what we really feel is a lack of heat. *Temperature* is the measurement of the amount of heat. From a scientific perspective, *heat* is defined as a form of energy. This energy is measured by temperature. Fundamentally, heat relates to the amount of molecular or atomic motion. As heat increases, molecular motion increases. The molecules in a piece of wood move much more slowly than when the wood is burning and releasing and transferring heat energy to the surrounding air. Water molecules move more slowly as heat is lost and the water freezes. On the other hand, as heat is put into water, as when we boil a pot of water, the motion of the water molecules increase to a point where they are colliding with each other and move apart to become steam. From this perspective, heat involves the speed of molecular motion and the collisions involved as molecular motion increases.

There are currently three major temperature scales that measure the amount of heat: Kelvin, Celsius (previously called Centigrade), and Fahrenheit:

Kelvin	Celsius	Fahrenheit
0°	−273°	−459.4°
233°	−40°	−40°
255.2°	−17.8°	0°
273°	0°	32°
283°	10°	50°
293°	20°	68°
303°	30°	86°
310°	37°	98.6°
373°	100°	212°

Kelvin is used within scientific and engineering fields. The significance of the Kelvin scale is that 0° is referred to as absolute zero. At *absolute zero*—which has not yet been achieved or observed—all but the absolute minimum of atomic and molecular motion stops. This point also is referred to as *zero-point energy*, where molecules have the least amount of energy.

The Celsius scale uses the same gradation as Kelvin, so that a rise of one degree Celsius is a rise of one degree Kelvin; the only difference is that they start at different points. Celsius is based on a zero point at the freezing point of water and 100 degrees at the boiling point of water at sea level and at a standard atmospheric pressure. This scale is the common international standard used everywhere as the public measurement of temperature, except for the United States. However, even in the United States, scientists use Celsius or Kelvin, but the general public still uses the Fahrenheit scale. This scale has a 180-degree difference between the freezing and boiling points of water.

Which has more heat energy, a bathtub full of luke-warm water or a lit match? The bathtub full of water has many more molecules colliding with each other than the lit match, so the bathtub as a total system has more heat energy. Heat is essentially the measure of molecular collisions. Let's consider the amount of heat in two bottles of water. *One bottle holds a gallon and the other holds a quart. If we pour boiling water into both bottles, which bottle contains the most heat energy?* If you suggested the gallon bottle, you are correct. Both bottles contain water that's 212° F or 100° C, but there are four times more molecules colliding in the gallon bottle than in the quart bottle.

What we have been discussing are the basics of thermodynamics, for which there are three laws:

- The *1st law of conservation of energy* states that we cannot create or destroy energy and that energy can only change forms. In most of our lives we are dealing with this law of thermodynamics. When we go outside to start our car, the burning or exploding gasoline goes from the chemical energy of burning to mechanical energy and heat energy, which is a loss to the system of the car. This heat is transferred from the piston chamber and exhaust system to metal and then to the air. Even walking to our car involves a transfer of energy as the biochemical energy we utilize to move is lost to the air as heat energy. Making breakfast and a cup of coffee transfers electrical energy to heat energy in an element to the energy of molecular collisions in the coffee and the hot eggs. When we hear about efficiency in various mechanical systems, such as a fuel-efficient car, we often think of how much gasoline the car uses. We commonly refer to how many miles per gallon our car gets. However, the real issue is how much of the chemical energy used in burning fuel is transferred to mechanical energy and how much is lost as heat. Some estimates of the efficiency of cars show that only about 25 % of the energy from combustion is used to actually move the vehicle, while 40 % is lost to the exhaust, 30 % lost through heat transfer to the coolant, and about 5 % lost to friction. Most of the losses or transfers out of the system are through heat.

- The *2nd law of thermodynamics* states that the entropy (see next paragraph for an explanation of entropy) of a system that is not in equilibrium will increase over time. In other words, the energy of a particular system will dissipate over time. A simple example is our home during the winter. If we turn on the heat and bring up the temperature to 68° F, then turn off the heat, the heat will gradually dissipate by transferring through windows, doors, and walls to the outside. When the inside and outside are at the same temperature, the system is said to be at equilibrium. Heat always moves from hot to cold, but not from cold to hot. The common expression, "close the door, don't let the cold in," is not accurate. We should say, "close the door, don't let the heat out."

- The *3rd law of thermodynamics* has to do with temperatures as they drop to near absolute zero. As this drop in temperature occurs, the entropy of a system approaches a constant minimum. *Entropy* is the tendency of systems to move from order to disorder. This is what happens to my office and science classroom as soon as I clean and organize them. In terms of thermodynamics, entropy has to do with the dissipation of energy in a system. The energy isn't destroyed, it just changes form or moves out of the system. When systems approach absolute zero the dissipation of energy reaches a minimal level, which remains constant.

Heat is transferred in three ways: conduction, convection, and radiation:

- *Conduction* is the transfer of heat through a solid. In addition, there are two ways conduction occurs. One way is through the *movement of free electrons*. This form of conduction is the most rapid and is characteristic of high thermal conductive materials, such as metals. The second form of conduction is through *collisions*, which is slower and characteristic of materials that are poor heat conductors. Electric stoves that have metals coils or that are flat with no visible heat coils work by way of conduction. Heat is conducted through the metal coil to the metal pot or pan.

- *Convection* is the transfer of heat through some sort of fluid, such as air or water. As a fluid is heated it expands, thus reducing its density. The less dense fluid rises and the more dense fluid sinks. This rise and fall of fluids sets up what are called convection currents. If you place a large beaker or glass pot of water on a hotplate or stove burner, you will begin to see the convection currents as wavy patterns in the water. The same convection currents can be seen while driving along asphalt highways on hot sunny days. The area above the highway appears to be blurry and moving. These types of visual occurrences have been called mirages, especially in desert settings. People walking through the desert may see what appears to be a lake or pool of water, but such mirages are due to convection currents in the air. Convection ovens work by using a heat source to set up convection currents.

- *Radiation* is the third way that heat is transferred. In this case, a medium is not required. Heat energy is transferred by electromagnetic waves. This type of energy transfer can occur through a vacuum, as well as through air or other mediums. Some examples include:

  - the Sun's heating of the Earth and other solar system objects;
  - the warm glow of a fire;
  - microwave ovens;
  - radiant heaters;
  - lasers.

With radiant heat transfer, we often encounter coinciding convection transfer, as with radiant heaters and fires. Radiant heat transfer also can heat up objects, which then transfer heat by convection or conduction.

Key Idea 4.7 Electrical Phenomena

The term "electricity" is widely used and misunderstood among children and most adults. In fact, physicists don't really like to use the term at all, because it brings up many different and contradictory concepts.

Sometimes we think of "electricity" as electrons flowing through a wire or our hair standing on end from static. Or, we may think of power plants generating electricity and batteries supplying electricity. These ideas suggest that electricity is a *substance* of some sort, but at the same time these ideas suggest that it is *energy*. However, we may find it simpler to refer to phenomena of the *electromagnetic spectrum* and associated concepts, such as electrical current, electrical charge, and so forth.

Basic Electrical Concepts

Electrical charge is the central concept involved in understanding how electrical phenomena work. An electrical charge is a property of matter that has to do with the difference between the forces of electrons and protons. From this perspective, electrical charge has substance and can be quantified, since each electron and each proton have the same but opposite charge. It is interesting to note here that protons have over 1,800 times the mass of electrons, yet they carry the same size charge as electrons. The basic laws of electrical charge include the following:

- *Like charges repel* each other and *unlike charges attract* each other. *Static electrical charges* demonstrate this property. If you rub a balloon against your hair then hold the balloon a few inches away from your head, your hair will move out towards the balloon.

In this case, the balloon has picked up free electrons from your hair, leaving more protons than electrons in your hair. If we rubbed two balloons against our hair then held the two balloons next to each other, they would move apart. The energy involved in electrical charges creates what is called an *electrical field*.

- Since electrical charge is based on the *fundamental charge* of one electron or one proton, all electrical charges are multiples of these fundamental charges. The quantity of electrical charge is named after Charles Coulomb, a French physicist born in 1736. This charge is described as $e = 1.602 \times 10^{-19}$ Coulombs. A *Coulomb* is the term for how much energy is in each electron. If we take this fractional number and invert it, we can find out how many electrons are in each Coulomb, which turns out to be about 6.24×10^{18} electrons or 6,240,000,000,000,000,000 electrons.

- *Electrical charge is conserved.* In a closed system, such as a cell phone circuit, the net charge of the system is constant, which means that the number of electrons and protons remain the same.

- *Static electrical charges* occur when there is a build up of electrons on an object. Many substances hold onto their electrons very tightly, while others can lose their electrons to other substances. Those that do not easily lose their electrons are referred to as *insulators*. These insulators are not good conductors of electrical charge. Some of these materials are used to wrap around wires. Good insulators include plastic, rubber, glass, and cloth. On the other hand, good *conductors* include most metals. Ironically, static electrical charges build up in insulators, not conductors.

Think about the statically charged balloon we discussed earlier. You can hold this charged balloon against a wall, which has a neutral charge. The balloon with a negative charge will push the electrons in the material of the wall away from the surface. As a result, the area of the wall near the balloon will take on a positive charge, which in turn will attract the negatively charged balloon. The balloon will stick to the wall.

Certain materials tend to give up or hold onto electrons more than others. In the following list, the materials at the top tend to give up electrons more readily, while those at the bottom tend to hold onto electrons. If you rub two of these materials together, one will give up electrons and become positively charged, while the other takes on electrons and becomes negatively charged. Try experimenting with different combinations.

- Skin → *gives up electrons = positive charge*.
- Glass
- Hair
- Nylon
- Wool
- Fur
- Silk
- Paper
- Cotton
- Hard rubber
- Polyester.
- Polyvinylchloride (PVC) plastic → *holds onto electrons = negative charge.*

Static electrical charges involve the build up of *huge* differences in charge (see the discussion of "volts" later in this section). If you have ever gotten a shock from household wiring, that shock was from a 110-volt system. The voltage of static electrical sparks are 10 to 100 times that of the household circuits. Lightning is an example of one of the largest static electrical discharges. Zapping someone with your finger after walking across a carpet usually involves a few thousand volts. On the other hand, a series of smaller electrostatic discharges are involved when our nerves carry a "message" and when our muscles contract.

Since such huge voltages are involved in static electrical discharges or sparks, they can be problematic. These discharges can damage computers and other sensitive electrical devices, or can ignite flammable fumes. Static electrical discharges are only a problem in dry conditions, such as on low humidity days and during the winter, when heaters dry out the air. When you approach you computer on dry days, you should touch something metallic before you touch your computer. The metal will dissipate the electrons that have built up in your body.

- An *electrical current* is the movement of electrical charge. Although we commonly hear about the flow of electrons in a current, like water flowing in pipes, current is primarily the flow of electrical charge. Electrons do move through wires in circuits, but their speed is rather slow—at a rate of about ¼ inch per minute. As electrons move through a wire, they collide with copper atoms, which create heat that is lost from the system. If electrical current was entirely the flow of electrons, when we turn on a switch for a room light we would have to wait hours for the light to come on. Electric current as the flow of charge or the flow of energy being transferred through wires is much faster. This flow happens at about 67 to 75 % of the speed of light. However, the typical representation of electrical current as a flow that uses the analogy of water in pipes is still useful for helping children develop understandings about electrical circuits.

- An *ampere* is a unit of electrical current and is named after a French scientist, Andre Marie Ampere, who worked with electricity in the latter part of the 18th century and early 1900s. The unit *ampere* or *amp* is the equivalent of the flow of 1 coulomb per second or 6.24×10^{18} electrons per second. To put this into context, a cell phone has a current of somewhere between 0.2 to 0.3 amps. A 60-watt light bulb in a typical North American house has a current of about 0.55 amps. Some other examples include:

    television = 2.5 amps
    microwave oven = 9.2 to over 20 amps
    iron = 10 amps
    hair dryer = 15.5 amps.

    Most household circuits provide for up to 15 amps of current for running lights, computers, televisions, and other devices. Homes also have 20 and 30 amp circuits for use with dryers, stoves, heaters, and other items that draw a great deal of current. These 15, 20, and 30 amp circuits have wiring that will accommodate this amount of current without the wires getting too hot. These circuits have either circuit breakers or old-time fuses that will break the flow of electricity, if the current exceeds these amperage limits and thus prevent fires.

- *Volt*—In order for an electrical current to occur, there needs to be some difference in the potential energy between two points. In a circuit with a battery, one end of the battery has a negative electrical charge and the other a positive charge. This difference in the potential for that electrical charge to move from one end of the battery to the other is what causes an electrical current to occur. The strength of this *potential difference* is measured in *volts*. The terms "volt" is named after Alessandro Volta, a physicist of the late 18th and early 19th centuries. AA, AAA, C, and D cell batteries are rated with a voltage of 1.5. If you refer back to our discussion about static charges, the potential difference or volts involved in a spark of static discharge can range from about 1,000 volts for the smallest spark to over 10,000 volts for bigger discharges.
- *Watt*—When an electrical system is set up with a potential difference and a current, this system can convert its electrical energy to *power*. This power is measured in *Watts*.
- *Ohm*—Another characteristic of electrical circuits has to do with the *resistance* of certain materials to electrical current. Resistance is often related to the size or diameter of the conductor, such as a wire. Thin wires provide more resistance to electrical flow than thicker wires. A useful analogy is when we drive along an interstate highway and come to a construction area where all of the traffic has to move into one lane. The narrower path for vehicles creates more resistance to the flow of traffic. In some cases, this resistance is used to produce heat and/or light. The elements in an electric stove and the filaments in a light bulb provide a great deal of resistance. When an electrical current passes through these elements and filaments, they heat up and glow. Fuses are made of materials with a specific resistance so that when too much current flows through them, they get hot and burn up so that the circuit is broken. The measurement of resistance is named after George *Ohm* (1789–1854).

The following list provides some of the formulas used in showing the relationships between volts (V), watts (W), amps (A), and ohms (Ω), with examples next to each formula:

- **W = V × A**
  60 W = 120 V × 0.5 A or *power* = potential difference × current.
  Analogy: You can water more of your lawn with a garden hose (*~watts*) if (*equals*) there is a lot of pressure (*~volts*) to deliver a great deal of water through the hose (*~amps*).
- **V = W / A**
  120 V = 60 W / 0.5 A or *potential difference* = power / current.
  Analogy: The difference in pressure from one end of a water hose to the other (*~volts*) is (*equals*) the amount of lawn that can be watered in a certain period of time (*~watts*) for each (*divided by*) quantity (e.g., gallons) of water that flows through the hose (*~amps*).
- **A = W / V**
  1 A = 120 W / 120 V or *current* = power / potential difference.
  Analogy: The amount of water that flows through your hose (*~amps*) is determined by (*equals*) the amount of watering that can be done in a certain period of time (*~watts*) per each unit of pressure that moves water through the hose (*~volts*).
- **Ω = V / A**
  240 W = 120 V / 0.5 A or *resistance* = potential difference / current.

Analogy: The resistance to the water flowing through the hose (~*ohms*) is equivalent to (*equals*) the amount of pressure (~*volts*) required to (*divided by*) move a certain amount of water through the hose (~*amps*).

- $V = A \times \Omega$

  120 V = 0.5 A × 240 W or *potential difference* = current × resistance.

  Analogy: The pressure that moves water through a hose (~*volts*) is equivalent to (*equals*) the resistance to the flow of water (~*ohms*) that affects (*times*) the actual flow of water through the hose (~*amps*).

- $A = V / \Omega$

  1 A = 120 V / 120 W or *current* = potential difference / resistance.

  Analogy: The flow of water through a hose (~*amps*) is determined by (*equals*) the pressure that moves the water through the hose (~*volts*) as it is affected by (*divided by*) the hose's resistance to water flow (~*ohms*).

Electrical Circuits

Electrical currents can take place only in what is called a *circuit*. This circuit allows an electrical charge to travel from one end of a source to the other, such as from the negative terminal of a battery to the positive terminal.

Most children and adults have misconceptions about how circuits work. Figure 4.23 shows a few examples of simple circuits using one battery, one bulb, and one piece of wire. The top left two examples show a straight line from one battery terminal to the bulb. In order for a circuit to work, the current needs to flow from one end of the battery to the other. In the top right two examples, a circuit is created, but the bulb is not a part of the circuit. The current flows

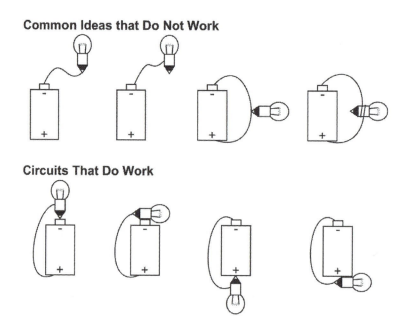

Figure 4.23 Top: Children's common ideas about how to use 1 battery, 1 wire, and 1 bulb to light the bulb, but do not work. Bottom: Four variations of circuits that do work to light the bulb.

directly from one end of the battery to the other without going through the bulb. The bottom four examples show complete circuits that include the bulb. In each of these examples, the wire touches one end of the bulb's circuit, while the battery terminal touches the other end. In order to understand how circuits work, it also is important to realize how a light bulb is constructed, which is a simple example of other electrical devices. Each end of the filament, which heats up and glows when an electrical charge passes through it, is attached to two posts. One of these posts attaches to the side of the base of the light bulb, while the other post attaches to the tip of the base. Notice that the tip and sides of the base are separated by an insulating piece of plastic. When a current contacts the tip or side it travels up the post across the filament and back down to the opposite part of the base.

This simple idea for an electrical circuit is the basis for understanding more complicated circuits. You can add switches, more bulbs, buzzers, motors with a fan, and other devices to this simple circuit. One of the common mistakes children make when adding additional devices, such as a switch, is that they lose track of the logic of the circuit, especially if multiple bulbs and switches are involved. For instance, in Figure 4.24, the intent is to make a circuit with one battery, two bulbs, and two switches. One switch turns off both bulbs, while the other switch only turns one bulb on and off when the first switch is off.

If you follow the circuit at the top of the figure from the negative end of the battery, the electrical charge will travel out along the wires until they reach both switches. The following list

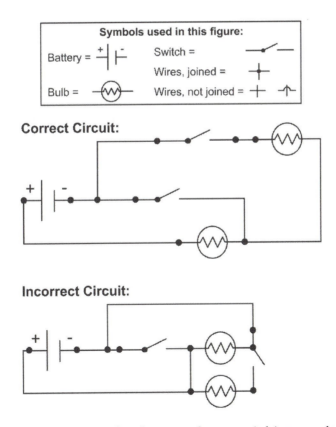

Figure 4.24 Two circuits, one correct and one incorrect, where one switch is supposed to turn both bulbs on and off and the other switch turns one bulb on and off when the first switch is "off."

shows the switch positions and the results. Keep in mind that when a switch is "on," it is referred to as being "closed," and when a switch is "off," it is "open."

- Top switch ON, bottom switch OFF = both lights ON
- Top switch ON, bottom switch ON = both lights ON
- Top switch OFF, bottom switch OFF = both lights OFF
- Top switch OFF, bottom switch ON = bottom light ON

If we do the same with the bottom, "incorrect" circuit, we get the following results:

- left switch ON, right switch OFF = both lights OFF
- left switch ON, right switch ON = both lights OFF
- left switch OFF, right switch OFF = top light ON
- left switch OFF, right switch ON = both lights ON

What occurs in this circuit is that the switches work incorrectly, because the switch on the left serves to bypass the light bulbs altogether when it is in the closed or "on" position. In other words, no matter what position the right switch is in, the left switch will allow the electrical charge to travel back to the positive terminal of the battery without passing through the bulbs. Even if the right switch is "on," the electrical charge will take the *path of least resistance*, which means not passing through the high-resistance bulb filament if there is an easier way to flow. If a house were wired this way, such a circuit could set off a circuit breaker or cause a fire. However, in a battery circuit, the wires will get hot and the battery will run down quickly if the left switch is closed.

The complexity of thinking through these kinds of circuits brings us to two basic types of circuits. One is called a series circuit and the other a parallel circuit (see Figure 4.25).

- *Series circuit*—is when a number of devices are wired together so that the electrical charge must pass through each device sequentially before returning to the battery or

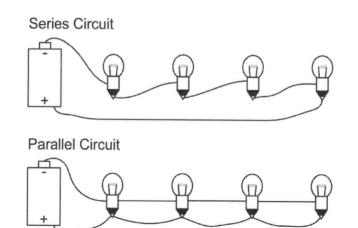

Figure 4.25 Series and parallel circuits.

other source. In the figure, you can see how the wires in the series circuit go to the side of the first bulb, then out from the tip to the side of the next bulb. The electrical charge is forced to pass through each bulb.

- *Parallel circuit*—is arranged so that the electrical charge will go to each device and pass through each one separately. In the figure, you can see how the wire from the negative terminal of the battery connects to the sides of all of the batteries, then another wire connects the tips of all of the bulbs as it returns to the positive terminal of the battery.

In a series circuit, if one bulb or device burns out, the entire circuit goes out. Christmas lights used to be wired in this way. The challenge was to find the bulb that was burned out so that it could be replaced. Today, Christmas lights are wired in parallel so that if one bulb burns out, the rest still work; and it's easy to find the burnt out bulb.

When you play around with batteries and bulbs, you will notice that if more than one bulb is in a series circuit, the bulbs do not glow as brightly as when one bulb is lit. If you recall the discussion on resistance, each bulb filament is characterized by high resistance. In a series circuit the current flows through each bulb in the circuit in sequence. The resistance of each bulb is added together to create the total resistance of the circuit. For instance, if you are using a 1.5 volt battery and the resistance of the bulb is 3 ohms, the current is 0.5 amps (1.5 v / 3 W = 0.5 amps). If you use two bulbs in this circuit, the voltage remains the same, but the total resistance changes, which in turn changes the current: 1.5 volts / 6 ohms = 0.25 amps. The change from one to two bulbs in a series circuit will change the amount of power that lights the bulb. If you recall that watts (power) equals volts times amps, we see the following change in power:

- 1 bulb in a circuit: 1.5 volts × 0.5 amps = 0.75 watts;
- 2 bulbs in a series circuit: 1.5 volts × 0.25 amps = 0.375 watts.

In a parallel circuit, the resistance of the circuit works differently. Instead of adding the resistances of each bulb as with a series circuit, the reciprocal of the resistances are added together. If we use the same two bulbs in a parallel circuit, the total resistance (R) is:

$$1/R = 1/3 + 1/3 = 2/3$$

If 1/R equals 2/3, then R = 3/2, which equals 1.5 ohms. If the resistance of each device is the same, then the total resistance is the same as the resistance of each device. In our example with two bulbs, the amps and watts remain the same—0.5 amps and 0.75 watts.

The circuits we have been examining are referred to as *direct current circuits*, such as those in a car or flashlight, the electrical charge moves in one direction from the negative pole of a battery to the positive pole. In *alternating current circuits*, such as those in our homes, the electrical charge moves back and forth at a rate of 60 cycles per second. Many countries outside North America have alternating currents at 50 cycles per second. The advantages of alternating current is that it is easier and cheaper to change voltages, so that we can have one power line coming into our homes, which can be used for both 220 and 110 volt circuits. At the same time, there is less loss of electrical energy over distance. Even though alternating current will degrade over distances, fewer transformers that boost the voltage as it degrades are needed to cover distances. For small devices and circuits, direct current is easy, portable (you can use batteries), and relatively inexpensive. For distributing electrical power across vast distances, alternating current is really the only way to do this effectively.

When we use electrical power in our home, unless we generate our own using wind, solar, or geothermal, we pay a utility company for the amount of "electricity" we use. This "electricity" is measured in kilowatts hours or in units of 1,000 watts times the number of hours. If we use a 100-watt light bulb for 10 hours, we have used 1-kilowatt hour of power. Let's say we pay an average of 5 cents per kilowatt-hour, then we have spent 5 cents for the use of the light bulb for 10 hours.

Electrical power can be generated in a number of ways: nuclear power plants, fossil fuel burning power plants, hydroelectric power plants, solar panel conversion, wind generators, and geothermal energy. With nuclear and fossil fuel power plants, the energy is used to boil water that creates steam, which in turn drives a turbine. The turbines turn a magnetic shaft that produces an electrical charge and current. In these power plants, nuclear or combustion energy is converted to mechanical energy, which is then converted to electrical energy. Hydroelectric plants use the flow of water through a dam to drive the turbines. Geothermal energy uses the heat from beneath the surface of the earth to use or create steam to drive a turbine. Wind is converted into mechanical energy that drives an electrical generator. Solar panels, on the other hand, convert energy from the sun directly into an electric charge. In other words, as photons from sunlight hit the material in the solar panel, they knock electrons loose and thus create an electrical charge. Solar panels that are used to provide electricity for homes are hooked up to a series of rechargeable batteries and a system to convert the direct current of the batteries to 60 Hz (cycles per second) alternating current and 110 and 220 volts.

Resources and References

Rosenthal, Jeffrey S. (2005) The magical mathematics of music. *Plus Magazine, 35.* Available at http://plus.maths.org/issue35/features/rosenthal/index.html.

Connexions—a cooperative educational site for authors, instructors, learners, available at http://cnx.org/.

Sound Waves in Air, available at www.sengpielaudio.com/calculator-wavelength.htm.

Refraction Simulator, available at www.ps.missouri.edu/rickspage/refract/refraction.html.

Section 5
Earth and Space

The National Science Education Standards addressed in this section are:

Content Standard D: Earth and Space Science

K–4:	1 Properties of earth materials
K–4:	2 Objects in the sky
K–4:	3 Changes in earth and sky
K5–8:	1 Properties of earth materials
K5–8:	2 Objects in the sky
K5–8:	3 Changes in earth and sky

Content Standard F: Science in Personal and Social Perspectives

K–8:	3 Types of resources

As we delve into discussion of the Earth and its place in the solar systems and universe, you will see that many of the essential concepts relate to each of the previous sections. Life on Earth (Section 2) has affected and continues to affect the nature of the Earth system and the Earth System has and continues to affect life. Ecology (Section 3) itself is the juncture of interactions between Earth and its living systems. The principles of physics and chemistry (Section 4) govern the Earth's systems and the nature and properties of its materials, as well as the behavior of the Earth, Moon, solar system, and the features of the universe beyond. As you read through this section, keep these other sections in mind and refer to them as needed.

Key Idea 5.1 The Structure of the Earth and Earth System

As we go about our daily lives, we rarely think about what we're walking on or what lies beneath us, unless we're gardening, experiencing an earthquake, or taking some sort of trip to a geological museum or site. Yet, we live on a planet that is quite complex. It also undergoes continuous changes, some of which are dramatic, such as earthquakes and volcanoes, while others are hardly noticeable, such as parts of the rock cycle and the continuous movements of the continental plates.

Layers of the Earth

When we examine the layers of the Earth, there are two basic approaches. One is based merely upon the *composition* of the layers. The other is based upon how different layers *function*. Figure 5.1 shows these two different approaches to viewing the layers of the Earth, which also are described below.

1. **Compositional View of the Earth's Layers**

   • *Crust*

      – We and other living things spend our lives on the crust.
      – The thickness of the crust varies between 4 to 25 or more miles (7–41 km). This relatively thin layer makes up the continents, which are the thickest portions, and the ocean floors, which are the thinnest portions.
      – Moving from the surface through the crust involves an increase in pressure and a decrease in temperature, as you may have experienced in hiking down through caverns.

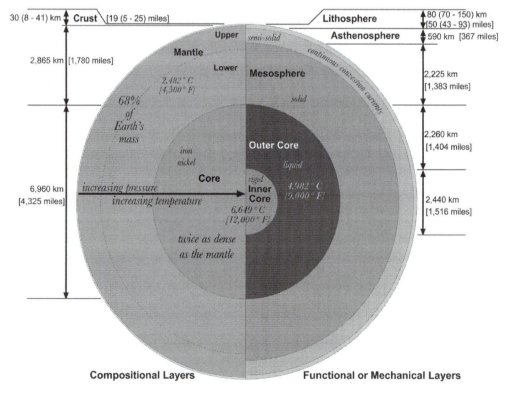

Figure 5.1 The compositional and functional or mechanical layers of the Earth.

- The compositions of the continental and oceanic crusts tend to be different:
- *Continental crust* is made up primarily of *granite*, an igneous rock (see later in this section), with large mineral crystals. This type of rock was formed from magma that was slowly pushed out from under the crust and allowed to cool very slowly.
- *Oceanic crust* is made up primarily of *basalt*. These rocks also are igneous, but were formed from volcanic eruptions, which cooled quickly with the resulting small crystal structures. Of course, you can find granite in the oceans and basalt on land, but they are not the most common in these areas.

- **Mantle**

  - The mantle lies below the crust and is about 1,780 miles (2,865 km) thick. It contains over two-thirds of the Earth's mass.
  - Silicates with some iron and magnesium are the primary materials in this layer.
  - Pressure and temperature increase from the upper to the lower portions of the mantle.

- **Core**

  - The core is about 4,325 miles (6,960 km) thick and is twice as dense at the mantle.
  - It is composed mostly of iron and nickel.

2. **Functional View of the Earth's Layers**

- **Lithosphere**

  - The upper part of the mantle is solid, like the crust. This solid portion of the mantle along with the crust is referred to as the *lithosphere.*
  - The lithosphere is the foundation for the continental and oceanic *plates* that make up the Earth's landmasses in a sort of jigsaw puzzle fashion. These plates of the lithosphere float on the next layer.
  - The thickness of the lithosphere ranges from 43 to 93 miles (70–150 km).

- **Asthenosphere**

  - This layer is composed of hot, semi-solid molten rock or *magma.*
    Convection currents occur continuously in this layer. As a result, the plates floating on top of this layer are "pushed" by these currents. The plates move towards, away from, or slide against one another. They move at a rate of 6/10 of an inch to 6 in (1.5–15 cm) per year.
    Example: Convection currents are noticeable when you heat water in a glass pot; currents of water can be seen moving from the bottom upwards and then cycling around.
    The term *plate tectonics* refers to the study of the structure and dynamics of these lithospheric plates, as shown on the map in Figure 5.2. The movements of these plates are important in understanding other aspects of the Earth system, including earthquakes, volcanoes, mountain building, and the rock cycle, which will be discussed later in this section.

- **Mesosphere**

  - Increased pressure and temperatures that average about 4,500° F (2,500° C).

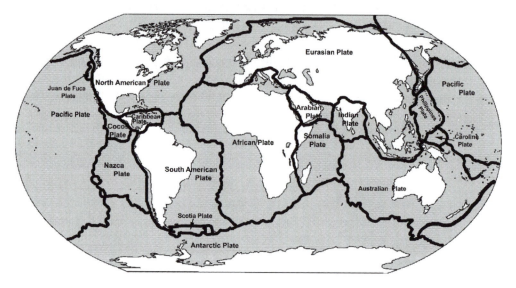

Figure 5.2 The arrangement of the plates that make up the lithosphere of the Earth.

Source: Adapted from University of Texas map collection (www.lib.utexas.edu/maps/world_maps/worldpol495.jpg).

- Solid, rigid layer.
- Thickness is about 1,383 miles (2,225 km).

- **Outer Core**

    - Although the pressure has increased, the outer core temperature is just under 9,000° F (5,000° C).
    - 1,404 miles (2,260 km) thick.
    - The Earth's rotational movement sets up a similar rotational movement of this liquid layer of iron and nickel.

- **Inner Core**

    - The solid *inner core* is even hotter (about 12,000° F or 6,650° C), but the increased pressure keeps this material in a solid state.
    - 1,516 miles (2,440 km) thick.
    - The interesting dynamic between the inner and outer cores is that they function like a giant electromagnet. As the Earth spins, it keeps the liquid outer core of iron and nickel spinning around the solid inner core of iron and nickel. It is this dynamic that produces the Earth's *electromagnetic field.*

Layers of the Atmosphere

If we move up from ground level into the atmosphere, we again move through a series of layers. These layers are shown in Figure 5.3. The content and ratio of gases that make up the first level of the atmosphere, the troposphere, remain the same. However, as you move up from sea level, as altitude increases, the atmospheric pressure decreases. The cruising altitudes of airplanes tend to be over 30,000 ft (9,144 m). At these altitudes, even altitudes over 15,000 ft (3,048 m), the pressure is so low that we cannot extract enough oxygen from the air to stay conscious or alive.

The *atmospheric pressure* at sea level is 14.7 psi (101.35 kPa). If you inflate your car's tires to 40 psi (275.8 kPa), you have taken the air at sea level and put more air into the tires, thus increasing the pressure bounded by the rubber. The ratio of gases has remained the same, but there is more of each gas within the tires. If you deflate these tires to 7.35 psi (50.68 kPa) (half the pressure at sea level), you now have the same ratio of gases, but with half as much of each gas. Breathing air at this pressure would make it difficult to stay conscious. Compared to sea level:

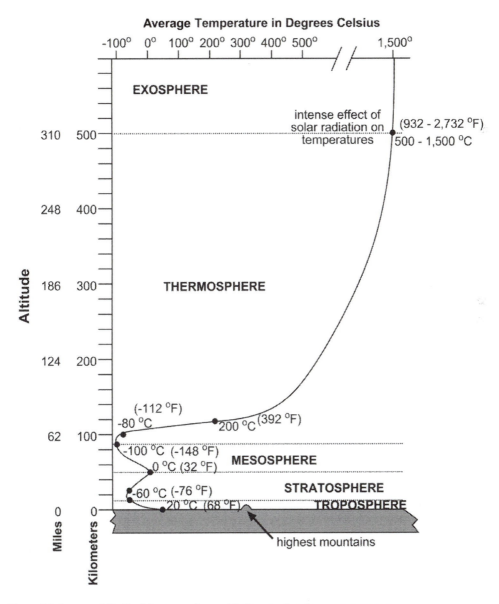

Figure 5.3 Layers of the Earth's atmosphere with the associated temperature ranges.

- at about 18,000 ft (5,486 m), the atmospheric pressure and oxygen are at about 25%;
- at 10,000 ft (3,048 m), the atmospheric pressure and oxygen content are about 50%;
- at 7,000 ft (2,133 m), the atmospheric pressure and oxygen content are about 67%;
- at 5,280 ft (1,609 m) or 1 mile, the atmospheric pressure and oxygen are about 75%.

Layers of the Atmosphere

1. **Troposphere**

   - We live in the troposphere, which extends upward to about

     - 22,000 ft (6,705 m) over the poles;
     - 58,000 ft (17,678 m) over the northern half of the United States;
     - 63,000 ft (19,202 m) over the equator.

   - The atmospheric pressure and the associated amount of available oxygen in the atmosphere decrease with altitude.
   - All weather systems and clouds develop in this layer, where the air is in constant motion.
   - Temperature also decreases with altitude. As you travel up from sea level, the temperature drops an average of 3.5° F for each 1,000 ft (305 m) up to the bottom of the next layer.

2. **Stratosphere**

   - The stratosphere contains the bulk of the ozone, which absorbs certain wavelengths of the Sun's radiation.
   - As a result, this absorption of heat radiation heats up this layer of the atmosphere. The temperature rises as you ascend through this layer.

3. **Mesosphere** (not to be confused with the layer of the mantle with the same name)

   - At the beginning of the mesosphere, the temperature again drops throughout its range in altitude from about 160,000 ft to 280,000 ft (48,768 – 85,344 m).

4. **Thermosphere**

   - At the beginning of the thermosphere, the temperature again increases to extremely hot temperatures at about 310 miles (499 km) high.

     - However, temperature is a tricky concept when considered in the thermosphere. Measures of temperature relate to the speed of particles and collisions of molecules. Since this layer has such a low density of oxygen, nitrogen, and other substances, the molecules move very rapidly when they absorb energy from the Sun's radiation. But the density of molecules is so thin that there are hardly any collisions between molecules—which would be the means of transferring energy that produces heat—so the atmosphere here would not "feel" hot.

   - This layer used to be called the *ionosphere*, since the Sun's radiation breaks molecules into separate ions.
   - The *auroras* (Northern and Southern Lights) take place in this layer as a result of these ionizations of molecules. The other effect of the strong ionization in this layer is that

radio signals can be bounced off them. HAM and AM radio signals can travel long distances by bouncing off this layer of the atmosphere.
- Some satellites and the International Space Station orbit in the upper regions of the thermosphere.

5. *Exosphere*

- The exosphere is the transitional layer above the thermosphere and outer space.
- This layer is made up of molecules and ions of air, as well as hydrogen and helium. These are the most common, but very sparsely distributed, constituents of this layer, which escape into outer space.
- The upper limit of the exosphere is about 6,200 miles (9,977 km).
- Many of the satellites we have in orbit are actually in this layer.

Forming Land and Landforms

As discussed in the previous subsection, the plates of the lithosphere floating on the slowly moving liquid magma of the asthenosphere account for earthquakes and a great deal of volcanic activity. The movement of the plates takes place in three basic ways:

1. Two plates move toward one another with one plate moving underneath. These areas are referred to as *convergent boundaries* and *subduction zones*. The three basic types of convergent boundaries are where:

   - an oceanic plate hits another oceanic plate;
   - an oceanic plate hits a continental plate;
   - one continental plate hits another continental plate.

     – Active volcanic mountains often occur along such convergent boundaries. In Figure 5.2, the convergent boundary between the Nazca (oceanic) and South American (continental) plates have resulted in the volcanically active Andes Mountains. As the Nazca plate is subducted underneath the South American plate, magma is released up into volcanic tubes. When oceanic plates are involved, volcanic mountains rise from the plate on top of the one that is being subducted. In addition, trenches occur at the boundary between the two plates.

2. Two plates move away from each other at *spreading or divergent boundaries*. These boundaries are usually found along the ocean floors, where underwater mountain ridges are located. Unlike the Rocky Mountains, the mountains that result from spreading are formed by escaping magma from the asthenosphere. As the plates move apart, magma rises along the ridge then cools creating new crust material along the ridge.

3. *Transverse boundaries* are those that occur along plates that are sliding past each other, such as where the Pacific and North American plates meet in California and Oregon. These boundaries are characterized by resistance that releases rapidly along *fault lines*. One of the most well-known fault lines is the San Andreas Fault that runs near the coast of California. Throughout this fault, the Pacific plate moves northward past the North American plate with rapid releases of stress, which we feel as earthquakes (which will be discussed in more detail shortly).

You can recognize faults through a number of visible clues in the terrain, such as:

- In Figure 5.4, each representation of a fault has a checkered band that represents the layers of earth we can see where cross-sections of the earth are exposed, such as in canyons, cliffs, river banks, and road-cuts.
- We also may run across a "discontinuity" in the landforms around us. We may be walking along a reasonably flat area, then come to a drop-off that extends across the area. This drop-off may be a fault line.
- Instead of a drop-off, we may come across a depression in the ground that runs along a linear path. This depression may be due to the washing away of loose rocks that broke away from movements of the *foot* and *hanging wall blocks* (as shown in Figure 5.4).

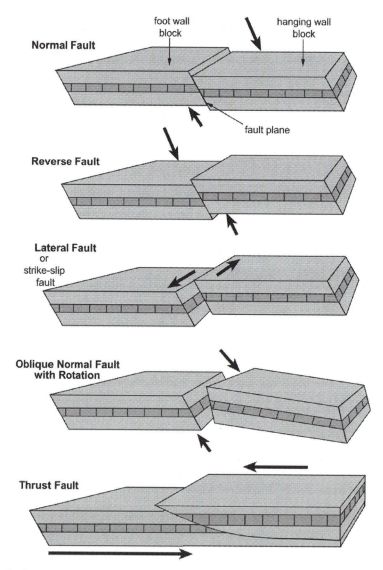

Figure 5.4 The five major types of faults.

- You may be walking along a stream or a dry wash and come across a shift in the path of the stream or wash. This shift may have occurred from movement along a fault line that intersects the stream.
- You also may come across changes in the patterns of plant growth in a specific area. Such a change in plant growth patterns are most easily recognized in farms and orchards where plants are grown in straight rows. When you come across a displacement of the rows, you may be looking at movement along a fault.

As the continental and oceanic plates crash into each other, pull apart from one another, and slide against each other, the effects include volcanic and earthquake activity. If you look at a map that shows worldwide earthquake and volcanic activity, such as in Figure 5.5, most of this activity is around the boundaries of the plates. In addition, as these plates move along major fault lines, the earth cracks at angles to these fault lines creating additional faults called *extensional faults*.

Earthquakes

As you have already read, earthquakes occur along plate boundaries and other fault lines that emanate from the primary fault lines. They occur when two plates or two rock walls on either side of a fault collide, pull apart, or slide along one another. However, a bit more about earthquakes needs to be explored. When the built-up energy is released as the two parts "slip" abruptly, the main point of this energy release is called the *focus*, which can occur at various depths, down to 62 miles (100 km) below the surface of the Earth. The point on the Earth's surface directly above the "focus" is called the *epicenter*. At the moment of energy release,

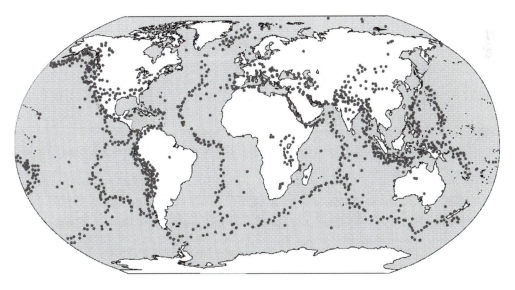

Figure 5.5 A map of earthquake and volcanic activity.

Source: Adapted from University of Texas map collection (www.lib.utexas.edu/maps/world_maps/world_pol495.jpg).

waves move through the Earth in all directions. These waves are called *seismic waves* and come in various kinds:

- *P-waves* or primary waves are *compression waves* (see Section 4 for additional discussions of waves). These waves move back and forth as they travel. The P-waves are the fastest of the seismic waves. If an earthquake rattles southern California at noon, the P-waves will hit the middle of the Indian Ocean or the approximate opposite side of the Earth at about 12:20 pm, California time—or 20 minutes to pass through the center of the Earth. The directions and speeds vary as the waves travel through different density materials that make up the Earth's layers.
- The *S-waves* or secondary waves are transverse waves that move from side to side. These waves are slower and cannot move through liquids, such as the outer core.
- *Love* and *Raleigh waves*, both of which are referred to as *L-waves*, move up and down and sideways along the surface of the Earth. These waves are the primary culprits in the damage and destruction that result from earthquakes.

Two scales are commonly used to describe earthquake intensity:

- The **Richter Scale** was developed to measure the intensity or magnitude of earthquakes. The scale that ranges from 1 to 8.8 (or 9.0 on some scales) is not a linear, arithmetical measurement, but one that is logarithmic. In other words, moving from 1 to 2 on the Richter scale is a 10-fold increase in magnitude or intensity. From 1 to 8 on this scale is an increase from 1 to 10,000,000 ($1 = 10^0$; $2 = 10^1$; $3 = 10^2$; $4 = 10^3$; $5 = 10^4$; $6 = 10^5$; $7 = 10^6$; $8 = 10^7$).
- The **Modified Mercalli Scale** was developed as a measure of an earthquake's destruction. Its scale is not based on measurements, but rather on observations. It has the following 12 levels:

  1. NOT FELT—not detected by seismographs.
  2. VERY WEAK—objects, such as chandeliers may swing; noticeable by a few people.
  3. WEAK—vibrations are like a passing truck or train; felt by a few people most of whom are inside.
  4. LIGHT—doors, windows, and other object rattle; many people inside of building feel the vibrations, but only felt by a few outdoors.
  5. MODERATE—doors move; object may fall off shelves and break; sleeping people are awakened; noticeable by almost everyone.
  6. STRONG—shrubs and trees shake; heavy furniture moved; walking is noticeably more difficult; books fall off of shelves.
  7. VERY STRONG—difficult to remain standing; poorly constructed buildings suffer moderate to heavy damage; plaster and loose bricks loosen and fall; small landslides along sloping ground; tap water becomes muddy.
  8. SEVERE—driving a car becomes difficult; branches of trees break and fall; chimneys and other tall structures break and fall.
  9. VIOLENT—extensive damage to buildings; underground pipes break; building foundations crack.

10. EXTREME—many cement and framed structures are destroyed; railroad tracks bend; many landslides; water from rivers and lakes is thrown onto the ground.
11. EXTREME (DISASTROUS)—bridges and most masonry and framed buildings are destroyed; railroad tracks are severely bent; all underground pipes and conduits are destroyed.
12. EXTREME (CATASTROPHIC)—nearly everything is destroyed; massive displacement of rock structures.

The earthquake that struck central Italy on April 6, 2009, had a Richter Scale magnitude of 6.3. The Modified Mercalli Intensity scale for this earthquake ranged from 5 to 8.3 depending upon the location. This earthquake resulted in the deaths of 287 people, with over a 1,000 injured, and over 10,000 buildings severely damaged or destroyed.

Volcanoes

As mentioned, many volcanic mountains occur along plate boundaries, where magma escapes between the edges of the plates. However, volcanoes appear in other locations as well, such as where the heat from the asthenosphere melts parts of the lithosphere and crust creating routes for magma to rise to the surface. These "hotspots" appear all over the world in both continental and oceanic plates. The following list describes the basic types of volcanoes present on Earth.

• **Shield Volcanoes:** Shield volcanoes are the largest volcanoes and have the typical look of a large mountain with a crater at the top. However, the sizes and shapes tend to vary from wide and relatively low to quite high. This type of volcano can occur along subduction zones and at "hotspots," where there are plumes from the asthenosphere through a thinner area of the lithosphere. The Hawaiian Islands have been built up from such hotspots. These types of volcanoes do not explode, except if large amounts of water somehow get into the crater. Instead of exploding, they exude streams of lava that flow down the sides of the mountain. However, in some cases, such volcanoes can produce cinder and spatter cones around the main vent of the volcano.

  – *Cinder cones* have been considered by many geologists to be a separate type of volcano, but are now considered a part of volcanic fields or companion structures to other types of volcanoes.
  – *Spatter cones* often occur in conjunction with other volcanoes. In these cases, a spatter cone develops around fissures or vents from the volcano. As lava spews up into the air, it lands, spatters, and fuses with the underlying cooled lava forming a new cone.

• **Strato Volcanoes** (previously called *Composite Volcanoes*): The most common volcanoes are strato volcanoes, which account for about 60% of the Earth's volcanoes. The lava in these volcanoes tends to be stiffer or more viscous than the basaltic lavas of shield volcanoes. Inside, layers of lava are interspersed with layers of other volcanic materials, such as gases and ash. The more viscous layers of lava tend to act like plugs that allow the gases below to build up pressure. As a result, these volcanoes often explode, spewing ashes into the atmosphere and for miles downwind. Mount St. Helens in Washington State, which erupted in 1980, is an example of a strato volcano. These types of volcanoes tend not to erupt often, because of the slow build up of magma, even though they do tend to occur along plate boundaries. On the other hand, they tend to cause more damage and loss of life than other volcanoes, which is probably due to the extent to which they spew extremely thick clouds of toxic gases and volcanic ash.

- **Rhyolite Caldera Complexes:** These volcanoes are the most violently explosive of all volcanoes, yet are barely noticeable. They have huge magma chambers beneath the surface of the earth. When they explode, they spew ash over great distances in all directions, then collapse in on themselves. The last of these eruptions occurred at Taupo, New Zealand, in 83 AD. There are very long periods (thousands of years) between the violent, major eruptions of these volcanoes. They usually have many vents across their areas. The smaller vents may release gases and ashes periodically. Yellowstone is an example of such a volcano, but is not likely to erupt over the next 10,000 years.
- **Monogenetic Fields:** Monogenetic fields are loosely organized areas of volcanic activity. These volcanoes tend not to look like volcanoes. Magma build up is very slow and tends not to have any set pathway of flow. When pressure builds up enough to erupt, it does not occur at any set location, thus the notion of "field." Some of these eruptions leave behind small mounds, called cinder cones. Monogenetic fields are found in Arizona, Oregon, Washington, Idaho, and California. In some places, vast lava flows are present, where lava, rather than just ash, streamed out of the cones, such as in the area of Sunset Crater near Flagstaff, Arizona.
- **Flood Basalts:** The evidence of these volcanoes used to be interrupted as evidence of huge rivers of fast moving lava covering large areas ranging over thousands of square miles with depths over 165 ft (50 m). However, these vast areas of basaltic lava seem to be built up from below. The most well-known flood basalt volcano is near the Columbia River in southeastern Washington State.
- **Mid-Ocean Ridges:** These volcanoes occur along the mid-ocean ridges at the boundaries between two oceanic plates. In these locations, the ridges are built up from molten basalt escaping between two oceanic plates as they diverge or move apart. The magma escapes upwards and cools, rapidly forming increasingly high ridges of basalt.

In addition to volcanic mountain building, there are three other types of mountain-building processes:

- *folded mountains* from the compression of rock layers as two plates collide;
- *uplifted* or *fault-block mountains* from the cracking and pushing up of rock layers along fault lines;
- *domed* or *upwarped mountain,* formed from upward forces that push and bend the layers above into mountains. This upward force can be from the intrusion of molten rock into areas below the layers that are bent upwards. Examples include the Black Hills of South Dakota and the Adirondacks in New York.

Erosion

Wind and water erosion are two of the primary *mechanical weathering* forces of change in land formations. Water flow in temporary and permanent rivers and streams erode away at the banks and bottoms of these streambeds and carry sediments downstream. Over time, these sediments build up in certain areas along the way, at the mouth of the river, or in bays and oceans. Water erosion also occurs as water runs off of slopes during rainstorms and recedes after floods. Beaches along coastal seashores undergo constant erosion from the waves and tides. During storms, these coastal regions can change more rapidly due to the increased tidal levels and intensity of wind and waves. Water erosion is a natural and ongoing process, but the problem is that people usually like to live where there is water—along rivers and streams, on the sides of hills with great views, by the seashore. Unfortunately, these are the very areas that are most subject to water erosion. Floods along rivers, mudslides on the hills, and hurricanes and other storms along the coast can damage and destroy buildings and other structures.

Wind also erodes away at landforms, but usually at a much slower rate than water. Strong winds can pick up and move small particles of sand and soil over fairly great distances. In addition to directly moving the land in this way, the airborne particles become erosive "weapons." We have sandblasting machines that will "clean" the sides of buildings by bombarding them with sand. In nature, the wind acts as a giant sand blaster, by picking up sand and soil and pounding landforms that rise above the ground.

Another form of mechanical erosion has to do with the *freezing of water* and *glaciers.* If you live in an area that goes through seasonal changes with snowy winters, you will notice that roads get new potholes and a variety of cracks after every winter. As snow melts, the water will penetrate into little cracks and holes in the surface of the roads. This melting process may take place during a sunny day. At night, the melted water freezes. When water freezes, it expands and cracks the road even further. As this process is repeated day after day, the road surface is broken up to the point where large parts of the surface are destroyed. This same process works on rocks. You also may notice that roads through rock-cuts have more rocks falling during the winter and early spring when the rocks along the sides of the cut are broken up by repeated melting and freezing.

Glaciers and other larger movements of ice will actually cut through the surface of the land beneath. During the end of the Ice Ages, as vast glaciers moved downhill they cut into and created many of the land formations we now have, including many lakes, river valleys, and "mountains" or mounds of rocks that were deposited at the melting ends of the glaciers. The glaciers that exist now, which are melting much too quickly from global warming, continue to cut through rocks and then carry away and deposit them. Many land formations of Canada and the northern part of the United States are the result of the last Ice Age glaciers' erosive actions and depositions.

Another effect of water has to do with its characteristic as a solvent and its role in *chemical weathering.* Many chemical compounds can dissolve in water. As water passes over certain types of rocks and minerals (which will be discussed shortly), it can actually dissolve parts of these materials. In addition, water with dissolved oxygen can act as an oxidizing agent. Oxygen can dissolve in water during rainfall, as water runs downstream, and from plant photosynthesis. If materials that contain iron come in contact with the oxygen in water, they will begin to oxidize or rust. If you see rocks that look reddish or brown, they are likely to contain iron that has oxidized from their exposure to dissolved oxygen in water. Water also can dissolve carbon dioxide during rain and from respiration of aquatic organisms. When carbon dioxide dissolves it becomes carbonic acid, which can initiate chemical reactions that actually change some substances with which it comes into contact. Rocks with potassium (feldspars) react with carbonic acid—the hydrogen ion in the carbonic acid removes the potassium, creating potassium carbonates, which then can be utilized by plants. Another example of chemical weathering occurs in rocks such as granite that contain feldspars and quartz. During chemical weathering, the feldspars are changed, while the unchanged quartz that does not react chemically will be washed away and eventually be broken up into sand particles.

Forces of Change

As we've seen, the major forces of change in land formations involve the "big" forces connected to plate tectonics. These "forces" include earthquakes and a variety of volcanic processes. Some of these forces result in the building of mountains, including islands, the raising of land as plateaus, and the building of deep oceanic trenches. The "smaller" forces of wind, water, and ice also make changes to land formations, including the building up of land with sediments and the destruction of land formations. All of these forces are both constructive and destructive. As you read further, you will see that these forces are involved in many of the processes of the rock cycle and in the creation of a variety of other land formations.

Key Idea 5.2 Earth Features

In this subsection, the major features of the Earth will be described briefly. These features have been created through a variety of the forces just discussed.

Continents

- Formation processes: plate tectonics.
- Continents are large landmasses, usually associated with a continental plate.
- Continents are not particularly well-defined other than by historical convention. However, the only two continents that do not sit on a specific continental plate are Europe and Asia. These two continents share a common continental plate.
- The seven continents include North America, South America, Europe, Asia, Africa, Australia, and Antarctica.
- India is often referred to as a sub-continent, since it sits on its own continental plate. However, Somalia, the Arab peninsula, parts of the Caribbean, and the Philippines also sit on their own continental plates.

Islands

Formation processes: volcanic, uplifting, and land subsidence.

- Islands are any land that is surrounded entirely by water.
- Types of islands:

– *Continental islands* are islands that arise from the continental shelf. Greenland, Cuba, Jamaica, Great Britain, Tasmania, and Sable Island (off of Nova Scotia, Canada) are examples of continental islands. Several subtypes include:

  ○ *micro-continental islands*, which arise as volcanic island from plates that are being pulled apart, such as New Zealand and Madagascar;
  ○ *cays* or *keys*, such as the Florida Keys, where sand deposits build up forming small islands;
  ○ *barrier islands* that form in similar ways as keys, such as the island communities along the coasts of New Jersey, Maryland, Virginia, North Carolina, and South Carolina.

• *Oceanic islands* are mostly volcanic formations. There are four basic types, with the first three having volcanic origins:

  – The first type are islands formed from volcanoes over hotspots, such as those that make up the Hawaiian Islands.
  – The second type involves volcanoes along plate subduction zones, such as the Aleutian Islands. These islands usually occur in an arc.
  – The third type, and last of the volcanic islands, occur along plate boundaries that are pulling apart, such as Iceland.
  – The fourth type occurs in rare circumstances where plate boundaries push up a landmass, forming an island, such as the Macquarie Island southeast of Australia along the southern boundary of the Australian Plate.

• *Tropical islands* include granite outcroppings and coral reefs. Islands from coral reefs are built up as sand and other sediments collect on top of the reefs and eventually create islands.
• *River and lake islands* occur from sediment deposition and erosion. In one stage of the aging sequence of rivers, the river follows a winding path. As time proceeds, it wears away at the inside of the bends. Eventually, it erodes through to the returning bend, leaving an island in the middle (see figure 5.7). Islands in lakes and some rivers were formed from hills or mountain peaks prior to the existence of the lake or river. These types of islands are common in human-made lakes where rivers have been dammed, which razed submerged towns as well as parts of surrounding hills or mountains.

Atolls

Formation processes: coral reef and sedimentation.

• Atolls are sandy islands that are generally circular, horseshoe, or oval shaped.
• Atolls have been built up over coral reefs. They usually form a ring around a lagoon of shallow saltwater. Most atolls are in the tropical Pacific Ocean, with others in the Indian Ocean, and only a few in the Atlantic Ocean.

Peninsulas and Capes

Formation processes: surrounding subsidence, uplifting, or erosion.

- Peninsulas and capes are landforms that extend out into the ocean or other large body of water and are connected to the mainland.
- *Peninsulas* are connected to the mainland by a narrow piece of land called an *isthmus*. Most of Florida is a peninsula.
- *Capes* are extensions of land into the ocean or other bodies of water, and are connected to the mainland, but not by land that is significantly narrower. Cape Cod, Cape Hatteras, and Cape Horn are examples of capes.

Plateaus

Formation processes: uplifting and occasional eroding

- Plateaus rise over 1,500 ft (457 m) above surrounding areas.
- Plateaus are flatlands with horizontal rock layers.
- Plateaus have at least one steep slope.
- Some plateaus are called "mountains" even though they are technically not any of the mountains described elsewhere in this chapter. Some plateaus formed from uplifting. Rather than crumple into mountains, these landmasses were lifted to higher altitudes while remaining relatively flat. Other types of plateaus were formed after the surrounding areas were eroded away.
- The highest plateau is the *Tibetan Plateau*, which formed about 55 million years ago when two plates collided and crumpled part of one plate to form the Himalaya Mountains. The other expanse of the plate was raised without folding or crumpling to form the Tibetan Plateau.
- In the United States, the *Colorado Plateau* covers an area that includes northern Arizona, eastern and southeastern Utah, western Colorado, and northwestern New Mexico.

Canyons

Formation processes: erosion from rivers.

- Rivers gradually cut through elevated landmasses, such as plateaus, to create canyons.
  Example: The Green, Colorado, and San Juan Rivers cut through the Colorado Plateau leaving behind extensive *canyons*, including the Grand Canyon. The layers of rock that have been built up over hundreds of millions of years are now exposed. In fact, at the bottom of the inner gorge of the Grand Canyon are igneous and metamorphic rocks that are almost two billion years old. On top of these rocks are layers of sedimentary rocks, which were built up when this entire area was under a sea until about 75 million years ago when the Colorado Plateau began uplifting. Up to the present point in time, the Colorado River has cut out the Grand Canyon to a depth of over 5,000 ft (almost a mile) (1,524 km), from 4 to 18 miles (6–29 km) wide, and about 277 miles (445 km) long.

Buttes and Mesas

Formation processes: eroded mostly from plateaus.

- Buttes are taller than they are wide.
- Mesas are wider than they are tall.
- Both have hard, flat, volcanic rock layers on top.
- Both have soft, sedimentary rock layers below.
- Mesas and buttes are similar to plateaus, but smaller. In certain areas, especially in the southwest United States, much of the land was once under a large sea. Over time, these areas built up many layers of sedimentary rock. After this area was uplifted above sea level, some parts were covered with lava from volcanic eruptions. Over time, erosion ate away at the underlying layers of sedimentary rock wherever they were exposed. Since the volcanic rock on top, called *cap-rock*, is much more resistant to erosion, the resulting formations were flat-topped "mountains." In some cases, the sedimentary rock beneath the cap-rock erodes away leaving an overhang, which eventually breaks off and falls.

Till

Formation processes: glacial erosion and deposition.

- A till is a collection of rocks piled up after being directly deposited by a glacier.
- Glaciers scrape and carry rocks as they move down hill. As they begin to melt, they drop the rocks they are carrying. The deposited rocks tend to be of different sizes and kinds.

Out-wash

Formation Processes: glacial erosion and deposition.

- An out-wash is a collection of rocks piled up after being deposited by a glacier and washed away.
- As opposed to till, the rocks are carried away from the glacier by the melted water.

Moraines

Formation processes: glacial erosion and deposition.

- Moraines are ridges of till.
- When glaciers disappear they can leave behind mounds of debris or till. These mounds can stretch out as long ridges.
- There are several types of moraine:

    - *lateral moraines* follow the linear edges of the glacier;
    - *end moraines* are deposited at the end of the glacier;

    – *terminus moraines* occur at the furthest point reached by the glacier;

    – *recessional moraines* are those deposited as the glacier receded;

    – *ground moraines* were laid down as glaciers receded and left a steady deposit of till, which created small, gentle rolling hills.

Outwash Plains

Formation processes: glacial erosion and deposition.

- Outwash plains are deposits of a mixture of silt, sand, and gravel that were laid down in layers from the glacial melt-water.
- In general, the layers of deposits in outwash plains are laid down in the order of weight of the material. The heaviest gravels are the lowest, followed by smaller and lighter gravel, then by sand, and finally by the fine particles of silt.

Kettle Holes and Lakes

Formation processes: glacial erosion and deposition.

- Kettle holes and lakes are depressions in the glacial deposits (till).
- On some occasions, large chunks of glacial ice dislodged from the glacier and then lodged deeply into the deposits of till. When these chunks melted, they left a large depression, which occasionally filled with water forming a lake.

Drumlins

Formation processes: glacial erosion and deposition.

- A drumlin is a long, smooth, sleek, and tapered mound; the steepest slope at the wider end was created at the end from which the glacier was moving; the gentler slope is at the end facing the direction of glacial movement.
- Drumlins range in height from about 50 to 200 ft (15–61 m), and tend to be about a quarter to a half mile long (0.4–0.8 km). They are almost always found in clusters, not as a single feature.

Eskers

Formation processes: glacial erosion and deposition.

- Eskers are long ridges of glacial deposited gravel and sand; they may be fairly low, in the range of several yards/meters high, but can extend for miles/kilometers.
- Current thinking suggests that eskers were deposited from glacial melting that formed tunnels in the ice at the bottom of glaciers. Eskers seem to take on the shape and size of these tunnels. In present day, eskers are a prime site for mining sand and gravel, which is leading to their destruction.

Kames

Formation processes: glacial erosion and deposition.

- Kames are steeply sloped hills of gravel and sand.
- Kames may be the result of dislodged glacial ice that deposited their contents of sand and gravel into mounds as they melted.

Alluvial Fans

Formation processes: water erosion.

- Alluvial fans are fan-shaped deposits of material found in mountainous deserts.
- Alluvial fans are deposits of material carried by water and deposited in some downstream location after the slope changes. They often occur where washes from mountains or canyons enter flat areas. As the water spreads out and slows down, the material it's carrying is deposited forming a fan shape. The heaviest and coarsest materials are deposited first, while the finer materials are found around the far edges of the fan.
- Alluvial fans are more commonly found in arid, desert environments where mountain washes flow into flatlands.

Inselbergs

Formation processes: water and chemical erosion.

- Inselbergs are steep-sloped granite outcroppings and mountain remnants in deserts.
- Inselbergs are part of the sequence of desert landscape changes. Over time, desert and mountain ridges are eroded away. Water breaks up and wears away granite through mechanical and chemical erosion along the mountain washes. Eventually, all that is left is a string of disconnected rock outcroppings and mountains.

Playa and Playa Lakes

Formation processes: water erosion.

- Playa are dry or occasional lakes in mountainous deserts.
- Playa are formed from water that runs further away from the alluvial fans in the desert basins, filling small depressions with water after rains. After the water evaporates, cracked muddy flats are all that are left.

Sand Dunes

Formation processes: wind erosion.

- Sand dunes are mounds of sand.
- Sand dunes are tapered gently toward the direction from which the dominant winds

blow—called the *windward* side. The *leeward* side, which faces away from the wind, is more steeply sloped. The wind moves the sand up into a gently sloped pile. At the top, the sand falls down as the wind swirls downward and back up along the leeward side of the dune.

- There are several types of dune:

  - *Barchan dunes* tend to occur where there are not great quantities of sand. They are usually individual formations that take on large crescent shapes with the pointy ends of the crescent pointing in the windward direction. These dunes also tend to migrate at up to about 50 ft (15 m) per year. Their size may reach 100 ft (30 m) in height and over 300 yards (274 m) wide from tip to tip of the crescent.

  - *Transverse dunes* occur as parallel ridges separated by troughs and form at right angles to the prevailing winds. They also occur where vast quantities of sand are not available. They tend to be common in along coastal beaches and in arid expanses.

  - *Longitudinal dunes* are ridges that form parallel to the prevailing winds. These dunes can vary from about 10 ft high and 100 ft long (3 m × 30 m) to almost 400 ft high and over 60 miles long (122 m × 96 km). These dunes are common in the Sahara Desert.

  - *Parabolic dunes* look like the reverse of Barchan dunes, but with fairly extensive plant growth. The steep slopes of these dunes point towards the windward, as opposed to the leeward side. The wind moves the sand from the windward side in a process of deflation, leaving the steeper slope pointing into the wind.

Deflation Hollows

Formation processes wind erosion:

- Deflation hollows are depressions that vary in depth and extent.
- Strong winds lift and transport fine particles, leaving behind heavier particles. As a result, depressions are left behind from the removal of material. These depressions range in size from about 3 ft deep by 10 ft wide (1 × 3 m) to 150 ft (45 m) deep by several miles/kilometers wide. Thousand of these deflation hollows can be found across the Great Plains of the central United States.

Craters

Formation processes: volcanic activity and meteor strikes.

- Craters are large circular depressions in the land with a surrounding ridge.
- The most common craters are from volcanoes, as discussed previously. Some extinct volcanoes leave craters behind, some of which have formed lakes, such as Crater Lake in Oregon.
- Meteors that reach the surface of the Earth create craters. These craters vary in size. From a ground-level perspective it is often difficult to see a crater. The area may look like the rest of the surroundings with trees, grasses, shrubs, and even buildings and farmland. However, the mark of a crater is a circular ridge of rubble, which may be covered with soil and full of vegetation. More complex craters have a mound in the

middle. The rocks in the rubble, which made up the original layers of rock, may show signs of partial melting. The original meteor may have vaporized or left bits and pieces mixed in with the rubble.

Oceans

Oceans cover over 70% of the Earth's surface. Although there is really only one continuous body of water, we've divided up this ocean into five primary oceans:

- Atlantic Ocean
- Pacific Ocean
- Indian Ocean
- Arctic Ocean
- Southern Ocean (which is often included within the Atlantic, Pacific, and Indian Oceans).

All of these oceans flow into one another, but at the same time, each one has its own characteristic currents and features. The Pacific Ocean is the largest and has the deepest points and highest underwater mountains. The deepest point at 35,798 ft orover 6.75 miles (10,911 m or almost 11 km) is in the western portion in the Mariana Trench. At the bottom of the Mariana Trench an object would experience almost 1,086 atmospheres of pressure.

In Figure 3.1 (Section 3), the middle diagram shows the zonation of the ocean. The abyssal zone is also referred to as the *abyssal plain*. As these plains begin to slope upwards towards the continents, they are called *continental rises*. When the slope dramatically increases as it moves up to the continental shelf, the slope is called the *continental slope*. The ocean floor also has deep trenches, underwater volcanic mountains, uplifted ridges at plate boundaries, and rifts, which are made of lava that has extruded from between plates that are moving away from each other.

Seawater Salinity and Temperature

Seawater is composed of a variety of different salts and other dissolved materials. Sodium chloride, the ingredient of table salt, is the major salt in seawater (Na^+ and Cl^- as ions). The other major ions from salts include: sulfates, magnesium, calcium, potassium, bicarbonates, bromide, borates, strontium, and fluoride. However, seawater can contain almost anything that can be found on Earth. The *salinity* of seawater is a measure of how much salt is dissolved in the water. Although salinities vary somewhat from location to location, the average is about 35, which refers to parts per thousand. Salinity used to be represented as 35‰. Salinities vary due to a number of factors:

- evaporation removes water, but leaves the salt behind, which raises the salinity;
- a river of freshwater entering the ocean lowers the salinity, as do heavy rains;
- the melting of icebergs adds freshwater and lowers the salinity, while the formation of icebergs and other ice increases salinity.

Inland bays and tidal pools experience a great deal more variation in salinity due to their shallow depth and reduced mixing.

The *temperature* of seawater varies depending on location, season, and depth. However, as you may recall from Section 4, the nature of water is different from most substances. As water cools, it reaches its maximum density at 4° C (39° F). As it continues to cool from this point down through freezing, it expands and becomes less dense. Saltwater modifies this pattern slightly by decreasing the freezing point. However, when water freezes, the salts are left behind. Seawater with a salinity of 35 freezes at –2° C (28.4° F). When water freezes it takes on a very tightly knit crystalline structure, which usually has no space to accommodate anything else, such as salt ions. As a result, when seawater freezes, its ice has no salt content. In terms of density, unlike freshwater reaching its maximum density at 4° C (39° F), saltwater is most dense just prior to its freezing.

The temperature of the vast majority of ocean water is between 0° and 4° C (32° and 39.2° F). Warming occurs in the top 3ft to 650 ft (1 m to 200 m) of the ocean that is affected by sunlight. Depending upon how clear the water is, sunlight may only penetrate a few yards into the water. Even with completely clear water, the water and other molecules absorb the sunlight so that by the time a depth of 650 ft (200 m) is reached, there is no further light penetration. In addition, sunlight striking the water at greater angles, as in the far northern and southern latitudes, does not penetrate as far. As water absorbs light, it also is absorbing heat energy. As a result, the water below the sunlight penetration level is cold.

Large-scale cycling of water from the surface to the deep ocean takes place when the water at the surface becomes denser, as with the cold North Atlantic waters. These waters not only become more saline as the seawater freezes, but also colder. Both of these factors increase the density of the water. As a result, this denser water sinks to the bottom and spreads out along the layers of water of equal density. At this point the temperature is about 3° C (37.4° F), with a salinity of about 34 to 35. This deep Atlantic water current flows toward the South then circles around the tip of Africa. At this point, some waters move up into the Indian Ocean while others move into the South Pacific. As these currents move northward they begin to warm, then rise to the surface and join the surface and shallow sub-surface currents shown in Figure 5.6.

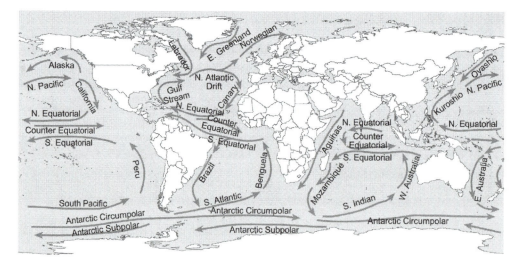

Figure 5.6 A map of the surface and subsurface currents of the Earth's oceans.

Source: Adapted from Wikipedia clickable world map (http://en.wikipedia.org/wiki/World/Clickable_world_map).

This deep water, *density-driven current* has been referred to as *conveyor belt cycling*. These deep ocean currents bring nutrients, including various parts in the marine carbon, phosphorus, and other cycles, from the bottom to the surface. In addition, the photosynthetic zone's oxygen-rich waters cycle downwards providing oxygen for deep-sea organisms where no oxygen is produced.

Ocean Currents

There are numerous surface and shallow sub-surface currents in the world's oceans. Many of these currents are "local" or "regional" and vary considerably with tides, between day and night, winds, temperatures, and seasons. However, there are major surface currents that may vary slightly during the year, but whose overall patterns remain stable. These surface currents, as shown in Figure 5.6, move in giant circular patterns, called *gyres*. They move counter-clockwise between latitudes 15° and 45° south, and clockwise between latitudes 15° and 45° North in the Atlantic and Pacific Oceans. The Indian Ocean doesn't extend far enough north to have a clockwise gyre. There also are opposing circumpolar currents around Antarctica, along with minor currents along the far northern parts of the Atlantic and Pacific Oceans. The currents in the northern hemisphere that move toward the North on the western sides of the oceans carry warm waters in relatively narrow, deep, and fast current streams. The currents that descend from the North along the eastern sides of the oceans carry colder waters in more shallow, wide, and slower current streams. If you have ever gone swimming on the east and west coasts of the United States, you probably have noticed that the ocean water along the east coast is much warmer than the water at the same latitudes along the Pacific Coast of California.

The major mechanism of the surface ocean currents or gyres has to do with wind, which, in turn, has to do with the sun's radiant heating of the surface of the Earth (this concept will be discussed in more detail later under the "Climate and Weather" subsection). This solar heating of the surface is not consistent in all locations, but varies with the surface, the latitude, and the season. These "big" patterns of wind movement remain fairly stable in each location. The basic pattern of wind movement has to do with heat and the spinning of the Earth.

Let's take a point at the bottom of the southern most gyre in the North Atlantic—at a point in the Northern Equatorial Current (see Figure 5.6). This point heats up a great deal more here, near the equator, than at its opposite point in the northern portion of the gyre (North Atlantic Drift Current). This heated air rises quickly. As it rises, the Earth's spin, which is towards the east, moves the rising air to the west. The air rising upward from a moving Earth will not keep up with the motion of the Earth's surface, but will "lag" behind, setting up a westerly movement. Since the surface of the Earth is moving faster near the equator than at points further north, the wind patterns above the oceanic gyres on either side of the equator move to the west and set up the dominant wind patterns, which in turn affect the gyres. These basic patterns of clockwise movements in the North and counter-clockwise movements in the South are referred to as the *coriolis effect*. This "effect" involves only large air and water masses.

In the Atlantic and Pacific Oceans there are currents that run along the equator in opposite directions in between the northern and southern gyres. These Counter Equatorial Currents occur as a result of the two westward movements of the gyres. Some of the water that moves westward on either side of the equator returns as the counter current, while the remaining water moves either northward or southward in the gyres. This counter current is similar to what happens if you sit in a bathtub and push water forward along both sides of the tub. You get a return flow backwards towards you in the middle of the tub.

Ocean Tides

Oceanic *tides* are a major factor in the dynamics of coastline ecology and environments. The gravitational pull from the Moon is the major force behind tidal movements. The Sun's gravity also affects tides, but is more of a contributing factor. As the Earth spins on its axis, the Moon's position changes continuously in relation to points on Earth.

Let's say the Moon is positioned above the western Atlantic Ocean in line with Florida's Atlantic coast at 5:00 pm on day one of our observations. The gravitational force of the Moon pulls on the ocean water, creating a bulge that creates a high tide along Florida's coast. As the Earth spins, this tidal bulge moves towards the west affecting the Gulf coast of Florida, then the west coast of the United States, and so on around the world. Since the Moon also moves in an easterly direction, by the time the Moon reaches the same point above Florida, it is about 50 minutes earlier, or about 4:10 pm the next day. The tidal bulge is on both sides of the Earth, the side nearest the Moon, as well as the opposite side. As a result, in most cases there are two high tides and two low tides in each 24-hour period. Tides tend to be highest where the Moon is directly above. Since the Moon's orbital plane does not line up with the Earth's equatorial plane, the location of the Moon varies from day to day. If you look at a tide table, you will notice that the tidal variation is not the same everyday.

The other factor that affects tides, as mentioned briefly, is the Sun. If the Sun and Moon line up on the same side of the Earth, we get the highest and lowest tides. The next highest and lowest tides occur when they line up on opposite sides of the Earth. Both of these alignments result in what are called *spring tides*. The smallest variations will occur when the Sun and Moon are at right angles to each other, which result in *neap tides*. Of course, this explanation of tides does not account for other variables. Winds blowing onshore at high tides will increase the height of the tide. This increase is especially large during storms, such as hurricanes, which can increase the heights of high tides so much that they cause widespread flooding and damage. These large tides are called *storm surges*. On the other hand, winds blowing out from land will suppress the size of tides. The other set of factors with tidal sizes has to do with specific coastal land formations. The Bay of Fundy lies between New Brunswick and Nova Scotia, in Canada, just north of the Maine coast. This bay is deep and narrow at its mouth, then proceeds to get shallower and narrower towards its northerly end. When the tides are flowing in, this bay's shape increases the tidal fluctuation. As a large amount of water enters the mouth at the beginning of the high tide, that same amount of water will reach the other end of the bay. It is kind of a sloshing effect, where all of that initial water piles up at the shallow and narrow end. In some locations around the world, the tidal variation may only be a few inches. However, in the Bay of Fundy, the tidal variation may be as much as 50 ft (8 m). The incoming high tides are so intense that in certain locations where rivers flow into the Bay, the tides actually push water back up the rivers in an event called a *tidal bore*. Tidal bores look like waves travelling upstream.

Ocean Waves

Ocean *waves* are mechanical surface waves. A detailed description of the dynamics and parts of these waves is provided in Section 4. Their particles move both up and down and back and forth longitudinally. A particle in a wave remains in a somewhat stationary position. This particle may rise and move forward along the crest, then down and backward along the trough with no net forward movement. If you are swimming in the ocean or if you watch something floating near the surface, you may notice its directional movement. This movement may be due to tides, wind, and/or currents. These currents may be moving in the same or different directions as the waves. Waves do not transport materials, but they do transport energy. As waves move, they carry with them energy that was transferred from friction with the wind. Ocean waves are formed by the action of wind blowing across the surface. Strong and sustained winds create larger waves, and larger waves carry more energy. As the bottoms of waves hit sand or rocks underwater, the circular pattern of energy movement is broken. This break in the circular pattern produces the classic crashing waves along beaches.

Many waves are caused by local winds or by a normal pattern of sustained winds. Other waves are caused by nearby storms or by storms that are thousands of miles away. *Tsunamis* are waves that are caused by earthquakes, not winds. Large earthquakes release a great deal of energy, which is transferred through these large waves. These waves may hardly be noticeable out at sea, but when they near land, they can release a great deal of energy and cause a great deal of coastal flooding and damage. Most ocean waves have short wavelengths and we can see them as rising and falling motions in the open sea and as breaking waves along the coast. However, tsunamis have long wavelengths. Although they are not particularly noticeable out at sea, they come ashore as a flooding wave, like a huge, rapid, high tide. In fact, they have also been called "tidal waves."

Freshwater Features and Systems

Many of the processes of freshwater systems have been addressed in Section 3, such as the water cycle (see Figure 3.8) and various freshwater habitats and ecosystems. In this section, some further aspects of the physical features and processes will be explored.

Most of the water on Earth is in the form of saltwater, which is not usable by many living organisms. Freshwater is much more limited. In fact, the estimates are that about 2.5% of the Earth's water is freshwater and 97.5% is saltwater. Of the available freshwater, just under 69% of this water is stored in glaciers and permanent snow cover. Just under 31% of freshwater is found as groundwater in soils, swamps, underground flows, and permafrost. Only about 0.3% of freshwater is found in lakes and rivers. As you have seen in Figure 3.8, evaporation from the oceans accounts for the vast majority of rain. As water evaporates from the oceans it leaves behind the salt. When it rains over land, a portion of this rain sinks into the soils (called *infiltration*) while the rest moves downhill as *run-off* to permanent or temporary streams and lakes, which eventually lead back to the ocean. The rate at which rain sinks into the soil is called the *percolation rate*. Soils that are more hard-packed and contain more clay and other fine-grained particles tend to have slower percolation rates and higher run-off rates. Soils that have higher water content that approach their *saturation points* also have greater run-off rates. Run-off in soils that become saturated may vary according to how much rain has occurred. After dry periods these soils may absorb a great deal of water, but once saturated, water just runs off. This situation can result in flooding if heavy rains continue. Some of the water that is absorbed into the soil joins the water table, while some water is drawn up into plants and some evaporates from near the surface of the soil. The water, which does not stay in the surface soil, does not evaporate, or is not used by plants, continues to make its way down into the level of soil that is completely saturated by water. This saturated level or *zone of saturation* of the soil, which may include rocks, sediments, and soil, is called the *water table*.

The Water Table

The area above the water table is referred to as the *zone of aeration*. The water table is not a level feature, but varies in its depth. It usually varies in a less dramatic fashion to the variations of the surface. As the surface land increases in altitude in the form of hills, the water table also increases from its previous depth.

The amount of water that can be stored in water tables and the rate at which this water flows varies according to how much space there is between the particles of soil and rock, which is referred to as the *porosity* of the material. Even though some materials may hold water, they may not allow water to pass through very easily. This capability is called *permeability*, where small the openings between particles reduce the flow of water and large openings increase the flow of water. As these openings get very small, the molecular attractions around the particles can prevent almost any flow from occurring. *Clay* is one such material that prevents water flow. If clay forms layers underground it may create what is called an *aquiclude* or a layer that prevents water from passing through and reaching the existing water table. As a result, this clay barrier can create a higher *perched water table*. These "raised" water tables tend to be common sources of springs. *Springs* are areas where groundwater moves out onto the surface. Springs are often the sources that feed natural ponds, lakes, and streams. Another term you often hear is "aquifer." *Aquifers* are highly permeable soils and rocks that allow groundwater to pass through easily. Watersheds, as discussed in Section 3, are those areas where water flows into central valleys and basins. Aquifers are the associated underground portions of watersheds.

Wells

Throughout history, human societies have used streams, lakes, and springs as sources of drinking water. However, such sources are not always available. In such cases, people have dug *wells*. Wells are drilled or dug down into the water table to depths that usually range from 20 to 600 ft (6–183 m), although deeper ones do exist. However, digging wells can be damaging to the water table. When water is extracted by a pump, it is removed from the water table. Depending upon the amount of water used, such usage can leave what is called a *cone of depression* in the water table. If the aquifer is not very permeable, it could take a very long time for water to refill this depression in the water table. In some cases, it may take a hundred years or more to return to its normal level. The rocks and materials underground do not always quickly distribute water from other parts of the water table into the areas where water has been removed by wells. Each well has its own characteristic refresh rate. Some rates may be fairly rapid, while others may be very slow.

Artesian wells are a special version of wells that tap into the groundwater. In these wells, the groundwater or aquifer is between two layers of impermeable rocks or clay. This layer of permeable rock, such as sandstone or limestone, is curved upward where it reaches the surface at some point along its layered band. This surface opening of the layer acts as an entry point for water, which flows down through the layer of rock. Depending upon where the artesian well is drilled, water from the underground layer will rise to the point of highest water in the layer, which could allow water to rise higher up in the well's pipe, which is called a *non-flowing artesian well.* If the water rises above ground, no pump is needed. The water could be stored in a tank that is located higher than the buildings that need water. Water can then be distributed by gravity. This type of well is called a *flowing artesian well.*

Hot Springs

Hot springs are variations of normal springs. In these cases, water in the aquifer circulates to great depths, where it is near hot igneous rock. These "hot" areas can be near volcanic plumes or other sources of contact with magma. Initially, these aquifers may become cooler with increasing depth from the surface. However, as it descends more deeply into the Earth's lithosphere, the temperature of the water begins to rise at about 0.6° C per 30 m (1° F per 100 ft). When this water reaches the surface of the land, it is considerably warmer than the surrounding air temperature.

Geysers are a type of hot spring. In such cases, water is contained in chambers of rock that extend down into hot igneous rock layers. The water at the bottom of these chambers is under a great deal of pressure from the water above it and is being heated continuously. Because of the pressure, some geyser water will need to heat to over 226° C (440° F) in order to boil, rather than the sea-level boiling point of 100° C (212° F). As the water heats and the pressure increases to the boiling point, it will push out onto the surface of the land. This geyser "eruption" releases the pressure, and the whole process starts over. The most famous geyser is probably Old Faithful in Yellowstone National Park, which erupts about once every hour. The process of geysers is also a model for scientists who are trying to tap into sources of *geothermal energy*, where water can be heated to create steam that would in turn be able to drive electrical generating turbines.

Streams and Rivers

On the surface of the land, *streams and rivers* are major features of water movement. As mentioned previously, many streams have springs as their sources. However, other sources for streams include melting snows and glaciers and water running from ponds and lakes. In some locations, especially in the desert southwest of the United States, you find *temporary rivers* that flow after heavy rains. These temporary rivers and streams are also referred to as *washes* or *arroyos*. Since desert soils tend not to absorb water, rain will run off into these washes. During particularly heavy rainstorms, these washes overflow and flood surrounding areas. Permanent rivers and streams have sources of water that flow throughout the year, even though this flow rate may vary depending upon rain and melting snow.

In all cases of streams, there is some gradient in the land that allows the water to flow downhill under the influence of gravity. Steep gradients have fast flowing streams with rapids and waterfalls, while low gradients have slower, meandering streams. *Stream flows* are measured as the *velocity* of the stream in kilometers or miles per hour. In general, the velocity of streams range from about a half a mile per hour (or 0.8 kph) up to about 20 miles per hour (or 32 kph). As streams wind their way across the land, every time a stream bends, the velocity of the water pushes water up against the far bend of the stream banks. The amount of erosion along stream banks is related to the stream's velocity. In addition to *erosion ability*, the velocity also determines the amount and size of *sediments that can be carried*. A faster moving stream can move larger and heavier materials than a slow moving stream. Streams with higher *sediment loads* also exert higher frictional forces.

The factors that affect velocity not only include the gradient, but also the amount of water being carried or the stream's *discharge*, the stream's *load*, and the shape and size of the streambed or *stream channel*. There are three basic types of stream channels:

- *Wide, shallow channels* have a relatively flat contour.
- *Semicircular channels* are more rounded in contour and consequently a bit deeper.
- *Narrow, deep channels*.

Of these three stream types, the semicircular channel stream has the least amount of contact between the water and the streambed, and therefore has the least amount of friction.

The *discharge* has to do with how much water passes through the stream. Discharge of rivers varies throughout the year, with peaks usually occurring in early winter and early spring in the United States.

As discussed, the "load" of a stream has to do with the amount of work a stream does in carrying materials. There are three types of load carried by streams:

- A *dissolved load* consists of chemicals that are dissolved in the groundwater or that are acquired along the stream's journey, such as salt run-off from roads during winter months, certain minerals in rocks and soils, and chemical pollutants.
- A *suspended load* consists of materials that do not dissolve, but remain as particles carried in the water—these particles may eventually settle out in calmer waters.
- A *bed load* consists of the materials that are too heavy to be carried in suspension and are moved along the bottom.

There also are materials that float on the water, such as leaves, branches, and other organic matter.

The other major aspect of the work of a stream has to do with its *carrying capacity*. The relationship here is quite simple: the stream's capacity is directly related to its amount of water or discharge. The sediments carried by streams may be deposited at different times and locations along the stream's path depending upon a number of factors. Some sediments are deposited in backwash areas as the stream bends. During floods, streams deposit the heaviest and coarsest sediments closest to its banks, while the finer sediments are deposited at the far reaches of the floodwaters. This effect builds what are called *natural levees* along the banks of streams and rivers. The area that is covered by floodwaters is called the *floodplain*, which usually occurs in some sort of valley. Earth scientists have further defined floodplains according to the projected frequencies or, more accurately, probabilities of floods in certain areas, such as 100-year and 500-year floodplains. However, the more accurate way of thinking about these floodplains is that in any given year there is a 1% chance of a flood in a 100-year floodplain and a 0.2% chance in a 500-year floodplain.

As mentioned previously in "Land Features," alluvial fans are the result of sediment deposits most commonly formed by temporary streams flowing out of desert mountains. The term *alluvium* refers to the material that is deposited when a stream's velocity is reduced. The final alluvial deposits of streams occur when they reach the ocean. When streams reach this point, their velocity drops rapidly as forward motion dissipates. When this happens, most of the sediment load is deposited in a pattern called a *delta*. Deltas are in the shape of a triangle or fan and may extend over hundreds of square miles for large river, such as the Mississippi.

The *aging process of rivers and streams* is shown in Figure 5.7. Young streams tend to follow relatively straight paths through the gradients of a particular terrain. As streams move from

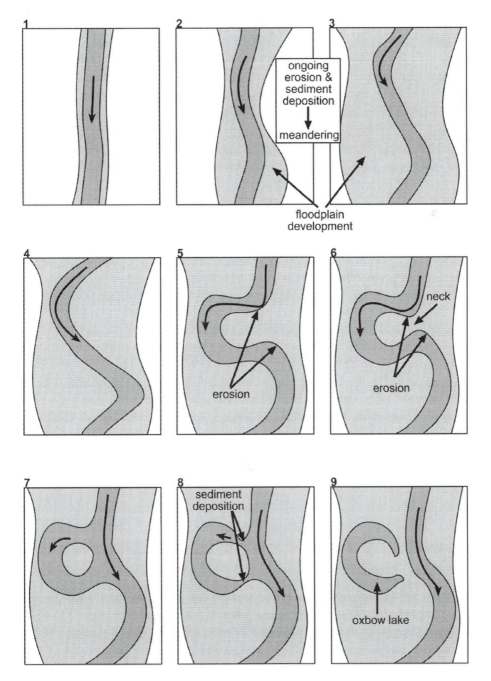

Figure 5.7 The stages in the development of rivers.

mountainous areas into the plains, they run across the surface of the land, cutting out a groove or streambed. As time goes on, periodic flooding occurs, as well as ongoing erosion and sediment deposition. The erosion that occurs during floods starts to cut out a floodplain that extends out to the higher slopes of the valley. In addition, every little turn in the streambed becomes an area where water that is running straight hits the banks of the stream and begins to erode away at that area. As the streams bend away from the flow, backwashes are created where the velocity of the current is minimized. Some sediments are deposited in these areas. As you can see in the Figure, streams begin to *meander* or wind through the floodplains. These meandering streams are signs of an older river. At a certain point the meandering becomes so pronounced that the water begins to erode away at the bases of the loops. Eventually the erosion connects the stream in a relatively straight line, while creating an island. However, the slower water that moves around the outside of the island deposits further sediments, which eventually cuts off the loop and creates what is called an *oxbow lake*.

If you look at Google Maps or Google Earth, you can find numerous examples of river aging, such as the Mississippi River with numerous oxbow lakes. The Colorado River that has cut out the Grand Canyon is an interesting example of how deeply rivers erode into the terrain. This river was once at the level of its current top or rim of the canyon. Now, the meandering Colorado River has cut down about 5,000 ft (1,524 m) into the canyon. You may wonder why more rivers haven't cut out deeper canyons. There are limits to how deeply a river can cut into the earth, which has to do with gravity. Rivers and streams run downhill. If there is a lake that a river flows into, the surface level of the lake is called the *local base level*. No upstream river can fall below that level. The ultimate base level is *sea level*.

Ponds and Lakes

Ponds and lakes are standing bodies of water. Streams may feed into them, as well as provide drainage from them. Some lakes were formed when they were cut out by Ice Age glaciers, such as the Great Lakes of the United States and Canada and the Finger Lakes of New York. Some lakes have formed from meandering rivers, as described above, while others formed when natural dams were created from heavy sediment deposits. And, still others formed in extinct volcanic craters, in limestone sinkholes that are relatively common in Florida, after earthquakes, and in other basins or depressions in the terrain. Of course, many present day lakes have been created when rivers have been dammed for electrical power generation or for the supplying of water to local communities.

Key Idea 5.3 Earth Materials and their Properties

Rock Cycle

The rock cycle is the major process of rock development and recycling (see Figure 5.8). As sediments are deposited, they build up in layers. Over long periods of time, the composition of these layers change as different materials are deposited, including the bones, shells, and other hard parts of dead organisms. As these layers build up on top of one another, the ones at the bottom are compressed due to the increasing pressure from the layers above. This pressure causes a process called *cementation* to occur. Part of this cementation process involves the precipitation of minerals that were dissolved in water in the areas between particles. Intermolecular forces (see types of bonds under "Atomic Structure" in Section 4.4) create a kind of bond between all of these materials, which result in what are called *classic sedimentary rocks, such as limestone and sandstone*. Two other forms of sedimentary rocks include *chemical sedimentary rocks*, which are precipitated from dissolved minerals, including halite and gypsum; and *biochemical sedimentary rocks*, which are formed from organic matter, such as coal and limestone. Later in this section we will examine the characteristics of these and other rocks and minerals.

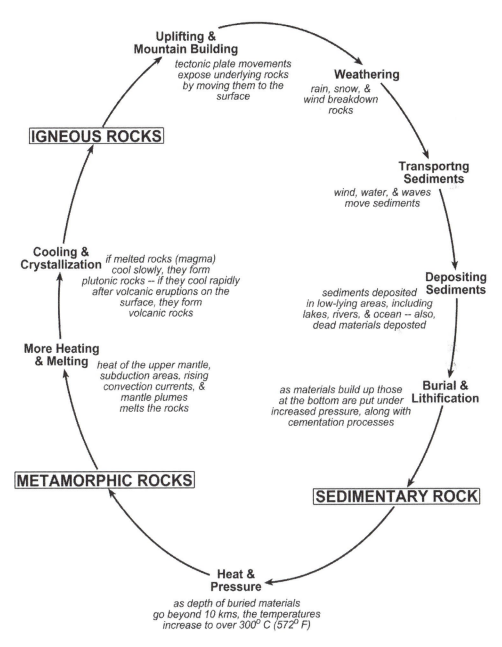

Figure 5.8 The rock cycle.

As these sedimentary rocks are formed and continue to be built upon, they incur even greater pressure as well as heat. This heat is associated with the increasing pressure from the depth as well as rocks nearing the bottom of the lithosphere where heat from the mantle is present. In sedimentary rocks, the materials that formed the rocks are clearly visible as rock particles. As these rocks heat, some of these materials soften and begin to lose some of their individual characteristics. At this stage of partially melted rocks, they are referred to as *metamorphic rocks*, or rocks between the two forms of sedimentary and igneous, such as slate, marble, and schist.

As these rocks increase in depth, they may become part of the upper mantle of molten rocks. As these molten rocks are pushed back to the surface through volcanic eruptions or other movements of materials from the mantle to the surface, they cool down and re-solidify as *igneous rocks*. Igneous rocks that cool quickly are referred to as *volcanic rocks*. The magma that cools slowly forms what are called *plutonic rocks*.

Earthquakes, weathering, and erosion can bring all stages of rocks back to the surface. In addition, the processes of weathering and erosion can break up igneous rocks and carry them off as sediments in rivers and the ocean, starting the rock cycle all over again.

Soils and Soil Profiles

Soils vary from one environment to another. Investigations of the soil and soil profiles, or the cross-section of soil, can tell us much about the history of the area. You can see *soil profiles* at the top of road-cuts and excavation areas. You also can dig down into the soil to a depth of several inches to a foot, meter, or more. In mature soils, you see distinct layers or soil *horizons*. In immature soils, these horizons may not be at all clear. Such *immature* soils have not been building up for very long, or they have been disturbed through excavation. The soil layers are:

- *Surface soil* or topsoil is the top layer This *"A" horizon* contains the largest amount of organic material, called *humus*, including dead leaves and other plant material, decaying animals and other organisms, and any eliminated materials from animal digestive processes. This layer also contains a variety of living organisms, including bacteria, mold, fungi, earthworms, various arthropods, and burrowing animals.
- The *subsoil* or *"B" horizon* is also referred to as the *zone of accumulation*. As the biological material from the surface soil is completely decayed and broken down, it becomes part of this layer.

  – These top two layers of soil are the richest layers in terms of their ability to supply nutrients for tree and plant growth. Roots from plants spread their way through these two layers of soils.

- The *"C" horizon* is the layer beneath the subsoil and is primarily composed of the material that was present before soil formation began. This material can be rocks, gravel, sand, or clay.
- Below this layer is the *bedrock layer* or *"D" horizon*, which can be granite, limestone, sandstone, or whatever rocks are indicative of the particular location.

Other common types of materials can mix with soils or can build up in their own separate layers. The list below describes some of these common types of particulate matter:

- *Sand*—coarse-grained particles of silicates, coral, and other materials. Grain size varies from fine (62 to 125 microns or 0.014 to 0.027 inch or less than 1/32 inch) to very coarse (1 to 2 millimeters or about 1/16 inch).
- *Silt*—a fine grained particle that ranges in size from 3.9 to 62.5 microns (a micron is one millionth of a meter or one thousandth of a millimeter). Silt is a common suspended sediment in streams and rivers.
- *Clay*—is a very fine particle that is less than 3.9 microns. Clay can be compacted into water-impermeable layers, such as those that create raised or perched water tables.
- *Loess*—fine-grained particles created by glaciation, which are blown by the wind and accumulate across the plains. Their particle size tends to be the same as fine silt. However, the angular sides of loess contribute to its unique properties. Loess can be eroded by wind and water, blown by the wind, and yet it can be dug out into cave-like homes. It also is very permeable and is a major part of highly fertile soils where it occurs. In the United States, loess deposits are most common in South Dakota, Nebraska, Iowa and along the Mississippi and Illinois Rivers in Illinois and Missouri.

Rocks and Minerals

The following charts describe some common rocks and minerals, along with some of their characteristics. These lists are not a complete list, but just an assortment of common examples of each type. If you are going to study rocks and minerals with children, you should buy a field guide of rocks and minerals.

Rocks

Rocks are combinations of various materials and minerals. Their formation was described previously in the "Rock Cycle" subsection. A few common examples are listed here:

Sedimentary	Metamorphic	Igneous
• Sandstone	• Slate	• Basalt
• Limestone	• Marble	• Granite
• Conglomerates	• Quartzite	• Pumice
• Shale	• Schist	• Obsidian
• Siltstone	• Gneiss	• Rhyolite

Minerals

Minerals are of two types: naturally occurring elements, such as gold, silver, and sulfur; and chemical compounds, such as those that make up quartz, calcite, and diamonds. The properties and characteristics of minerals include:

- *Crystals*—Some minerals form crystals, which are a result of the way in which their molecules arrange themselves in a solid state where they can form without spatial restrictions. Some minerals form from a dissolved state and have molecular structures that will form crystals as they precipitate out of solution. However, most often the conditions for crystal growth are not good enough for crystal formation.

- *Color*—Colors are always quite noticeable, but they are not usually a very good characteristic upon which to identify a mineral. Yellow for sulfur is a good identification criterion. However, color for a mineral like quartz is not very reliable. Other substances in quartz crystals can make them pink, purple, white, and black.
- *Streak*—Streak tests are made by rubbing a mineral on a plate of unglazed porcelain. Even though a mineral may appear one color, the color that is made from a streak test tends to be much more accurate. This test was once very common among geologists. However, now it is not used very often.
- *Luster*—This characteristic relates to the quality of light reflection off a mineral. Metal ores are described as having a metallic luster. Luster descriptions of other minerals include: vitreous or glassy, pearly, silky, resinous, and earthy or dull. These qualities are not measurable.
- *Hardness*—From the more technical perspective, hardness relates to how resistant a mineral is to abrasion and scratching. Again, this quality is relative, with no absolute measurement. However, there is a scale of hardness referred to as *Mohs Scale*, which goes from softest (1) to hardest (10):

Hardness	Example
1	Talc
2	Gypsum
3	Calcite
4	Fluorite
5	Apatite
6	Orthoclase
7	Quartz
8	Topaz
9	Corundum
10	Diamond

Higher numbered minerals can scratch those with lower numbers. For comparison, a fingernail has a hardness of 2.5, a penny is 3.0, and a piece of glass is 5.5.

- *Cleavage*—Cleavage relates to how a mineral will split apart along lines that involve weaker molecular bonds. Cleavage is described by the number of planes a mineral has, along with the angles at which these planes meet. Mineral cleavage varies from no cleavage at all, to poor cleavage, to well-defined smooth cleavage planes. If you found a piece of mica, which is a flat, silvery mineral, it has one cleavage plane. You can separate sheets (the one plane) of mica with a knife or fingernail.
- *Fracture*—Fracture occurs when a mineral is hit hard enough. The common types of fracturing include:
  - irregular;
  - conchoidal, which is similar to how glass breaks with smooth, curved surfaces;
  - splinters;
  - fibrous, like asbestos.

- *Specific gravity*—Specific gravity is another term for density, or the ratio of the weight of the mineral to its volume (see section 4 for further information on density). Most minerals have specific gravities of about 2.6. However, some may be less, while other may be quite a bit higher.

At this point, we know of about 2,000 types of minerals. However, only about 20 are commonly found.

Natural Resources

In addition to the complex interactions and interrelationships among living and nonliving parts of our world, human beings have taken advantage of a wide range of earth's materials throughout their history. We refer to the useful materials as *natural resources*. These resources have become essential for the maintenance of our lives and for further development and progress. However, we are now finding that unlimited and blind use of these resources can be very damaging, with both current and future repercussions.

There are two sources of natural materials: those from biological sources, and those from non-biological sources. However, some seemingly non-living natural sources may have originated from biological sources, such as limestone, coal, oil, and some carbon dioxide.

The following list provides a partial overview of some of these natural resources. As you read through this list and think about our natural resources, keep in mind the discussion of energy costs from Section 3. All of these natural resources take energy to produce. Whether this energy is biochemical or geological, the energy used for the initial production is a one-way process. Even though we may think of some materials as renewable resources, they still take energy to produce naturally and take both energy and monetary costs to produce for our use.

Materials from biological sources include:

- *Wood*—used for construction and fuel, wood pulp in papers and cardboards.
- *Plant fibers*—wood fibers for paper and construction materials; cotton, hemp, and other plants for clothing, fabrics, and some papers.
- *Plant products*, such as oils, saps, and waxes—latex, cooking oils, linseed oils for wood finishes, some rubbers, some paints.
- *Animal fibers*—wool for clothing and fabrics.
- *Animal skins and other parts*—leather goods, lard, tallow for candles.
- *Natural sponges*—bathing and cleaning sponges.

Non-living materials from or produced by previously living sources include:

- *Coal, oil, and natural gas*—fuels, plastics, synthetic fibers and textiles.
- *Limestone and other calcareous rocks* from shells and other skeletal materials—construction products, lime production, marble from naturally or artificially "metamorphized" limestone for construction, used in cement.
- *Shells, bones, coral*—calcium nutritional supplements, decorative constructions.

Non-living materials include:

- *Metal ores*—metals and alloys for construction, technology, and other goods.
- *Clays*—ceramics, pottery, porcelain, bricks, tiles, an ingredient in some cements.
- *Sand and related materials*—used in the production of glass, ingredient in cements, other construction uses.
- *Rocks*—construction materials.
- *Other minerals (elements)*—some are used in nutritional supplements; used in the manufacturing of a wide variety of materials, including metal alloys, glass, and technologies; uranium and other radioactive elements are used in energy production, medical imaging and treatments, and weapons.

Key Idea 5.4 The History of the Earth

The study of our planet's history is based on two basic methods. One method, *relative dating*, is based on understandings of how the Earth's materials are made, such as how sedimentary, metamorphic, and igneous rocks are formed. These understandings are the based on two major principles:

- *Law of superposition* states that lower layers are older than higher layers.
- *Principle of original horizontality* states that sediments are deposited in horizontal layers. Any changes to the original horizontal positions must have occurred after the layers were deposited and are caused by some event, such as earthquakes, uplifting, or some other change to the crust.

The other method, *absolute dating*, involves radioactive dating (see Section 4.5 for additional information). Radioactive substances occur naturally and decay at known rates. Based on these rates of decay and the radioactive isotopes' changes into stable elements, as well as what we know about how common these radioactive elements are in nature, we can determine with a fair amount of accuracy how old certain substances are. As discussed in Section 4, carbon-14 is used to date materials that were once living. However, carbon-14 can only be used to date back to 50,000 years based on the relatively short half-life of carbon-14 (about 5,730 years). Table 5.1 provides the names of some common radioactive isotopes, along with their half-lives, end-products, and what materials they are used to "date."

Table 5.1 Radioactive Isotopes Used for Geological Dating

Isotope	Half-Life (years)	Stable End-Product	Objects of Dating
Carbon-14	5,730	Nitrogen-14	Previously living materials, such as bones, mummies
Uranium-235	704 million	Lead-207	Pitchblend, uraninite, zircon, monazite, apatite
Potassium-40	1.26 billion	Argon-40	Potassium feldspar, muscovite, amphibole, glauconite
Uranium-238	4.47 billion	Lead-206	Pitchblend, uraninite, zircon, monazite, apatite
Rubidium-87	48.8 billion	Strontium-87	Many different rocks and minerals

At present, the Earth is estimated to be 4.6 billion years old. The Earth and other planets and solar system objects formed as materials started to coalesce around the Sun. As the Earth took its shape and position, the first part of its history, called the *Hadean Eon* from the idea of Hades or hell, was characterized by the dominance of molten rock across the surface. Because of the presence of molten rock, we have very little information about this period.

After the Earth cooled over the next 600 million years, rocks began to form, water accumulated, oxygen appeared, and the first life on Earth began. The *Archean Eon* that spanned a period from 2.5 to 4.0 billion years ago is the source of our oldest known rocks that are still in existence today. Some of these rocks contain the oldest known fossils of life that began during this time. As the Earth cooled, the atmosphere was mostly made up of nitrogen, hydrogen, carbon, and low levels of oxygen. Water vapor was also a major component of the atmosphere. The oceans formed along with the beginnings of the continental plates. The first prokaryotes (see Section 2 for further information) arose during this time. These organisms resembled bacteria, which, by the end of this eon, developed photosynthetic abilities. These first organism were not only the ancestors for all life that followed, but also became the first major organisms to affect the Earth and its atmosphere. They were responsible for adding oxygen to the oceans and the atmosphere and for regulating oxygen levels in the atmosphere.

The next eon, the *Proterozoic Eon*, extended from about 542 million years ago back to the beginning of the Archean Eon at 2.5 billion years. During this time, eukaryote life forms with membrane covered internal structures and nuclei arose, as well as the first multicellular organisms. Plate tectonic activity began with major mountain building occurring during four distinct periods of activity. The first widespread glacial activity also took place near the end of this eon. The latter part of this eon used to be called the *Precambrian Era*, which preceded the *Paleozoic Era* (the first era of the next eon).

The *Phanerozoic Eon* is the one that extends from the end of the Proterozoic Era, 542 million years ago up to the present day. From the beginning of this eon, life forms diversified with representatives in most of the major groups (phylums) that exist today. Five mass extinctions occurred during this eon, as well:

445,000,000 years ago	*Ordovician Period*	~ 65% of all species lost
365,000,000 years ago	*Devonian Period*	~ 72% of all species lost
250,000,000 years ago	*Permian Period*	over 95% of all species lost
210,000,000 years ago	*Triassic Period*	~ 65% of all species lost
65,000,000 years ago	*Cretaceous Period*	~ 76% of all species lost

It is believed that the causes of these extinctions have had to do with major environmental changes, such as those caused by collisions with a huge meteorites or comets or by huge increases in global volcanic activity. These types of events can cause major changes in the environment, through which many organisms were not able to survive. At the same time, these extinctions left the door open for all kinds of new organisms to arise, including the earliest human ancestors about 5.3 million years ago. Further details of these eons, eras, periods, and epochs can be explored at the Smithsonian Institute's *Geological Time: The Story of a Changing Earth* (http://paleobiology.si.edu/geotime/main/).

Fossils

Fossils have provided evidence of the history of life on Earth. However, it is important to realize that fossilization is not a common process. Most living things that die leave no evidence at all. However, under certain conditions, fossilization does occur. There are twelve general types of fossilization:

1. *Permineralization*: These types of fossils often contain some of the original bone or plant fiber material. This fossilization process occurs when groundwater flows into the areas where the materials have been deposited and buried. The minerals in the water penetrate into the pores and other spaces in the bones, teeth, and fibrous tissues where they precipitate out. These stony fossils take the three-dimensional shape of the original body parts. Petrified wood was produced in this way.

2. *Replacement*: This process occurs when water dissolves the original material, while the dissolved minerals in the water replace the original material. These replacements processes usually take a long time, but they do reproduce fine details of the original structures at the microscopic level. If these processes occur rapidly, they reproduce the overall shapes, but without the detail. These fossils are also three-dimensional. The minerals most typically involved in replacement processes are calcite, silicates, pyrite, and hematite.

3. *Molds and Casts*: After organisms die and are buried in sediments, fine sand, clay, or other materials are compacted around the organism. If no mineral replacement occurs, such as in waters with low mineral content, the material of the organism dissolves leaving a detailed mold or cast of its external features. In other cases, the sediments fill the inside of a shell or other hollow structure and forms an internal mold.

4. *Tar*: The La Brea Tar Pits in Los Angeles, California were once a collection area for unwitting animals that happened to stumble into them. After stumbling into these pits and dying, the bones and teeth and the exoskeletons of insects were preserved, while the soft body parts decayed and dissolved.

5. *Carbonization or Distillation*: This process involves the softer parts of plants, animals, and other organisms that are likely to decay quickly, which is exactly what happens. However, as these parts decay, the original carbon in the material is left behind. Frequently, these dark colored materials leave a relatively detailed outline of the organism on the surface of rocks.

6. *Chemical Fossils*: These "fossils" are not the visible types that we tend to think of. Rather, these fossils are chemicals that have been left behind as evidence of the organisms that have existed and the chemical processes that have taken place during the history of the Earth. Some substances exist in rocks that are the results of the breaking down of photosynthetic materials. When these substances are found, such as in Proterozoic rocks, we know that photosynthesis had been taking place during that time period. Coal, oil, and natural gas deposits are another form of chemical fossilization of organic matter.

7. *Polymerization or Fossil Resin (Amber)*: This process involves the conversion of tree saps into a natural plastic-like polymer, which is often called amber. Insects, bacteria, archeans, fungi, and other organisms are often trapped in the sap, which tends to preserve the fine details of soft-bodied organisms.

8. *Simple Burial*: In some cases, organisms and parts of organisms, such as pine cones, are buried and preserved without very much change over time. Peat bogs have been a source of various plant parts that have been preserved for tens of millions of years with little change due to the presence of tannic acid. Various mollusks and ammonites have been preserved for many years as well.

9. *Imprints*: These fossils are similar to the molds (see #3 above). Shells may leave impressions in sand and clay that are then preserved. Certain events are also preserved in this way, such as ripples in the sand from wave action and rain drops in mud.

10. *Trace Fossils*. These fossils are similar to imprints (see #9 above). These fossils are not preservations of the organisms, but are preserved evidence of certain activities. Such activities include worm burrows, footprints and tracks, coprolites or fossilized fecal droppings, burrows, snail tracks, nests and nesting sites, and other activities.

11. *Freezing*. These rare types of preservations occur when animals fall into some area in which they are frozen before any decay occurs. The remains include internal organs, skin, hair, and other features. At this point, the only frozen remains have been fairly recent—since the last Ice Age.

12. *Desiccation or Drying*: In arid areas, some animals die and then dry out without decay, similar to mummification without the wrappings.

Fossils have been a tremendous source of information about the history of our Earth. This history includes the life forms, activities, and physiological and chemical processes that have occurred. It is from such sources that we have been able to determine the make-up of the atmosphere, when photosynthesis occurred, and what organisms lived during certain periods of time.

Fossils most commonly occur in sedimentary rocks, including various types of shale and limestone, sandstone, siltstone, and mudstone. If you are looking for fossil collecting areas, these types of sedimentary deposits can be likely locations.

Key Idea 5.5 Climate and Weather

When we talk about *weather*, we are referring to the conditions of the atmosphere at a particular time. These conditions are changing constantly. *Weather forecasts* are attempts at predicting what will be happening at some point in the future. *Climate*, on the other hand, has to do with the types of conditions that are typical for a particular area over long periods of time. We may say that the weather tomorrow in northeast Missouri is going to be clear and sunny with temperatures in the mid-70s, humidity at 60%, and winds out to the southeast at 5–10 miles per hour. The *climate* in Missouri may be referred to as "temperate" or with climatic conditions that are typical of mid-range northern latitudes in the central part of the United States. Such a climate has four distinct seasons with rain and snow, as well as higher than usual probabilities for tornadoes than other parts of the country. In either case, weather and climate are described using the same sorts of information about temperature, wind, humidity, and atmospheric pressure. All weather and climatic conditions involve and arise out of the interactions of these four factors.

Earth–Sun Relationships and the Seasons

If asked, most people, even highly educated people, have misconceptions about how the seasons occur. At the same time, seasonal changes affect most people in non-tropical regions worldwide. *How do you think the seasons happen?*

The first idea we need to understand is that the Earth orbits around the Sun. However, the Earth's axis does not sit at a perpendicular position in relationship to the plane of its orbit around the Sun. Instead the Earth's axis is tilted at a 23.5-degree angle from the vertical. In Figure 5.9, the Earth is shown slanting towards the Sun in a position that occurs on the northern hemisphere's summer *solstice*. At this point in time, the Sun's light rays are coming directly from the vertical at latitude 23.5° North, which is also called the *Tropic of Cancer*. The *Tropic of Capricorn* is at 23.5° South. The Arctic and Antarctic Circles occur at latitudes 66.5° North and South, respectively, which are 23.5° from the poles at 90° North and South.

An important part of the Earth's tilt is that its orientation is maintained throughout the orbit around the Sun. In Figure 5.10, you can see how the northern hemisphere tilts toward the Sun during the summer in the northern hemisphere, while the southern hemisphere tilts toward the Sun in their summer and our winter. During the spring and fall *equinoxes*, the Sun's light rays hit the equator at the vertical or perpendicular.

If we look at Figure 5.9 and imagine that the winter sun is hitting the Earth from the left side of the figure, we can see that the Sun's rays are hitting the Tropic of Capricorn rather than the

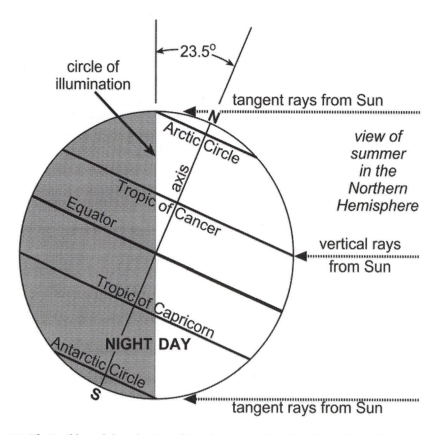

Figure 5.9 The Earth's angle based on its orbital plane around the Sun, along with the layout of latitudes.

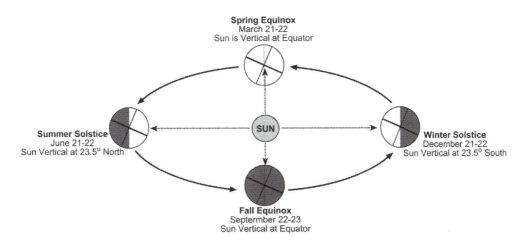

Figure 5.10 The Earth's orbit around the Sun with seasonal positions.

Tropic of Cancer. The rays hitting the Tropic of Cancer during the winter are coming from a 66.5° angle (90° minus the 23.5° change in the angle of the axis) rather than from a 90° angle during the summer. There are two major effects of the change in angle of the sun's light rays during the winter: the amount of atmosphere the light travels through at different latitudes, and the dispersal of light due to its angle of approach. The northern hemisphere points towards the Sun during the northern hemisphere summer. In this position, from the equator to the mid-ranges of the northern latitudes, the Sun's light travels through the least amount of atmosphere. However, even the Tropic of Capricorn and the Arctic Circle get much more direct light than at the southern latitudes, from the mid-range to the Antarctic Circle. Since molecules in the atmosphere absorb the Sun's light energy, travelling through more atmosphere decreases the amount of the Sun's energy that reaches the Earth's surface. The second issue of light dispersal has to do with the angle at which the light hits the surface of the Earth. In Figure 5.9, the light rays hitting the Earth as shown are coming directly from the vertical. As you move towards the North and south, the angle at which the light hits the Earth increases. The effect at both extremes in latitude is similar to how the Sun's light strikes us just after sunrise and just before sunset.

The other effect of these dynamics between the tilt and angles of sunlight involves the length of the days or the length of time the Sun's light is striking the surface of the Earth. The length of a day at the equator is the same year round, at 12 hours. As you move North or South from the equator, the length of daylight changes depending upon the time of year, as shown in Table 5.2. At the summer solstice, the days never end in the Arctic Circle, but remain 12 hours long at the equator. Even though the polar region gets less sunlight because of the angle and the amount of atmosphere through which the light passes, the overall exposure to the Sun is longer in the summer.

Radiation and Heat

The Sun's radiant energy that crosses the spectrum of electromagnetic radiation, including the visible light range (see Section 4), strikes the Earth's atmosphere. Part of this energy is reflected

Table 5.2 The Length of Daylight at Different Latitudes and Different Times of Year (times are in hours and minutes, unless noted)

Latitudes (degrees)	Summer Solstice	Winter Solstice	Equinoxes
0 (equator)	12:00	12:00	12:00
10	12:35	11:25	12:00
20	13:12	10:48	12:00
30	13:56	10:04	12:00
40	14:52	9:08	12:00
50	16:18	7:42	12:00
60	18:37	5:33	12:00
70	2 months	0	12:00
80	4 months	0	12:00
90 (poles)	6 months	0	12:00

back into space, while some is absorbed or scattered. The total average amount of sunlight that is reflected back into space by the outer layers of the atmosphere is about 30%. Certain gases absorb specific wavelengths of light. Oxygen (O_2) and ozone (O_3) absorb radiation in the longer wavelength ultraviolet range, which is why "holes" in the ozone layer are problematic. As mentioned before, most of the ozone is in the stratosphere, which is the reason why the temperatures are so high in this layer. The other major absorber of ultraviolet radiation in the shorter wavelength range is water vapor. About 20% of the total absorption of solar radiation is due to ozone, oxygen, and water vapor. As it turns out, almost all of the visible range of solar radiation passes through the atmosphere without being absorbed.

Only about 50% of the Sun's total *radiant energy* hits the Earth's surface. As the surface warms from the radiant energy, it reflects back some of this heat energy, which, in turn, heats the air. At night, the heat loss is not regenerated by continued sunshine. As a result, the atmosphere cools. At higher altitudes, this difference between daytime and night-time temperatures can be quite extreme. In higher mountainous regions, this day-to-night difference in temperature can range between 25 to 45° F (3.8–7.2° C). In the summer, this means that during the day the temperature may be 80° F (26° C), but at night the temperature can be in the 40s (4° C). The day-to-night temperature differences in any location can be moderated if there is a cloud cover. As heat radiates from the Earth's surface at night, the clouds reflect back some of this heat, thus keeping it warmer at night. This re-absorption of heat energy by water vapor molecules in the atmosphere is what is referred to as the *greenhouse effect*. Without this effect, the Earth may not have been able to support life or, at the very least, life on Earth would have been dramatically different in terms of how organisms would have to be adapted for very cold climates.

Different types and colors of objects will absorb and reflect different amounts of heat energy from the Sun. Freshly fallen snow, as you may suspect, reflects 80–90% of the Sun's radiant energy. For old, dirty snow, this percentage drops to 45–70%. Green meadows, forests, and croplands reflect between 5 and 25% of the Sun's light. Black-topped roads reflect about 5–10%, while concrete reflects 15–30%. Clouds reflect back a certain portion of light depending upon how thick they are: thin clouds of less than 500 ft (152 m) reflect between 25 and 63%, while thicker clouds that are over 1,000 ft (304 m) thick reflect between 59 and 84% of the

Sun's radiation. Of course, the angle of the Sun in relation to its penetration of the atmosphere and to hitting the Earth's surface is a major factor in the amount reflection off of some objects and surfaces. A body of water reflects only about 5% of the light when the Sun is directly overhead. However, this percentage increases to more than 60% when the angle of the Sun is very low in the sky. In addition, rough seas reflect less sunlight than calm seas.

As we saw in Section 4, *temperature* is the measurement of heat energy. The common temperature and statistics that are recorded include:

- temperatures taken throughout the *day and night at regular intervals*;
- *daily mean temperatures* as the average of the low and high temperatures;
- the *monthly mean* is the average of the daily means for the month;
- *annual mean temperature* is the average of the monthly means for the year;
- *temperature ranges* for months and years.

All of these temperature statistics allow comparisons to be made over longer periods of time and to note extremes in temperatures and other long-term patterns.

As we continue to examine weather it is important to realize how heat is radiated by different substances. If you have spent any time around the oceans, you may notice how the climate and temperature on land are affected by the temperature of the ocean water. Along the Atlantic coast, air temperatures are moderated by the ocean temperatures even though these temperatures vary from summer to winter. In the winter the air near the coast is a bit warmer, and in the summer it is a bit cooler. On the Pacific coast where the water is cooler, the air temperatures near the water are always cooler. In California, where the monthly mean temperatures do not vary nearly as much as on the east coast, the coastal air temperatures are moderated from those further inland. Water also tends to hold onto its heat longer than does the land. Since light penetrates more deeply into water, more water is heated per unit area than the same area of land. Basically, it takes a great deal more energy to heat water than it does to heat the same volume of air. While water takes more energy to heat, it also loses energy more slowly. As we look at climate patterns, including global warming, it is the *heat capacity* of water that plays a key role.

Humidity, Clouds, Fog, and Precipitation

As mentioned in the previous subsection, a major component of the atmosphere is water vapor. Water vapor not only is important as an absorber of ultra violet radiation, but also is a major store of water in the water cycle (see Section 3).

Water's ability to change state to and from liquid, vapor, and solid at ranges of temperature that are common on Earth make it a unique substance for supporting life on Earth. Up to this point, we have seen how freezing water becomes less dense and therefore floats, which allows life to continue to exist in lakes during the winter. We also saw how water in the oceans moderates coastal weather due to its heat capacity. This "heat capacity" relates to how much heat energy is required to change the temperature of water, which turns out to be 1 *calorie* of heat energy to raise 1 g or 1 cm³ of water by 1° C. On the other hand, to change 1 g of water to water vapor through simple *evaporation* takes 600 calories of heat energy. This heat energy is needed to speed up the motion of the water molecules to the point where they escape as vapor. When the vapor returns to the liquid state as *condensation,* this heat energy is released. When water evaporates from the oceans in the tropics and condenses as clouds, the release of huge amounts of heat energy can result in violent storms, such as *hurricanes,* which is the name used for Atlantic Ocean storms, or *typhoons,* which is the name used for Pacific Ocean storms. Condensation on surfaces is called *dew* or *frost,* and condensation in the atmosphere results in *clouds* or *fog.* In order for frozen water to melt, it takes about 80 calories of heat energy to *melt* 1 g of water. In reverse, *freezing* water releases about 80 calories of heat per gram of water. Although we typically think of water's changing to different states as linear steps from solid to liquid to gas and vice versa, there are instances where the liquid states are skipped. When frozen water as ice or snow skips the liquid phase, it is called *sublimation.* The amount of energy required for sublimation is equal to the amount needed for melting plus the amount needed for evaporation, or 680 calories. In *deposition,* when water vapor skips condensation into a liquid state and becomes a solid, as with frost, 680 calories are released into the atmosphere.

Humidity is the term we use to talk about the amount of water vapor contained in the atmosphere. There are two ways of referring to humidity:

- *Absolute humidity* refers to the actual amount of water vapor in the air, which is measured in as grams of water per cubic meter. This term is not commonly used.
- *Relative humidity* is the percentage of water in the air in relation to its maximum capacity to hold water vapor. This maximum capacity is the *saturation point.* The saturation point changes with temperature. The "relative" aspect of relative humidity refers to the amount of water vapor in the air at a specific temperature at a specific altitude. In other words, 80% relative humidity will contain different amounts of water vapor at different temperatures. At sea level, 80% humidity at 20° C (68° F) has almost twice the amount of water vapor as 80% humidity at 10° C (50° F).

A related concept we hear about in weather reports is the dew point. *Dew point* is the temperature at which the air with its water vapor content will need to be in order to reach 100% relative humidity. Let's say that the temperature outside is 86° F (30° C) and the absolute humidity is 9.381 grams of water vapor per cubic meter. The relative humidity for this absolute humidity at 86° F (30° C) is 30.7% and the dew point is about 48.7° F (9.3° C).

Condensation occurs on surfaces when the atmosphere is at the saturation point. Dew is condensation that occurs on surfaces of cars, grass and other plants, and other natural and human-made objects. *You may be thinking that clouds and fog are condensation, so how can water vapor condense in the air?* This condensation in the air would not happen if there were only particles of the gases present. However, there are all kinds of particles floating in the air that act as surfaces for condensation, such as those in smoke, dust, and even salt. These tiny particles are called *condensation nuclei.*

The primary types of clouds are described in the list below. In distinguishing these clouds it may be helpful to know the meanings of the root words. "Cirrus" has to do with hair-like or feathery shapes, like a lock of wavy hair or a downy feather. "Cumulus," like "accumulate," has to do with piling up puffs of clouds. "Stratus" has the same root as "stratified" as with sheet-like layers. The other common word root is "nimbus," which means "cloud" in Latin and refers to clouds that result in precipitation.

- *Cirrus*—high and feathery: fair weather.
- *Cirrocumulus*—high, small, puffy, and wavy (may look like fish scales): fair weather.
- *Cirrostratus*—high, thin sheets: may precede rain or snow storms.
- *Altostratus*—mid-level altitude, thin, and evenly spread: may produce light rain, drizzle, or snow flurries.
- *Altocumulus*—mid-level altitude, medium sized puffs of scattered clouds that may appear in bands: may develop into cumulonimbus and rain.
- *Stratus*—low, flat, and evenly spread out; they may range from thin to thick and have fuzzy borders: possible steady rain or drizzle, which may last for days.
- *Stratocumulus*—low, spread out broad, flat bottomed, and puffy topped clouds; larger than stratocumulus: light precipitation.
- *Nimbostratus*—low, very spread out, dark, flat clouds that have no real distinctive features: steady rain that may last for days.
- *Cumulus*—puffy clouds that pile up vertically from low to higher altitudes: fair weather when small, but severe weather when they pile up to high altitudes.
- *Cumulonimbus*—huge, puffy clouds that range in altitudes from near the ground at the bottom of the cloud to over 75,000 ft (22,860 m) (very high): thunderstorms, potential for tornados, possible heavy rain and hail.

There are other variations of these clouds, as well as unusual clouds that form under certain conditions. Some of the unusual clouds include *lenticular* clouds that form around mountains and look like smooth rounded lenses or flying saucers, and *Kelvin-Helmholtz* clouds that look like spirals of cirrus clouds or rib-cages.

The forms of precipitation include:

- *Rain*—*raindrop* formation is not well understood. The droplets that make up clouds are very tiny. If you lined up seven or eight of these droplets, they would be about the same thickness of a hair. It takes about one million of these droplets to make up an average sized raindrop. At this tiny size, the droplets could take a couple of days to fall to the ground, but they would evaporate before they did reach the ground. Somehow these droplets join with others, which may involve some increased motion that allows them to collide and join with one another.
- *Sleet* occurs during the winter when raindrops form in clouds above a sub-freezing layer of air. As the raindrops fall, they freeze into ice pellets that proceed to fall to the ground.
- *Freezing rain* is a similar winter form of precipitation, except that the sub-freezing layer is near the ground. As the raindrops fall through this layer, they don't have time to freeze until they hit the ground.
- *Hail*, on the other hand, falls during thunderstorms from cumulonimbus clouds. Hail stones begin as rain falling, but the intense updrafts of air that occur in these clouds take the raindrops up to levels where the temperatures are sub-freezing. The frozen droplets may fall and be lifted again while accumulating new layers of ice. The stronger the storm the larger the hailstones can get. Most hailstones are between a quarter of an inch and an inch (0.6–2.5 cm) in diameter. However, they may reach the size of baseballs and weigh over a pound (0.45 kg).

- *Snow—snowflakes* form when water vapor in clouds drops to sub-freezing temperatures. As the droplets of water vapor begin to coalesce and freeze, they form the characteristic crystalline shapes of snow flakes. The formation of these structures is very
sensitive to all sorts of factors, such as wind, temperature, and dust particles. The con-
tinual variations that occur among all of these factors produce snowflakes that are
uniquely different. However, there are several common patterns of snowflakes that
form in different temperature ranges:

  - hexagonal plates from 25–32° F (–4 to 0° C)
  - needles from 21–25° F (–6 to –4° C)
  - hollow columns from 14–21° F (–10 to –6° C)
  - indented hexagonal plates from 10–14° F (–12 to –10° C)
  - lacy hexagonal shapes or dendrites from 3–10° F (–16 to –12° C).

Pressure, Wind, and Storms

Change in *atmospheric pressure* is a critical factor in weather activity and weather
forecasting, yet, compared to other weather factors, changes in pressure are hardly, if at all,
noticeable. As discussed in subsection 4.2, atmospheric pressure is measured in *kilopascals*. In
the past, this pressure was measured in "inches of mercury," with normal sea level atmospheric pressure at 29.92 inches of mercury. However, the common measurement used now by
weather forecasters is *millibars*, where 1 millibar equals 100 newtons per square meter of pressure. In this scale, normal atmospheric pressure at sea level is 1013.2 millibars. This normal
pressure drops as altitude increases (as discussed previously). In addition to altitude, pressure
changes when changes occur in the density, moisture content, temperature, and mass
of the air.

If you can think of air masses as three-dimensional bodies of air, the air masses that are less
dense have lower pressures than those that are denser. The primary factor or variable that
affects air pressure is the *Sun's uneven heating of the surface of the Earth*. As the air heats up it
expands and becomes less dense (with lower pressure). For any air mass, there is a gradient of
pressure as it moves away from the center of a pressure system. These *pressure gradients* are
shown on weather maps as what are called *isobars*. These isobars are drawn as concentric lines
with each one representing a specific pressure. These lines are not static, but represent winds
at specific pressures circling the high- and low-pressure centers. The "steeper" the gradient,
the faster the winds, as shown in Figure 5.11. In this figure, there is a 4-millibar difference
between each isobar (line). As the pressure decreases, the force of the pressure gradient
increases. As a result, the winds are very light and very mild between 1024 and 1020. The winds
increase slightly between 1020 and 1016; and slightly more between 1016 and 1012. The pressure gradient increases more rapidly as the pressure decreases from 1012 to 996 and lower.
Consequently, the winds increase greatly over this pressure gradient range, which we all have
experienced as low pressure systems move into our areas.

If the Earth did not spin, creating the Coriolis Effect, and there were no frictional forces on
the air masses, the air in high pressure areas would flow directly into low pressure areas.
However, the Coriolis Effect creates air flows in circular patterns around the centers of low and
high pressures. The two types of circular airflows are (see Figure 5.11):

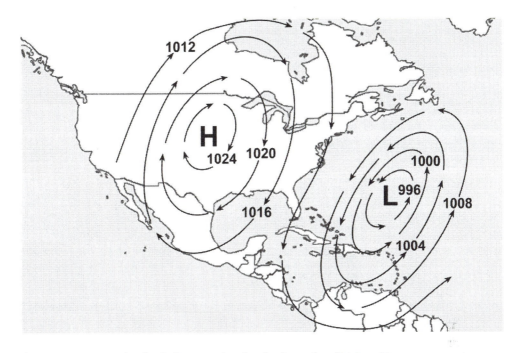

Figure 5.11 An example of an isobar map showing the dynamics of high and low pressure systems.

Source: Adapted from University of Texas map collection (www.lib.utexas.edu/maps/world_maps/world_pol495.jpg).

- *anticyclonic* systems, in which winds move around high-pressure centers in a clockwise direction—the outer streams of air move out and around the outer flows of the cyclonic systems;
- *cyclonic* systems, in which winds move around low-pressure centers in the counter-clockwise direction.

In general, air that rises is connected with clouds and precipitation. Air that descends is connected with sunny and mild conditions. In low-pressure situations where air is moving around a central low in a tightening spiral, the area of the air mass tends to get smaller. These situations are referred to as *horizontal convergences*. When this occurs, the air that was spread out builds up on top of the lower level air mass. If this building up remains constant, a low-pressure system should counteract itself very quickly. However, when the surface air converges and pushes air upward, the opposite pattern occurs at higher altitudes in the air mass. As the air rises, it *diverges*—it spreads out and pulls more air upward from the surface. This rising air can occur very slowly as low-pressure systems build. In fact, the surface level air may take over a day to rise 3,000–4,000 ft (900–1,200 m). If this diverging air maintains an equal movement to the converging air below, the low-pressure system maintains itself. If the divergence is greater than the convergence, it can pull even more air up into the system and intensify a storm system. In high-pressure systems, the surface level is diverging and the air mass above is converging. As the air descends into the system it compresses and warms. These *anticyclones* do not produce clouds and precipitation.

Hurricanes and Tornadoes

Hurricanes and tornadoes are both associated with strong low-pressure systems. *Hurricanes* (in the Atlantic) and *typhoons* (in the Pacific and Indian Oceans) develop over warm ocean waters with temperatures above 80° F (26.5° C). These warm waters develop both the *rain capacity* of the storm and the *energy capacity* from the rising warm air. The early stages of these storms are called *tropical disturbances*. As they develop wind speeds over 38 mph (61 kph), they are classified as *tropical storms*. Hurricanes are storms with sustained winds of 74 mph and above. The Saffir-Simpson scale of hurricane categories are based on sustained wind speeds:

CATEGORY	WIND SPEEDS	EXAMPLES
I	74–95 mph (119–153 kph)	Cindy (2005); Gaston (2004)
II	96–110 mph (154–177 kph)	Erin (1995); Isabel (2003)
III	111–130 mph (178–209 kph)	Rita (2005); Katrina (2005)
IV	131–155 mph (210–249 kph)	Charley (2004); Hugo (1989)
V	156 mph (249 kph) and above	Camille (1969); Andrew (1992)

As intense low-pressure systems, hurricanes spin in a counter-clockwise direction around the central low-pressure area, called the *eye*, where air descends into about a 20 to 30 mile (32–48 km) wide and eerily calm area in the middle of the storm.

Tornadoes, by definition, develop over land mostly from cumulonimbus clouds. During strong low-pressure systems as the air warms in the spring and summer, a tornado can develop from strong, spiral, uplifting winds, which create a funnel cloud that extends from the cumulonimbus cloud to the ground. These storms develop from intense thunderstorms where powerful downdrafts drag increasingly strong circulation of winds down to the ground. Most tornadoes have winds that range from 40 to 110 mph (64–177 kph) with a ground level diameter of about 225 to 300 ft (68–90 m). However, much bigger storms can occur with winds in excess of 300 mph (480 kph) and a diameter of over a mile (1.6 km). Smaller tornadoes also occur that may only be a few feet in diameter. *Tornadic waterspouts* are tornadoes that pass over water, while sucking up the water underneath. These events are not the same as *waterspouts* and their land relatives, *dust devils*, which are not associated with clouds.

Lightning

Lightning usually occurs in conjunction with strong low-pressure systems and the build up of cumulonimbus clouds. Current understandings of lightning suggest that small particles of water in clouds collide and interact in ways that create charges. Larger particles tend to take on negative charges and stay near the bottom of clouds, while smaller particles take on positive charges and are blown to upper parts of the clouds. This separation of charge creates a huge electric potential in the range of millions of volts (see Section 4 for more details on electrical charge). When this electrical potential is discharged, lightning can occur:

- from one part of the cloud to another part in the same cloud;
- from one cloud to another;
- between the Earth and the cloud.

Each lightning flash usually consists of about four or more pulses or strokes. The heat generated by lightning can reach 20,000° C (about 36,000° F), which is about three times as hot as the surface of the Sun. This rapid expansion of the air from such heating and the subsequent rapid cooling of the air results in a sound wave, or *thunder*. I'm sure you have noticed the lag time between lightning and subsequent thunder. Lightning flashes travel at the speed of light, and the sound travels at about one millionth of that speed (see Section 4 for more information on the speeds of sound and light). Essentially, we see the lightning instantaneously, and have to wait for the sound to arrive. An easy estimate for how far away you are from the lightning strike is to measure the time it takes to hear the sound. A close estimate is about 5 seconds per mile (1.6 km). The discharge of lightning occurs like a giant spark, where the charge from the cloud moves along a path of air that ionizes this air along the way. As this discharge moves close to the ground, the ionized area on the ground may discharge towards the descending lightning. In other cases, where there is a tall object rising from the ground, the discharge may begin from the object instead of the cloud. Lightning can be extremely dangerous. Although many people survive being struck by lightning, they do suffer significant injuries.

Wind Patterns

From the previous discussion, the wind patterns around low- and high-pressures systems are due to differences in pressure as air either spirals downward or upward along the pressure gradient isobars. At a larger scale, winds tend to flow in certain directions between latitudes 0° to 30°, 30° to 60°, and 60° to 90°, which are shown as *prevailing winds* in Figure 5.12. Most of the time, these prevailing winds blow in the directions indicated. The major reason for these wind patterns has to do with heating from the Sun, which creates three major air movement cycles (see Figure 5.13):

- *Hadley Cells*

  - The Sun's heat is most intense along the equator, where the air rises as it heats.
  - As the equatorial air rises, it creates a cyclonic or counter-clockwise low-pressure system at the surface level.
  - However, once the air rises instead of flowing outward in multiple directions, these air masses move toward the poles (either the North or South Pole, depending on which side of the equator).
  - As the air moves in a polar direction, it cools and descends creating a high-pressure system at the surface level and moves back towards the equator.
  - This cycling of air from the equator northward or southward occurs between North and South latitudes 0° and 30°.

- *Polar Cell*

  - At the poles, the cold air sinks and spreads southward.
  - The Coriolis Effect from the spinning of the Earth moves this southward moving air in a westward direction.
  - These airflows are called "easterlies." In meteorology, winds are named after the directions from which they come—easterlies come from the east and move toward the west.

- As this air moves southward toward 60° latitude, it begins to warm and then collides with the westerlies that move from 30° to 60° latitudes.
- The colliding air masses mix as the warmer air rises, which again create low-pressure systems at the surface.
- Part of this rising air moves northward, then cools and descends at the pole.

- *Ferrell Cells*

  - The air in Ferrell cells circulate in opposite directions to the Polar and Hadley Cells and occur between 30° and 60° latitudes.
  - These cells are not well understood.

The other patterns of wind circulation are shown in Figure 5.12 as the seasonal oceanic wind patterns. These oceanic patterns are sustained by the prevailing winds. In addition, these air circulations mutually interact with the oceanic currents (as depicted in Figure 5.6). The air currents drive the ocean currents and the ocean currents through their heating dynamics affect the air currents.

There also are a variety of *localized wind patterns* that may vary over a 24-hour period. An example of such localized patterns is the winds that blow from the ocean towards land during the day and from the land toward the ocean at night. This pattern is again driven by heat. The surface of land heats and cools more quickly than the surface of the ocean. In fact, there is hardly any change in water temperature over a 24-hour period. Over the same period of time, the land surface temperature can vary considerably. As a result, the hot air over land rises and then descends as it cools over the ocean. The cool air blows back towards land, then heats and

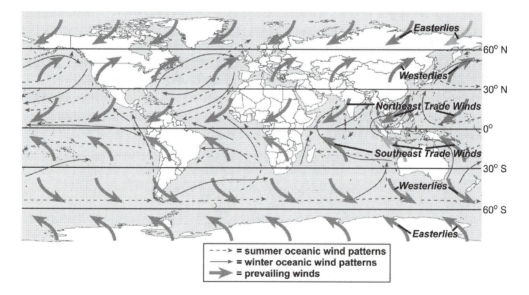

Figure 5.12 Map of the dominant wind patterns at different latitudes and the summer and winter oceanic wind patterns.

Source: Adapted from Wikipedia clickable world map (http://en.wikipedia.org/wiki/World/Clickable_world_map).

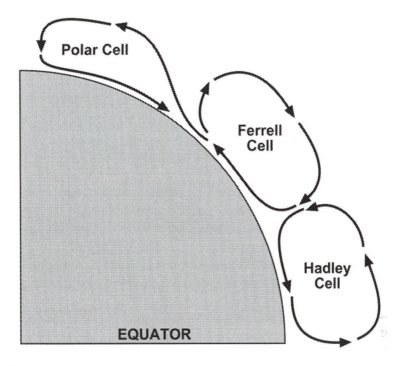

Figure 5.13 Atmospheric wind patterns.

rises. At night, the pattern reverses. The air warms over the ocean at night and rises, then descends over the cooler land and blows back towards the ocean. Similar types of winds occur around mountain ranges, where air ascends on one side of the mountains. Humid air will condense and produce clouds and precipitation on the windward side. As the air passes over the mountains and descends, it dries out as it warms and compresses. In the Rocky Mountains these dry, warm winds are called *Chinooks*, and in the Alps they are called *foehn*. Daily cycles of winds also occur in mountains and valleys, where warm air rises along the sides of valleys creating *valley breezes*. At night, the air cools and travels back down along the sides of the valleys creating *mountain breezes*.

Jet streams are another wind pattern we hear about in weather forecasts. These rather narrow tubular patterns of wind are at high altitudes, which can be as high as the border area between the troposphere and the stratosphere. There tend to be two jet streams in each of the northern and southern hemispheres. Meteorologists are not quite sure how these winds operate, but suspect that they are driven by a combination of solar heating, temperature differences, and the Earth's rotation. These streams of air occur between air masses of very different temperatures, such as those around the poles and those around the mid-latitudes. They typically occur at altitudes where the atmospheric pressure is around 250 millibars. The northern jet stream is the one that meanders across much of North America, Europe, and Asia, while the southern polar jet stream tends to circle Antarctica. The subtropical jet streams occur around the 30° North and South latitudes. On weather forecasts, these streams are represented as continuous flows around the planet that seem to change shape like a slow-motion wave of rope. However, jet streams can start and stop. They can split into two or more streams, then combine into one stream, and even flow in the opposite direction. As with other wind patterns, these streams of air are driven along pressure and temperature gradients. Steeper gradients result in faster winds. Jet streams typically move at about 50 mph (80 kph), but can exceed speeds of 240 mph (385 kph). These air streams also affect the direction and speed of weather systems, such as low-pressure (cyclonic) systems ranging from mild low-pressure storms to hurricanes.

El Niño and La Niña are terms that we hear frequently in weather reports. These terms refer to the counter-equatorial currents in the Pacific Ocean (see Figure 5.8). Under normal conditions, the Peru Current brings cooler water to the equatorial ocean off of the northwest coast of South America. The south-equatorial current takes this cooler water westward to the mid-Pacific before it begins to warm significantly. In *El Niño* years, the counter-equatorial current strengthens so much that it creates a wide "belt" of warm water across the entire Pacific Ocean and pushes the cooler Peruvian current water southward. In *La Niña* years, the opposite pattern occurs. The counter-equatorial current weakens, while allowing the south equatorial current to carry colder water almost all of the way across the Pacific. These kinds of variations occur seasonally, but in El Niño and La Niña years the seasonal variations are exaggerated, so that winter patterns are displaced by summer patterns and vice versa. As a result of these two major variations in ocean currents and temperatures, North American weather is affected dramatically. The effects of these two patterns are most evident during the *winter*. These winter effects in North America include:

- *El Niño*

  - warmer temperatures than normal from southern Alaska down through the north central Untied States;
  - warmer than usual in the northeast and eastern Canada;
  - cooler and rainier than normal in the southeast and southwest United States.

- *La Niña*

  - warmer than normal in the southeast United States;
  - cooler than normal in the northwest through north central United States.;
  - dry and warm in the southwest and Gulf Coast states.

Other Weather Features

During the winter, we often hear about *wind chill* in weather reports and forecasts, and we certainly have felt the effects of wind and cold weather in most parts of the United States. Our bodies will lose heat at an increasing rate as the temperature of the environment drops. Additional heat loss occurs as wind speeds increase. Wind chill tables provide the equivalent temperature with no wind.

Heat index tables are used during summer months. Instead of our bodies losing heat, the problem becomes one of the body's ability to cool itself through the evaporation of sweat. As relative humidity increases, the ability of the air to "hold" more moisture decreases. As a result, our ability to cool from evaporation is reduced. Heat indexes, like wind chill tables, provide equivalent temperatures that take into account the effect that relative humidity has on our perception of temperature.

Weather Patterns and Climate

The major issues that we face have to do with climate change and global warming. These issues may be the most important ones ever faced by human beings. Climate change affects all aspects of our lives, including:

- economics and livelihoods, including costs of living and jobs;
- agriculture;
- transportation;
- living situations, including the very existence of certain cities, towns, and even countries;
- water availability and use;
- food availability and supplies;
- national and international politics, including higher potentials for civil unrest and warfare;
- health and welfare, including increased potential for starvation and disease.

As we have seen in parts of this section, the Sun's radiation is the source of energy both for many weather, environmental, and physical processes and for most of life on Earth. However, solar radiation can be problematic. Damage to the ozone layer has damaged our shield against ultraviolet light, which in turn has resulted in increased incidences of skin cancers. In addition, excessive heat can lead to all kinds of unpredictable changes in our environment. We have seen how ocean currents and atmospheric patterns of winds and storms are closely interrelated. At the same time, glaciers and "permanent" snow and ice coverage are important stores in the water cycle. Global warming has been changing the dynamics of the entire global system. Glaciers are melting at unprecedented rates, reducing our water stores, raising sea levels, and changing global oceanic water currents. As a result, these changes can affect weather patterns, storm activity and intensity, such as hurricanes, and global air temperature patterns. Unpredictable extremes in temperatures can occur, where one location may be much hotter than usual, while another is much colder than normal. Some locations may get more flooding, while others endure long droughts.

Key Idea 5.6 Earth, Moon, and Solar System

Since early in the history of humankind, people have watched the Sun, Moon, and stars. They described and named constellations. They used these objects for the development of cultural mythologies and for the construction of calendars and clocks. Although some of their under-standings were naïve—such as the Earth being at the center of the universe—other under-standings were incredibly accurate. These understandings led to systematized agricultural practices, the first calendars and sundials, navigational practices and devices, and a wide vari-ety of cultural practices and mythologies.

The Sun as Seen from Earth

In this and other sections, we have seen how important the Sun is to life and to many of the physical processes on Earth. As seen in Figure 5.10, the relationship between the Earth's rotational angle and the Sun is critical to understanding the seasons. From our position on Earth, the Sun's daily "path" across the sky changes throughout the year. Although the Sun does spin on its axis and the whole solar system is moving along with the rest of our galaxy, it does not move around the Earth. Its apparent movement across the sky is due to the spinning of the Earth. The change in the Sun's apparent path is due to the Earth's orbit around the Sun. Since the Earth spins at an angle to its orbital plane, for those of us living in the northern hemisphere, the Sun appears lowest in the sky during the winter and highest in the summer. Of course this "path" across the sky varies depending on the latitude at which you live.

In general, the Sun rises later and sets earlier and follows a path lower towards the southern horizon during the winter. A difference in latitude exaggerates this pattern. During the winter at higher latitudes, the days are shorter and the Sun is much lower in the sky than at lower latitudes. Let's take two locations in the United States: Walhalla, North Dakota at about 49.5° N, and Key West, Florida at about 24.5° N. These two locations are approximately 25° apart. During the summer, the Sun is almost directly overhead in Key West at about 89° from the southern horizon. In Walhalla, the Sun is about 64° from the southern horizon. During the winter, the Sun is about 48° from the South at noon in Key West and about 23° in Walhalla. However, the time the Sun is above the horizon in these two locations varies more than may be indicated by the latitude difference alone. Since the Earth is a sphere, the difference in latitude makes a bigger difference in the length of days due to the position of each location on the sphere. In the summer, less of the Earth is in the way of the Sun at higher latitudes, therefore the days are much longer than those at lower latitudes. The *lengths of daylight* in summer and winter in each location are:

	Walhalla, ND	Key West, FL
June 21	16 hrs 11 mins	13 hrs 28 mins
December 22	8 hrs 15 mins	10 hrs 25 mins

In Walhalla, there is about almost an 8-hour difference between the length of days in summer and winter, whereas in Key West, the day length only varies by about 3 hours between winter and summer. This 5-hour difference between the summer and winter differences in day lengths is due to a difference in 25 degrees of latitude.

The Moon

The Moon's orbit has been the basis for calendars in a variety of historical and contemporary cultures. Yet, we hardly notice the Moon's presence. Many people think the Moon is only "out" at night. Others think the phases of the Moon are caused by the shadow of the Earth. In the well-known American children's book *Goodnight Moon* (M. Wise Brown, illus. C. Hurd, 1947, Harper), the little boy says "goodnight" to the Moon every night, and every night the Moon is in the same position in his bedroom window. However, if we spend time observing the Moon, we find these statements don't really make sense.

When asked, *which way does the Moon orbit the Earth*, most people say from the east to the west, where it sets just like the Sun. However, this is the way it appears to move because of Earth's rotation towards the east. The Earth's spin is what makes both the Sun and Moon appear to rise and move across the sky to the west. We know the Sun doesn't orbit the Earth, but the Moon does. If we observe the Moon carefully, we find that it "rises" later each day. The Moon rises later because it has moved further to the east than it had been the day before. If we observe this process from outer space, the *Moon makes a complete 360° orbit* in 27.32 days, which is called the *Sidereal Period*. However, from our perspective on Earth, the time it takes from full Moon to full Moon is 29.54 days, which is the *Synodic Period*. The difference has to do with Earth's orbit around the Sun. What we tend to forget about when thinking of the phases of the Moon, which we'll discuss shortly, is that the Earth is orbiting the Sun as the Moon orbits the Earth. Each day, the Moon moves about 13.2° eastward around the Earth. At the same time, the Earth moves about 0.99° eastward around the Sun. Let's assume that on day one, the Moon is full. After the Sidereal Period of 27.32 days, the Moon has moved 360° around the Earth. However, the Moon is not quite full again, because the angle between the Earth and the Sun has changed by about 27°. It takes the Moon just over 2 more days to make it back to the point where the Moon, Earth, and Sun are aligned for a full Moon again.

A *lunar eclipse* occurs when the Earth is directly in between the Sun and the Moon. If the Moon's orbital plane were on the same plane as the Earth's orbital plane, we would have a lunar eclipse every month instead of a full Moon. However, the 5° tilt off the Earth's orbital plane creates a situation where lunar eclipses occur less frequently.

Figure 5.14 explains how the phases of the Moon occur. In the figure, the Sun's light is coming from the right side. On the inner circle with the arrows showing the direction of the Moon's

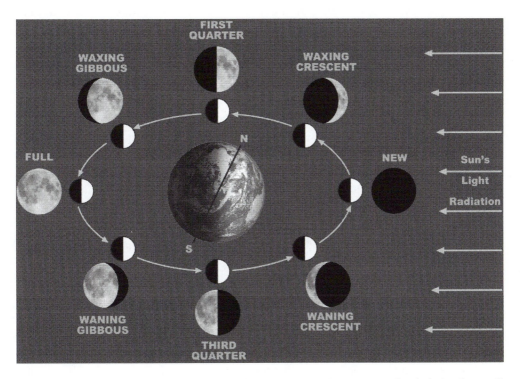

Figure 5.14 The phases of the moon with views from outer space (inner ring with side facing the Sun lit up) and as they appear from Earth (outer ring).

Source: Adapted NASA image (http://veimages.gsfc.nasa.gov/249/globe_west_540.jpg). Earth image modified (rotated and brightness adjusted); Moon from author's photo.

orbit, the side facing the Sun is lit. The outer circle shows the "face" of the Moon as it appears in each phase. If you examine the "face" of the Moon carefully in each phase around the outside, you notice that the "face" doesn't change position, but only gets covered by darkness to different degrees. What this means is that the same side of the Moon always faces the Earth. In other words, the Moon rotates in sync with its orbit. As the Moon moves around the Earth, it rotates on its axis at a rate that allows the same side of the Moon to always face the Earth.

Another issue in the orbit of the Moon around the Earth has to do with its relationship to the angle of Earth's axis. You can see that the angle of the Earth is tilted as discussed previously. In addition, the Moon's orbital plane it tilted 5° off the Earth's orbital plane. In other words, the Moon' orbit varies from 28.5° to 18.5° from Earth's equatorial plane. The Earth is tilted 23.5° to its orbital plane, therefore the Moon's orbital plane varies 5° to either side of this plane. From our perspective, we can see the Moon rising very far to the NNE one day and then far to the ESE another day within the same month.

The Solar System

The center of our solar system is the *Sun*, a rather small star as stars go. There are larger stars, which live hot and die quickly, and smaller stars. The Sun, as we've seen, is vital to life and many of the processes on Earth. Compared to everything else in our solar system, the Sun is huge. The diameter is over 100 times that of Earth, and by volume you could fit over 130,000 Earths into the Sun. The Sun is currently about 70% hydrogen and about 28% helium, along with a variety of other elements making up the remaining 2%. The Sun is a giant fusion factory, where hydrogen is used to create helium while releasing incredible amounts of energy in the range of 386,000,000,000,000,000,000 megawatts, or the equivalent of about 3.86^{24} 100-watt light bulbs.

- This fusion process takes place in the *core*, which has a temperature of about 15,600,000° K (Kelvin). The pressure in the core is the equivalent of about 250,000,000,000 Earth atmospheres or 3,650,000,000,000 psi. The surface, on the other hand, has a temperature of only 5,800° K.
- Outside of the core is the *photosphere*, which absorbs and converts the initial gamma radiation from the core to visible light range radiation.
- A thin *chromosphere* lies above the photosphere.
- The *corona*, which is only visible during eclipses, extends millions of kilometers beyond the surface of the Sun. The temperature of the corona is greater than that at the surface and is in the range of 1 million° K.
- The *magnetosphere*, the Sun's magnetic field, extends beyond the solar system.

Sunspots, which are not well understood, are areas of the Sun's surface that are cooler (3,800° K) and thus appear darker by comparison. In addition to emitting light and heat radiation, the Sun also emits steady streams of mostly electrons and protons, which comprise what is called the *solar wind*. These particles travel at a rate of about 1 million mph (400 kilometers per second) and create the "tails" of comets. During *solar flares*, where the solar wind becomes more intense and includes other more high-energy particles, we experience the effects as *auroras* and as radio wave interference and power surges.

Solar eclipses occur when the Moon moves in between the Sun and the Earth. The shadow of the Moon covers a certain portion of Earth. If you are in the middle of this shadow, the Moon just happens to cover the entire disk of the Sun, with the exception of the corona. If you are nearer to the edges of the shadow, only a portion of the Sun's disk is visible.

As we know, a shake-up to our solar system model occurred in 2006, when Pluto was demoted from planet status. The International Astronomical Union unanimously redefined the term *planet*. Pluto was excluded because its orbit is elliptical and crosses the orbit of Neptune. Planets have orbits with no obstructions, such as another planet's orbit. As a result, we now have eight planets in our solar system, with four dwarf planets and a number of other objects, including asteroids. Table 5.3 provides a list of planets and dwarf planets with basic information about size, distance, rotation, and orbits. Table 5.4 provides additional information about these planets. All of the planets and dwarf planets orbit in the same direction as the Earth. All of the planets orbit in almost circular paths. The dwarf planets have elliptical orbits. The rotations of these objects all move in the same direction from west to east with the exceptions of Venus and Uranus.

Other objects in the solar system include Kuiper Belt objects, asteroids, and comets. The *Kuiper Belt* lies outside the orbital path of Neptune and contains a variety of objects, most of

Table 5.3 Planets and Dwarf Planets in the Solar System: diameters, distances, and orbital and rotational periods

Object	Diameter (km)	Mean Distance from Sun (km)	Orbital Period (object's "year")	Rotational Period ("day")
Sun	1,390,000.0			*Variable:* 25 days at middle 36 days at poles
Mercury	4,880.0	57,910,000	87.97 days	175.94 days
Venus	12,103.6	108,200,000	224.70 days	– 116.75 days
Earth	12,756.3	149,600,000	365.26 days	24:00:00 hours
Mars	6,794.0	227,940,000	686.98 days (1.88 years)	24:39:35.24 hours
Ceres	*975.0*	*413,787,616*	*4.6 years*	*9:00:00 hours*
Jupiter	142,984.0	778,330,000	4,332.71 days (11.86 years)	9:55:33 hours
Saturn	120,536.0	1,429,400,000	10,759.50 days (29.46 years)	10:29:33 hours **still uncertain**
Uranus	51,118.0	2,870,990,000	30,685.00 days (84.01 years)	– 17:14:24 hours
Neptune	49,532.0	4,504,300,000	60,190.00 days (164.79 years)	16:06:36 hours
Pluto	*2,274.0*	*5,913,520,000*	*90,550.00 days (247.91 years)*	*6 days 9:17:00 hrs.*
Haumea	*996 × 1,960*	*6,482,916,000*	*285.4 years*	*3:54:00 hours*
Makemake	*1,300–1,900*	*6,850,333,600*	*309.9 years*	*unknown*
Eris	*2,500.0*	*10,123,147,760*	*557.0 years*	*> 8:00:00 hours*

Notes: In Rotational Period, "–" = retrograde or rotation in the east to west direction.

Planets are in boldface.

Dwarf Planets are in italics.

Table 5.4 Other Information on the Planets and Dwarf Planets

Object	Moons	Rings	Percent of Earth's Gravity	Atmosphere
Mercury	0	No	38	None
Venus	0	No	90	CO_2
Earth	1	No	100	N_2 & O_2
Mars	2	No	38	CO_2
Ceres	*0*	*No*	*2.28*	*None*
Jupiter	63	Yes	264	Hydrogen, Helium
Saturn	60	Yes	93	Hydrogen, Helium
Uranus	27	Yes	89	Hydrogen, Helium
Neptune	13	Yes	112	Hydrogen, Helium
Pluto	*3*	*No*	*6*	*Methane*
Haumea	*2*	*No*	*4.5*	*None?*
Makemake	*0*	*No*	*5.1*	*Possibly methane*
Eris	*1*	*No*	*8.2*	*Possibly methane*

Note: Planets are in boldface.
Dwarf Planets are in italics.

which are composed of rock and ice. The *asteroid belt* lies between Mars and Jupiter. Ceres is a particularly large asteroid, which is now considered to be a dwarf planet. The thousands of objects in the asteroid belt are made of varying sized pieces of rock. Some asteroids are round, while others are irregularly shaped. Some astronomers think that the asteroids are the leftovers of a planet that was destroyed in that particular orbital location. *Comets* are another category of objects that travel in orbits around the Sun. These objects are large balls of ice and dust. As comets near the Sun, the solar wind evaporates part of the surface of the comet, which results in its "tail."

Throughout the solar system there are other materials, such as: the rare molecules of oxygen and other elements; dust and interstellar dust; meteoroids; and increasing amount of space junk from our explorations and missions into space. The "space" in "outer space" is far from empty. It's just sparsely inhabited. Beyond the solar system, there are many other stars, planets, and galaxies, but we do not have the space in this book to cover this material.

Resources and References

Celestia, downloadable freeware, 3–D space simulation, available at www.shatters.net/celestia/.
Dennis Mollet and James Kistner's *Lightning* from Arizona State University, available at www.public.asu.edu/~gbadams/lightning/lightning.html.
Jeff Haby's *The Weather Prediction*, available online at www.theweatherprediction.com.
iTouch Maps (find latitude and longitude of specific locations by touching the map), available online at http://itouchmap.com.
Smithsonian National Museum of Natural History, *Geologic Time: The Story of a Changing Earth*, available online at http://paleobiology.si.edu/geotime/main/.
Stellarium, downloadable freeware, "a planetarium on your computer," available at www.stellarium.org/.
United States Geological Survey, *This Dynamic Earth: The Story of Plate Tectonics*, online edition available at http://pubs.usgs.gov/gip/dynamic/dynamic.html.

Index